CONTOURS OF JUSTICE

Cases, Crises and the Quest for Judicial Autonomy

CONTOURS OF JUSTICE

Cases, Crises and the Quest for Judicial Autonomy

GALDA VERLAG 2025

Bibliografische Information der Deutschen Nationalbibliothek
Die Deutsche Nationalbibliothek verzeichnet diese Publikation in der Deutschen Nationalbibliografie; detaillierte bibliografische Daten sind im Internet über https://dnb.de abrufbar.

ISBN 978-3-96203-483-2 (Print)
ISBN 978-3-96203-484-9 (E-Book)

If you have any questions about product safety, please contact us at the following e-mail address : contact@galda.com

TABLE OF CONTENTS

Part Two:
Systemic Challenges To Access Justice

Part Three:
From Challenges To Change – Forging A Fairer Justice System

CONTRIBUTOR PROFILES

Mohamed A. Bangura is the Prosecution Legal Adviser/Evidence Officer at the Residual Special Court for Sierra Leone, The Hague. Previously, he served as a Trial Attorney in the Office of the Prosecutor at the Special Court for Sierra Leone, where he was involved in prosecuting all four of the court's trials. He holds an LLM from the University of London and an MSc in Property Law from London South Bank University.

Ronald Gidwani is a Barrister and Solicitor of the High Court of Sierra Leone working with Halloway & Partners, Inner Chambers, as the Deputy Head of Chambers and a Lecturer at the University of Sierra Leone, assigned to the Department of Law, Faculty of Law, Fourah Bay College. He holds a Bachelor of Arts (BA Hons) in History and Political Science from Fourah Bay College, University of Sierra Leone, a Bachelor of Laws (LLB Hons) from Fourah Bay College, University of Sierra Leone, a Master of Laws (LLM) in International Human Rights Law from the Central European University (CEU), and a BL Hons certificate (Utter Barrister) from the Sierra Leone Law School. He has been a Legal Practitioner and Lecturer for 13 years. He served as Director and Supervisor of the Human Rights Clinic, Fourah Bay College, under the Open Society Justice Initiative (OSJI) Project.

Kadija Kabba is a seasoned lawyer with 18 years of experience, currently serving as the Head of the Legal Affairs Department in a leading financial institution. She previously served as Director of Legal at the West African Monetary Institute (WAMI) for four years. She holds a Bachelor's and Master's degree in Law, a Master's degree in Peace and Conflict Resolution and International Relations, and a Bachelor of Arts degree. Her research has been published in prestigious journals, including those affiliated with the University of London's School of Advanced Study, United Kingdom, and the University of Tromsø, Norway. With 18 years as a legal practitioner, Ms. Kabba blends academic rigour with practical expertise. Beyond her professional endeavours, she finds solace in classical music and literature.

Saramba Kandeh is a Barrister and Solicitor of the High Court of Sierra Leone with over a decade of experience in International Human Rights Law, International Law, and Women, Peace, and Security. She has been a Legal and Gender Advisor for AIDS-Free World since 2016 and is part of the legal team pursuing a civil action against former Gambian President Yahya Jammeh on behalf of individuals living with HIV/AIDS. Her prior experience includes roles with The Advocates for Human Rights in Minnesota, Timap for Justice as Deputy Director, and AdvocAid Sierra Leone as Duty Counsel. Ms. Kandeh holds an LL.M in International Human Rights Law from the University of Notre Dame, a Bar License Certificate from the Sierra Leone Law School, and an LLB (Hons.) from Fourah Bay College, University of Sierra Leone.

Commissioner Victor I. Lansana is the Vice Chairman of the Human Rights Commission of Sierra Leone and a Barrister & Solicitor of the Superior Courts of Judicature. An Associate Partner at the Law Firm of Kanu & Associates, he has extensive experience in public interest litigation and pro bono legal services. He is the founder of Legal Aid for Consumers & Employees (LACE), dedicated to addressing economic and labor injustices. With a BA (Hons.) and LLB (Hons.) from Fourah Bay College, an Utter Barrister Degree from the Sierra Leone Law School, and an MPA from IPAM, USL, Commissioner Lansana has also lectured extensively and contributed to human rights advocacy in Sierra Leone.

Conrad Lisk is a legal professional with LLB degrees from the University of Sierra Leone and the University of London, as well as an LLM in Human Rights and Civil Liberties from the University of Leicester. He is a qualified barrister and solicitor at the Sierra Leone Bar and a solicitor in England and Wales. Currently, he serves in the UK government legal service, leveraging his extensive expertise in law and human rights.

Augustine Sorie-Sengbe Marrah is a civil and commercial litigator, constitutional expert, and democracy activist. He graduated at the top of his class from the Sierra Leone Law School in 2009 and has over a decade of legal practice experience. Augustine has worked on international commercial arbitrations and human rights cases, including representing the Association of Ebola Survivors against Sierra Leone at the ECOWAS Community Court of Justice. He runs Marrah & Associates, his law firm, and has held several prominent positions, including Secretary of the General Legal Council and a member of Sierra Leone's Pharmacy Board. Augustine holds memberships in the Sierra Leone Bar Association, the International Bar Association, and the Commonwealth Lawyers Association.

Millicent Stronge is a legal professional specializing in Civil and Corporate Law, International Arbitration, and Regulatory Compliance. A member of the Sierra Leone Bar Association, the International Bar Association, and the Chartered Institute of Arbitrators, she graduated with a BA from the University of Sierra Leone and later obtained her law degree from the University of London. Millicent has extensive experience in legal transactions across sectors, including energy, mining, and finance, making her a sought-after counsel for both regional and international clients.

Yada Hashim Williams is a highly experienced barrister and solicitor with over 30 years of legal practice in Sierra Leone. He holds an LLB (Hons.) from the University of Sierra Leone and an LLM from the University of London. Yada has played a pivotal role in developing Sierra Leone's legal framework, serving as Lead Appeals Counsel at the Special Court for Sierra Leone and as Chairman of the Law Reform Commission. He has also been President of the Sierra Leone Bar Association and a member of the Judicial & Legal Service Commission. Yada Willaims continues to shape Sierra Leone's legal landscape as the current Chairman of the Law Reform Commission.

The views expressed in this book by all authors are strictly personal and do not represent or reflect the positions, opinions, or policies of their current or former employers, affiliated organizations, or any other entities with which they are associated.

Editors

Rowland Cole is a legal practitioner, former judicial officer and a rule of law, human rights and transitional justice expert. He has led several law reform initiatives and facilitated the drafting and enactment of several laws including in relation to legal aid, anti-corruption, prison reforms, judicial reforms, local government and alternative dispute resolution in Botswana, South Sudan, Liberia and Malawi. He holds a Doctor of Laws degree from Stellenbosch University, South Africa. He also holds an LLM degree from the University of South Africa and an LLB (Hons) from the University of Sierra Leone. He is a former Fellow of the Hague Academy of International Law. He has published several scholarly articles in peer reviewed journals in the areas of international law, international human rights law, procedural law and law reform.

Abdul Tejan-Cole is a legal practitioner with over 30 years of experience, specializing in transitional justice, human rights, and the rule of law. He holds degrees from the University of Sierra Leone and University College London and has practiced law since 1991. As a lecturer at the University of Sierra Leone, he teaches the Sierra Leone Legal System and Transitional Justice. Abdul was a prosecutor at the Special Court for Sierra Leone and has held pivotal roles in transitional justice processes, including consultancy work with the UNDP in South Sudan, The Gambia and Liberia. He has also contributed to the reform of Sierra Leone's justice system through the Justice Sector Development Project, a DFID-funded initiative. Abdul has managed numerous projects and is adept in both quantitative and qualitative research methodologies. His extensive work with human rights organizations and his contributions to transitional justice frameworks have earned him international recognition, including as a Yale World Fellow and recipient of the Human Rights Watch Annual Award.

ACKNOWLEDGEMENTS

A note of thanks and deep gratitude to all the chapter authors for their trust in joining this journey, first in shaping the vision for this book and then in generously sharing their experiences and reflections. We acknowledge the efforts and dedication of the authors to make time amidst many urgent and competing demands, and their determination in working through rounds of feedback and revision, as well as patience and understanding in bearing with the inevitable challenges of working virtually.

We extend heartfelt appreciation to our peer reviewers, whose careful reading and thoughtful comments sharpened the arguments and strengthened the clarity of this book. Special thanks go to Dr Annette Mbogoh of the University of Nairobi's Faculty of Law for her invaluable time and insights.

This book has also benefited from the ongoing support of colleagues in our respective organisations. Their assistance, both big and small, was essential at every step, from convening discussions to helping with drafts, and from coordinating workshops to preparing the manuscript for publication.

We are also grateful to the editorial and production teams who guided this book through to completion, offering patience, advice, and technical skill. Their contributions ensured that the final product reflects the quality and seriousness the subject deserves.

Above all, this book is dedicated to the communities, practitioners, and advocates whose work and courage animate its pages. It is our hope that their struggles and determination for justice will continue to inspire and guide all those committed to building fairer societies.

FOREWORD

Justice is never static. It is built, tested, and renewed through the choices of judges, lawyers, and citizens. This book, Contours of Justice, captures that truth with clarity. It presents not only cases and controversies but also the wider struggles to protect judicial independence in Sierra Leone.

My own journey through the law has shown me how fragile justice can be when courts lose their autonomy. As State Counsel, High Court Judge, Appeal Court Judge, and finally Chief Justice, I saw how political pressures, limited resources, and public skepticism tested the system. Yet I also witnessed judges who stood firm, lawyers who argued with courage, and citizens who refused to lose faith in the rule of law.

The chapters in this volume take us through landmark trials and systemic challenges. They reveal the dangers of executive overreach, the persistence of corruption, and the consequences of unfair trials. They also point to reforms, from truth and reconciliation processes to legal aid and judicial review, that can restore trust. In doing so, the authors remind us that justice requires more than legal texts. Justice depends on integrity, vigilance, and the courage to defend constitutional principles, even when doing so is unpopular or dangerous.

This book comes at a time when Sierra Leone, like many nations, continues to search for a judiciary that is both independent and accountable. Its value lies not only in its detailed analysis but also in the questions it asks of us all. How do we ensure fair trials in politically charged cases? How do we protect judges from undue influence? How do we make the courts accessible to the poorest and most vulnerable?

I commend the authors and editors for their thoughtful contributions. By reflecting on past failures and proposing practical reforms, they offer guidance for the present and hope for the future. It is my belief that a judiciary that is faithful to its oath and shielded from interference remains the strongest safeguard of democracy.

I invite every reader to engage with these pages with an open mind and a critical spirit. The lessons here belong not only to lawyers or judges, but to every citizen who values fairness, accountability, and the promise of justice.

Umu Hawa Tejan-Jalloh
Former Chief Justice of Sierra Leone

LIST OF ABBREVIATIONS

ACC	Anti-Corruption Commission
ALR (SL)	African Law Reports (Sierra Leone Series)
CJ	Chief Justice
CPA	Criminal Procedure Act
CRC	Constitutional Review Committee
DfID	Department for International Development
DW	Defence Witness
EALR	East African Law Reports
ECOWAS	Economic Community of West African States
EIDHR	European Union Initiative for Democracy and Human Rights
GIZ	German International Cooperation
HRCSL	Human Rights Commission of Sierra Leone
JA	Justice of Appeal
JLSC	Judicial and Legal Service Commission
JSC	Justice of the Supreme Court
JSDP	Justice Sector Development Programme
PW	Prosecution Witness
RSCSL	Residual Special Court for Sierra Leone

TASOA	Treason and State Offences Act (TASOA)
TRC	Truth and Reconciliation Commission
UNDP	United Nations Development Programme
UNIPSIL	United Nations Integrated Peace Building Office in Sierra Leone
WAMI	West African Monetary Institute

INTRODUCTION

Since Sierra Leone became a republic in 1971, it has taken full control of its justice system. A significant step in this transition was replacing the Privy Council with the Supreme Court, which was endowed with the highest authority over judicial matters. This marked a new chapter for Sierra Leone's judiciary, tasked with upholding the rule of law and serving as a guardian of constitutional principles.

However, the evolution of the judiciary has been fraught with challenges. Initially operating under a cabinet system of government with limited separation of powers, the judiciary's independence was formally guaranteed by the Constitution. Yet, as Sierra Leone transitioned to a quasi-presidential system, the expansion of executive powers rendered the judiciary increasingly vulnerable to political interference. The Truth and Reconciliation Commission (TRC) aptly described this erosion:

> 'By the early 1990s, greed, corruption, and bad governance had led to institutional collapse, through the weakening of...the judiciary...By the time of the conflict, successive regimes had rendered the country devoid of governmental accountability. Institutions such as the judiciary...had become mere pawns in the hands of the executive...The independence of the judiciary was systematically destroyed.'[1]

This indictment underscores the judiciary's inability to safeguard its independence and highlights how political interference has compromised its

---

1 Sierra Leone Truth and Reconciliation Commission, Final Report (Sierra Leone: Sierra Leone Truth and Reconciliation Commission, n.d.), accessed April 2, 2025, www.sierraleonetrc.org/index.php/view-the-final-report/download-table-of-contents.

impartiality. Forced retirements, politically motivated dismissals, and executive manipulation of judicial appointments are just a few of the mechanisms used to subordinate the judiciary to the executive branch.

Judicial independence, defined as freedom from external pressures or interference, whether from the executive, legislative branches, or other societal forces, is fundamental to democracy and the rule of law. Without it, courts cannot act as impartial arbiters of justice or checks on government power.

Aniagolu JSC, in the Nigerian Supreme Court case *Oba Lamidi Adeyemi (Alafin of Oyo) and others v Attorney General, Oyo State and Others,*[2] articulated this principle emphatically:

> 'It cannot be too often repeated...that the jurisdiction of the courts must be jealously guarded if only for the reason that the beginnings of dictatorships in many parts of the world had often commenced with the usurpation of the authority of courts...It is in this vein that the courts must insist, wherever possible, on a rigid adherence to the Constitution of the land and curb the tendency of those who would like to establish what virtually are Kangaroo courts, under different guises and smoke-screens of judicial regularity.'[3]

Sierra Leone's judiciary has not been immune to such encroachments. The Constitution of 1978, which established a one-party state, granted the president unchecked power over judicial appointments and dismissals, effectively undermining judicial autonomy. Judges who resisted executive influence faced dismissal or other reprisals, fostering a culture of compliance that eroded public trust in the judiciary.

The adoption of the 1991 Constitution marked a significant shift, introducing reforms aimed at insulating the judiciary from executive interference. Judges' appointments were now subject to recommendations from the Judicial and Legal Service Commission and parliamentary approval. Additionally, section 120(3) of the Constitution explicitly declares that the judiciary '*shall not be subject to the control or direction of any other person or authority.*'

While these provisions represent progress, their implementation has been uneven. Judicial independence, as the TRC noted, is not guaranteed merely

---

2 1 SCNLR 525 (1984).

3 *Adeyemi v Attorney General,* 1 SCNLR 605 (1984).

by constitutional provisions but by the commitment of all three branches of government to uphold it. The TRC highlighted:

> 'Judicial independence ultimately depends on the will of individuals in the three branches of state to adhere to the Constitution. Judges themselves, above all others, must be committed to the building of an independent and impartial judiciary...This requires judges to possess courage and integrity.'

Unfortunately, these ideals have often been undermined by systemic corruption, political interference, and resource constraints.

Throughout Sierra Leone's history, the judiciary has been implicated in several high-profile miscarriages of justice. Aminata Forna's *The Devil That Danced on the Water*[4] recounts the treason trial of her father, Mohammed Sorie Forna, as a stark example of judicial complicity in political persecution. Forna's case is emblematic of a broader trend in which courts have failed to resist executive overreach, delivering rulings that appear to align more with political expediency than legal principles.

More recently, the judiciary's handling of constitutional crises, such as the dismissal of Vice President Alhaji Samuel Sam-Sumana, has raised questions about its impartiality and ability to act as a check on executive power. The Supreme Court's ruling in this case, which validated the president's unilateral dismissal of the vice president, was criticized for its expansive interpretation of presidential authority and its disregard for procedural fairness.

These cases illustrate how judicial subservience has not only eroded public trust but also perpetuated governance failures. Citizens, skeptical of the courts' ability to deliver impartial justice, often turn to alternative mechanisms or extrajudicial means to resolve disputes, further undermining the rule of law.[5]

An independent judiciary is indispensable for safeguarding democratic principles. As the African Commission on Human and Peoples' Rights observed in *Civil Liberties Organisation v Nigeria*,[6]

---

4 Forna, Aminatta. The Devil That Danced on the Water: A Daughter's Quest. Atlantic Monthly Press/HarperCollins, 2002.

5 Truth and Reconciliation Commission of Sierra Leone. Witness to Truth: Report of the Truth and Reconciliation Commission.

6 *Civil Liberties Organisation v Nigeria*. 45/90, African Commission on Human and Peoples' Rights, 27 Apr. 1997.

> 'A government that governs truly in the best interest of the people...should have no fears of an independent judiciary. For a government to oust the jurisdiction of the courts on a broad scale reflects a lack of confidence in the justifiability of its own actions, and a lack of confidence in the courts to act in accordance with the public interest and the rule of law.'

Judicial independence not only upholds the rule of law but also serves as a bulwark against authoritarianism. In the absence of an independent judiciary, power becomes concentrated in the executive, weakening democratic institutions and enabling abuses of power.

This book critically examines Sierra Leone's judiciary, unpacking the systemic failures that have undermined its independence and exploring pathways for reform. Through a rigorous analysis of judicial precedents, legislative enactments, and historical context, this study advocates for restoring the judiciary's role as a bulwark of justice and accountability in Sierra Leone.

The challenges are formidable, but as this book demonstrates, they are not insurmountable. Drawing on examples from Sierra Leone and comparative jurisdictions, it offers a roadmap for building a resilient judiciary that embodies the principles of independence, impartiality, and integrity. The judiciary's transformation is both a legal duty and a moral necessity, vital for building a just, democratic, and prosperous Sierra Leone.

Abdul Tejan-Cole

PART ONE:

LANDMARK LEGAL CONTROVERIES

UNDER THE GAVEL – FRANCIS MINAH AND THE QUANDRIES OF SIERRA LEONE'S LEGAL SYSTEM

MOHAMED A. BANGURA

1. Introduction

In the past three decades or more, there has been an increasing desire and willingness on the part of countries with advanced legal systems to carry out an introspection of their justice systems to ascertain the extent to which they attain fairness in dispensing justice.

Concerns about patterns of injustice against marginalized groups, such as the poor and underprivileged, have prompted action in many countries.[1] These nations have opened legal channels to revisit completed cases. New evidence, unavailable during the original trial or appeal, can now be presented. This evidence must demonstrate the potential for exoneration or acquittal. Most impactful in driving this change is the advancement in the use of DNA evidence as well as other scientific methods of investigation. The results have been phenomenal. Many high-profile convictions have been overturned and persons wrongfully convicted have been compensated for the injustice wrought upon them.[2]

Some countries established national institutions to address the issue of miscarriage and wrongful punishment. In the UK, the Criminal Cases Review

1 World Justice Project, WJP Rule of Law Index 2023 (Washington, D.C.: World Justice Project, 2023), accessed December 31, 2024, https://worldjusticeproject.org/rule-of-law-index/.

2 Samuel R. Gross, Maurice Possley, and Klara Stephens, "Race and Wrongful Convictions in the United States" (The National Registry of Exonerations, 2017), accessed September 19, 2024, https://www.law.umich.edu/special/exoneration/Documents/Race_and_Wrongful_Convictions.pdf.

Commission (CCRC)[3] is an example and in the US, the Innocence Project,[4] a non-profit organization that works to free the innocent, prevent wrongful convictions and create fair, compassionate, and equitable systems of justice for everyone has been in the lead on this subject.[5] Lately, also, there has been the National Registry of Exonerations.[6] Analysts believe that the issue of miscarriage of justice, especially in multi-racial societies, will never fully be addressed, particularly in the US, where what has been achieved presently is probably only the tip of the iceberg.[7] Nonetheless, it is incredibly reassuring that injustice of this kind is getting the highest consideration it deserves by way of redress as more countries follow these examples.

Sierra Leone is no exception to judicial mishaps of this kind. The country's post-independence political history is replete with accounts of a steady erosion of judicial independence and a decline in the rule of law, mainly from an overreach by the executive arm of government, in gross disregard for constitutional principles. The Truth and Reconciliation Commission (TRC) outlined the root causes of Sierra Leone's 11-year civil war. It highlighted several judicial problems. Political interference, corruption, and inept officials weakened the judiciary. The lack of functional independence reduced justice quality. These issues eroded public confidence in fair justice delivery.[8] Although that dark image of its functionality may have improved somewhat since the pre-conflict period, public perception remains grim about the Judiciary's record in dispensing fair justice. Thus, examining some of its judgements

---

3 Criminal Cases Review Commission," Wikipedia, last modified September 19, 2025, https://en.wikipedia.org/wiki/Criminal_Cases_Review_Commission.

4 Innocence Project, "About," accessed December 31, 2024, https://innocenceproject.org/about/.

5 Innocence Project, "About.

6 National Registry of Exonerations," Wikipedia, accessed December 31, 2024, https://en.wikipedia.org/wiki/National_Registry_of_Exonerations.

7 Samuel R. Gross, Maurice Possley, and Klara Stephens, Race and Wrongful Convictions in the United States (report, National Registry of Exonerations, Newkirk Center for Science and Society, U. of CA Irvine, March 7, 2017), accessed December 31, 2024, https://www.law.umich.edu/special/exoneration/Documents/Race_and_Wrongful_Convictions.pdf. The report noted that 'African Americans are only 13% of the American population but 47% of the 1,900 exonerations listed in the National Registry of Exonerations (as of October 2016), and the great majority of more than 1,800 additional innocent defendants who were framed and convicted of crimes in 15 large-scale police scandals and later cleared in 'group exonerations.' ... The main reason for this racial disproportion in convictions of innocent drug defendants is that police enforce drug laws more vigorously against African Americans than against members of the white majority, despite strong evidence that both groups use drugs at equivalent rates. African Americans are more frequently stopped, searched, arrested, and convicted, including in cases in which they are innocent. The extreme form of this practice is systematic racial profiling in drug-law enforcement.'

8 Sierra Leone Truth and Reconciliation Commission, Final Report (Freetown: The Commission, 2004), 3A: Chapter Two, Governance: Introduction, paras. 27–34.

over the years, especially those involving human rights, accords well with this global movement of self-scrutiny. Furthermore, the treason trial of Francis Mischeck Minah,[9] arguably the most widely critiqued in the jurisprudential history of Sierra Leone's Judiciary, makes, *inter alia*, an excellent choice for this analysis.

It is essential to highlight a fundamental limitation this work suffers from the outset. For reasons that are too well known about the state of public records keeping in Sierra Leone, it was impossible to lay hands all the original court records for this analysis, such as transcripts of the trial in the High Court or the Notices of Appeal filed by the convicted persons both in the Court of Appeal and Supreme Court. Thus, this work has relied on the Appeals Judgement of the Supreme Court as the primary source of information regarding the entire trial process. Admittedly, this limits appreciation of the full scope of the submissions made at trial by the accused as well as the Trial Judge's summing-up to the jury. Similarly, the work has not benefitted from the originality in assessing the actual grounds of appeals as formulated by the appellants. Reliance on the Supreme Court Judgement means that the arguments analysed in this work are based entirely on the Supreme Court judges' understanding of those arguments and their prioritization of the issues raised for consideration.

Notwithstanding this shortcoming, faith should be maintained that being professional judges sitting in the highest court of the land, they would have kept to their oaths of allegiance to the Constitution of the Republic and acted fairly and justly to all manner of people as by law required. Furthermore, from discussions with some of the key players who worked on the case in defence counsel, reasonable assurance was received that the issues ventilated in this work from the Supreme Court Judgement affecting, in particular Francis Mischeck Minah, are a fair reflection of what obtained in the courtroom some three and a half decades ago.

2. Francis Mischeck Minah - 1925–1987

Francis Minah was a prominent politician who later became vice president of Sierra Leone in the 1980s.[10] Born on August 19, 1929, in Sawula, Pujehun District, in the Southern Province of Sierra Leone, Minah was

---

9 *The State v Gabriel Mohamed Tennyson Kaikai and 17 Others,* [1989] SLSC 9 (29 September 1989), https://sierralii.gov.sl/akn/sl/judgement/slsc/1989/9/eng@1989-09-29.

10 Magbaily C. Fyle, Historical Dictionary of Sierra Leone, 3rd ed. (Lanham, MD: Scarecrow Press, 2006).

highly educated. After completing secondary school at Methodist Boys High School in Freetown, Sierra Leone, he studied at King's College of London University in Britain. On his return home, he worked as a Development Officer in the Civil Service of Sierra Leone in the 1950s. He later returned to Britain to study law, graduating from Gray's Inn in 1962. He returned to Sierra Leone and established a private legal practice for a short period. In 1967, he entered politics as a Member of Parliament for Pujehun South Constituency.

Minah did not declare for the Sierra Leone People's Party (SLPP) in the 1967 elections, despite expectations for southern politicians. Instead, he later joined the All Peoples' Congress (APC) government under Siaka Stevens as a minister. He served in various roles, including minister of foreign affairs, health, and justice, as well as attorney-general. Ultimately, he became vice president of Sierra Leone. Not long after President J. S. Momoh, Siaka Stevens' successor, took office, Minah, as Vice President, was implicated in a plot to overthrow the government. He was arrested, tried, convicted of treason and executed.[11] Minah's political career and its potential influence on his trial, conviction, and execution will be explored in a separate discussion within this work.

3. The Treason Charges

By an instrument of indictment entitled *The State v Gabriel Mohamed Tennyson Kaikai and Others*,[12] Francis Mischeck Minah and 17 other persons were charged with four counts of treason, misprison of treason and murder. Gabriel Mohamed Tennyson Kaikai (aka 'GMT Kaikai') was a senior police officer and mastermind of the alleged coup. He was the first accused, while Francis Minah was Fifth Accused. The two were the most prominent figures indicted. Minah was charged with one count of treason. Also indicted were relatives of both GMT Kaikai and Minah.[13]

All 18 accused persons were arraigned before the High Court in Freetown in June 1987 on the four-count indictment. Count 1 charged the first 16 accused persons with the offence of treason contrary to S. 3(1)(a) of the Treason and State Offences Act, No. 10 of 1963. Two of the 18 were charged

---

11 Fyle, Historical Dictionary, p.132.

12 *The State v Kaikai*, [1989] SLSC 9.

13 Solomon E. Berewa, A New Perspective on Governance, Leadership, Conflict and Nation Building in Sierra Leone (Bloomington, IN: AuthorHouse, 2011).

with the offence of misprision of treason contrary to law, while four were also charged with the offence of murder contrary to law.[14]

The case for the prosecution was that between June 1, 1986, and on divers days between that day and March 23, 1987, Gabriel Mohamed Tennyson Kaikai, first accused and 15 others committed the offence of treason, in that they prepared to overthrow the Government of Sierra Leone by unlawful means. Four among them were also charged with the murder of one Mohamed Adama Rogers, a State Security Division (SSD) Officer, and two others were each charged with the offence of misprision of treason.[15]

The count on treason was supported in the particulars of offence by twenty-six overt acts,[16] which in themselves became the subject of challenges by the accused regarding the form of the indictment at trial and on appeal. Four of those overt acts contained information that supported the charge against the fifth accused. The overt acts implicating Francis Minah read as follows: [17]

> '1. On the 16 June 1987 and on divers days between that day and the 23rd day of March 1987 in Sierra Leone the said Gabriel Mohamed Tennyson Kaikai, Prince Deen Kaikai, Joseph John Harding, Daniel Sulaiman Kaikai, Francis Mischeck Minah, David Abu Samu, Francis Augustine Ensah, Francis Massaquoi, Amara Allieu Tarawallie, Josephus Abiodun Williams, Patrick Benedict Kaikai, Hassan Morlai Conteh, Conrad Innis, Kazim Allie, Raymond Brima Dorwie and Haruna Vandy-Jimmy conspired together and with other persons unknown to overthrow the Government of Sierra Leone in that they agreed:
>
> (a) To lay ambush, attack and kill the President of Sierra Leone Major General Dr. Joseph Saidu Momoh.
>
> (b) To make a broadcast over the Sierra Leone Broadcasting Service announcing the dissolution of Parliament, the suspension of the Constitution of Sierra Leone,

[14] *The State v Kaikai,* [1989] SLSC pp.43-51.

[15] *The State v Kaikai,* [1989] SLSC p.51.

[16] *The State v Kaikai,* [1989] SLSC p.43.

[17] *The State v Kaikai,* [1989] SLSC p.44.

the disbanding of the Recognized party[18] and the formation of a National Reformation Council.

(c) To impose a dusk-to-dawn curfew in Sierra Leone.

(d) To overthrow and take over the Government of Sierra Leone by unlawful means.

2. Francis Mischeck Minah on a date unknown between the 1st and 23rd March 1987 in Freetown, incited Jamil Sahid Mohamed and Gabriel Mohamed Tennyson Kaikai and others unknown to overthrow the Government of Sierra Leone by unlawful means.

3. On a date unknown between the 1st July 1986 and 23rd March 1987 Francis Mischeck Minah incited Haruna Vandy-Jimmy to solicit and collect contributions in furtherance of a plot to overthrow the Government of Sierra Leone by unlawful means.

4. On a date unknown between the 1st February, 1987 and 21st March, 1987 Haruna Vandy-Jimmy collected from inhabitants of Wonde Chiefdom, Bo District in the Southern Province of Sierra Leone and other persons unknown – the sum of Le 80,000 (Eighty Thousand Leones) on behalf of Francis Mischeck Minah in furtherance of a plot to overthrow the Government of Sierra Leone by unlawful means.'

Several acts of preparation were laid in the overt acts, including the allegation of conspiracy implicating all the accused persons to overthrow the Government in that they agreed, *inter alia*, to ambush, attack and kill the President of the Republic of Sierra Leone, disband the recognised party declare a dusk to dawn curfew, form a National Reformation Council and take over the Government by unlawful means.[19]

The prosecution further alleged that in the act of preparation to overthrow the Government, several persons were solicited and incited to join the plot,

---

18 The Constitution of Sierra Leone, Act No. 12 of 1978, S. 5 states that '(T)he Recognised Party' is a constitutional expression referring to the APC Party as the sole recognised political party in Sierra Leone under the then 1978 One Party Constitution.

19 *The State v Kaikai,* [1989] SLSC p.51.

monies were collected from individuals and paid to others in pursuit of the plot to overthrow the Government by unlawful means and that arms and ammunition were collected from persons and stored in places, while orders were issued to some of the accused in furtherance of the plot.[20]

The defence, represented by counsel, advanced several critical arguments to challenge the prosecution's case against Minah, emphasizing procedural and evidential deficiencies to contest his conviction. These arguments are particularly relevant to the article's focus on judicial integrity and the rule of law, as they highlight potential political interference and procedural lapses in Sierra Leone's judiciary, issues central to the non-assignment of cases and broader access to justice.

The defence primarily argued that the prosecution failed to prove Minah's direct involvement in the alleged treasonous plot beyond reasonable doubt, as required by Sierra Leone's criminal procedure. The indictment listed specific overt acts, including Minah's alleged incitement of Jamil Sahid Mohamed and Gabriel Mohamed Tennyson Kaikai to overthrow the government and his incitement of Haruna Vandy-Jimmy to collect contributions for the plot. However, the defence contended that the evidence was insufficient, relying heavily on uncorroborated accomplice testimony from prosecution witnesses, e.g., PW18, PW21, PW33, which required a judicial warning about the dangers of conviction without corroboration. The defence asserted that the trial judge, Williams JA, failed to adequately direct the jury on this rule, risking a miscarriage of justice, as uncorroborated accomplice evidence is inherently unreliable.

Additionally, the defence challenged the admissibility of certain evidence against Minah, arguing that hearsay and improperly obtained statements were wrongly admitted. Specifically, they contested the prosecution's reliance on statements allegedly made by co-accused, which were inadmissible unless Minah expressly or implicitly adopted them. The defence argued that no such adoption occurred, and the trial judge's failure to instruct the jury to disregard these statements prejudiced Minah's case. Furthermore, they questioned the prosecution's use of circumstantial evidence, asserting that the trial judge did not sufficiently clarify that the burden of proof remained on the prosecution to establish guilt beyond reasonable doubt, particularly given the political context of Minah's high-profile roles as a former minister and vice president under Siaka Stevens' APC government.

---

[20] *The State v Kaikai*, [1989] SLSC p.51.

The defence also highlighted the political dimensions of the trial, suggesting that Minah's conviction may have been influenced by his prominent political career, a point the article notes for separate discussion. As a former Attorney-General and Justice Minister, Minah's involvement in the APC government made him a target for political retribution, potentially undermining the trial's fairness. This argument aligns with the article's critique of political interference in the judiciary, as noted by the Truth and Reconciliation Commission, and underscores how such dynamics contribute to judicial failures like non-assignment of cases.

4. Procedural Matters: Trial, Conviction, Sentences and Appeals

The trial proceeded before Williams, J.A.[21] and a jury in the High Court in Freetown from 1st June 1987 and was concluded on 17th October 1987. The prosecution called thirty-six witnesses, some of whom gave evidence on their behalf, while others made statements from the dock. In total, there was a total of forty-four exhibits.

At the close of the case for both the prosecution and the defence, and after a lengthy summing-up by the learned trial Judge, which lasted several days, the jury returned a unanimous guilty verdict in respect of all the accused. The death sentence was passed on the first 16 accused, while the 17th and 18th accused were sentenced to terms of imprisonment of 4 and 7 years, respectively.

The Court of Appeal allowed the appeals of the 7th, 11th, 14th and 15th accused but confirmed all the other convictions and sentences handed down by the High Court. The fourteen convicted prisoners, including the first and fifth accused, filed further appeals to the Supreme Court from the Judgement of the Court of Appeal. Many grounds of appeal were filed on behalf of each appellant, but they were substantially identical or had common ground with those filed on behalf of the other appellants. The Supreme Court, in a unanimous judgement, affirmed the Court of Appeal judgement in respect of the fifth accused and many others, which in effect amounted to upholding the conviction and sentence against Minah.

---

[21] Justice D.E.M. Williams JA was sitting judge of the Court of Appeal when he got assigned/was selected as the trial judge of this case.

5. Claims of Injustice Against Minah, What Validity?

Francis Minah's indictment, conviction, sentence and execution for treason is arguably the most critiqued criminal trial in the history of the Judiciary. The Judiciary of Sierra Leone tried several treason cases of questionable validity and fairness. Notable examples include the 1975 trial of *Mohamed Sorie Fornah and 14 Others.*[22] Earlier, the 1971 trial involved former army commander *Brigadier John Bangura and Others.*[23] Never before had an alleged coup leader held such a senior government position as in this case. After all, Minah was the sitting Vice President of the ruling APC Government, the second gentleman of the Republic. That, plus the nature of the evidence adduced at trial to support the charge against him, made the mere thought of Francis Mischeck Minah being involved in a coup preposterous and astounding.

There were thus widespread skepticism and incredulity, short only of an uproar when it became clear that Minah had been charged as one of the coup plotters. That skepticism did not, however, give way to public sympathy for him or the others for several reasons. In a bid to put down the coup once state authorities had become aware of it, they were confronted by some of the coup makers in a gunfight in which one state security personnel, Special Security Division (SSD) officer Mohamed Adama Rogers was killed.[24]

Secondly, the first accused, G.M.T. Kaikai, a senior police officer and former *aide de camp* (ADC) to President Siaka Stevens, had had a public spat with his boss, the Inspector General of Police James Bambay Kamara, which led to his demotion in rank for insubordination after a disciplinary committee hearing.[25] Kaikai's attitude toward his superior officer earned him significant public opprobrium. But beyond this, Minah's political style of ruthless ambition within the APC party[26] bought him little public sympathy despite the incredulity of his involvement in the coup. He was intolerant to the opposition and was known to have acted with random brutality, even against his constituents in Pujehun District.[27]

---

22 *Mohamed Sorie Fornah and Others v The State*, Cr. App. 31/74, judgment delivered April 30, 1975 (unreported); See also, Forna, Devil That Danced on the Water.

23 *The State v Brigadier John Bangura and Others*, (unreported).

24 *The State v Kaikai*, [1989] SLSC p.51.

25 Berewa, A New Perspective, p. 84.

26 Berewa, A New Perspective, p. 105-106.

27 Cocorioko SL Newspaper, "Why all the fuss about Minah?," February 10, 2008, http://cocorioko.net/why-all-the-fuss-over-f-m-minah/.

Minah may have set the tone for this widespread criticism of unfairness in his allocutus before the trial judge, Justice D.E.M. Williams. In response to the question whether he had anything to say before being sentenced, Minah tersely stated, 'I cannot help but convince myself that this is an orchestrated allegation that has been levied against me to get rid of me.'[28] Rightly or wrongly, this theme of injustice came to be echoed reverberatingly by writers, journalists, poets, researchers, scholars and even musicians, within and outside Sierra Leone, in most cases without any factual or legal basis to support the claim.

The TRC, in its final report, described it as 'an improbable coup'[29] Solomon E. Berewa, lead Counsel for Minah in the High Court who later became Vice President of Sierra Leone, wrote in his book that he felt 'the allegations were flimsy and preposterous and that it was unlikely that a jury would convict Minah on those charges.'[30] Another of Minah's defence counsel, Garvas Betts, speaking to the New York Times, described the whole issue thus: 'The whole thing is pretty hollow … I don't think you can connect some of the characters.'[31]

In academic dictionaries and encyclopedias, it is recorded of Francis Minah that 'In 1987, he was falsely accused of plotting a coup against President Momoh.'[32] ExecutedToday.com, an online news outlet that chronicles historical executions worldwide, called it a 'farcical trial,'[33] while John Musa, a US-trained lawyer, in an article a four-part series, highlights the unfairness of the charges and trial thus:

> 'It is my contention that Minah was wrongly charged and the Trial Court, the Court of Appeal and the Supreme Court erred or deliberately conjoined in the alleged conspiracy to juridically murder an innocent man. Courts invariably err and judges act politically especially in treason trials where the evidence is often times picayune.'[34]

---

28 Sierra Leone Live, "Was Francis M. Minah Guilty of Treason?," July 30, 2001, https://sierraleonelive.com/was-francis-m-minah-guilty-of-treason-part-4/.

29 Sierra Leone Truth and Reconciliation Commission, Final Report, para. 95.

30 Berewa, A New Perspective, p. 85.

31 New York Times, "At a Trial in Sierra Leone, a Script for a Coup," October 11, 1987, https://www.nytimes.com/1987/10/11/world/at-a-trial-in-sierra-leone-a-script-for-a-coup.html.

32 Academic Dictionaries and Encyclopedias, s.v. "National Registry of Exonerations," accessed December 31, 2024, https://en-academic.com/dic.nsf/enwiki/6085635.

33 ExecutedToday.com, "1989: Francis Minah, Vice President of Sierra Leone," October 7, 2016, https://www.executedtoday.com/tag/francis-minah/.

34 Sierra Leone Live, "Was Francis M. Minah Guilty? Part II.

Sierra Leonean poet Omar Farouk Sesay in a recent piece titled 'Memory Markers for the Dead of Yesterday,'[35] wrote:

> 'At the gallows of the prison, we will plant memory markers
>
> To mark the spot where, on October 7, 1989, Francis Mishak Minah,
>
> Gabriel Mohamed Tennyson Kaikai and others were executed
>
> After a treason trial that is still on trial in the court rooms of
>
> Our consciences.'

Perhaps not to be outdone in this national outcry over injustice against Minah, popular Sierra Leonean traditional musician Salia Koroma produced an album recorded around 1987-1989, titled, 'The Country Sierra Leone is an Older Woman.'[36] The song highlights issues about the trial.[37]

Some of this outcry is simply a re-echo of the unsubstantiated claims about alleged injustice against Minah. Others, it has to be said, coming from more informed minds about the process, deserve much closer and careful scrutiny. Determining whether the alleged unfairness rises to the level of a miscarriage of justice requires a dual approach. The first involves an analysis of the legal process itself to see where the injustice or unfairness lies. The other approach will involve examining the several non-legal theories and unsubstantiated statements that would appear to give some motive why anyone would want to cook up a coup against no less a person than the second gentleman of the Republic. Greater weight will be accorded to the findings from the former analysis than the latter, the analysis in the former being based on facts, evidence and legal principles that were before the court

---

35 Sierra Leone Telegraph, "Memory Markers for the Dead of Yesterday," November 25, 2021, https://www.thesierraleonetelegraph.com/memory-markers-for-the-dead-of-yesterday/.

36 Nikiibu Notebook, "Salia Koroma on Francis Minah: 'The Country Sierra Leone is an Older Woman,'" December 1, 2014, https://nikiibu.wordpress.com/2014/12/01/salia-koroma-on-francis-minah-the-country-sierra-leone-is-an-older-woman/.

37 Koroma, known for his topical songs addressing social and political issues, drew from older 1950s and 1960s compositions to craft a poignant commentary on Minah's case, portraying Sierra Leone as an 'older woman' deserving respect and fairness. The song reflects widespread belief in Minah's innocence, fueled by allegations of political vendetta under President Joseph Saidu Momoh's regime, and served as a cultural protest against judicial bias and lack of transparency. This artistic response underscores how Minah's trial, amid Sierra Leone's history of politicized justice, resonated beyond the courtroom, contributing to eroded public trust in the judiciary and echoing the Truth and Reconciliation Commission's critiques of systemic corruption (TRC Report, Volume 1, page 27). Koroma's work exemplifies how cultural expressions amplified calls for accountability, paralleling the article's examination of non-assignment delays in contemporary cases.

and adjudicated upon. Those are facts, evidence and legal principles that are ascertainable and justiciable.

6. The Facts, The Evidence and the Law

i) *Challenges against the indictment: Overt Acts*

In the Supreme Court, Minah and the other appellants contended that the laying of overt acts in the indictment is not permissible under S. 3 (1)(a) of the Treason and State Offences Act (TASOA), 1963, there being no reference to overt acts in any of the provisions under the Act. They also contended that laying several overt acts under the same count rendered the count duplicitous and void. Thirdly, they argued that since the repeal of the Treason Act of 1351 by virtue of S. 19 (2) of the Treason and State Offences Act (TASOA), 1963, the inclusion of overt acts in a charge of treason ceased to have any place in Sierra Leone's criminal laws, referring in particular to Section 74 of the Courts Act. No. 31 of 1965 and the Criminal Procedure Act, 1965 (Hereafter, CPA, 1965), S.3, Part 1, captioned, 'General Provisions Procedure.'[38]

The most serious contention on challenges to the indictment was the permissibility of laying overt acts under Sierra Leone treason laws. All the convicted persons challenged this practice at trial and on appeal. They relied on the Judgement of the Court of Appeal in the Treason Appeal of *Mohamed Sorie Fornah and Others v The State.*[39] The Appellants in Fornah's case had similarly raised the issue before the Court of Appeal as to whether there was any legal basis under Sierra Leone law for the inclusion of overt acts in charges under the Treason and State Offences Act (TASOA), 1963. However, this reliance on Fornah's case turned out to be of no real value to Minah and his colleagues as that the issue was never decided in that case but was left open only to resurface now.

In Fornah's treason trial, Luke J.S.C sitting in the Court of Appeal gave the following insightful historical background about the inclusion of overt acts in charging treason:

> 'The necessity for overt acts in information or Indictment of Treason was first introduced by the Treason Act, of 1351.

---

[38] *The State v Kaikai,* [1989] SLSC.

[39] Mohamed Sorie Fornah and Others v. The State, Cr. App. 31/74, judgment delivered April 30, 1975 (unreported); See also, Forna, Devil That Danced on the Water.

> According to the statute that requirement related only to the species of treason of 'Being adherent to the King's enemies in his realm', and not to any other species of treason. That species of treason was required to be proved by "open deed," which in more modern times has been defined as, "any act manifesting the criminal object."[40] In the 17th & 18th centuries, the Courts by judicial interpretation, extended the requirement of an overt act to all species of treason. But the Treason Act of 1351 is no longer applicable in Sierra Leone. It was repealed by S. 19 (2) of the TASOA, 1963. The question then is: are overt acts necessary in Indictments for the species of treason created by the TASOA, 1963? That is an arguable question, but it is not necessary to decide it in this appeal because the State chose to lay overt acts in the indictment in the instant case.'

In coming to a decision on this issue in Minah's trial, therefore, the Supreme Court, S.M.F. Kutubu CJ, Presiding, first considered the ordinary lexical meaning of the term 'overt act' which from various sources generally carried a sense of openness, unconcealed, not covered, open to view or knowledge, plain, evident, not a secret, an open act, one consisting of something stronger than mere words, and like connotations. Some sources also pointed out that its use is principally connected with treason and conspiracy.

Next, the law justices looked to statutory sources for authority permitting the use of overt acts in charging treason. The Treason and State Offences Act (TASOA), under which the charges were brought had no provision relating to overt acts nor the Constitution.[41] The CPA, 1965,[42] which regulates criminal proceedings in Sierra Leone, also did not contain any provision specifically authorizing the use of overt acts in charging offences.

They then examined the provisions of Sect. 51 of the CPA, 1965, which relates to the preferring of charges. It states:

> 'Every information or indictment shall contain and shall be sufficient if it contains a statement of the specific offence or offences with which the accused is charged, together with

40 *R v Thistlewood* (1820) 33 St. Tr. 681.
41 Act No.12 of 1978 (as amended), S. 125.
42 Act No. 32 of 1965.

> such particulars as may be necessary for giving reasonable information as to the nature of the offence charged.'

They also considered Rule 3(4) of the indictment rules, which reads:

> 'After the statement of offence particulars of such offence shall be set out in ordinary language in which the use of technical terms shall not be necessary.
>
> Provided that (a) where any rule of law or any Act or statute limits the particulars of an offence which are required to be given in an information or indictment, nothing in this rule shall require any more particulars to be given than those so required. (b) It shall be sufficient if only the words of the section of the enactment creating the offence are set out in the particulars of the offence.'

And finally Rule 3(5), which states:

> 'The forms set out in the Appendix to these rules, or forms conforming thereto as nearly as may be, shall be used in cases to which they are applicable; and in other cases, forms to the like effect or conforming thereto as nearly as may be shall used, the statement of offence and the particulars of offence being varied according to the circumstances in each case.'

Following these references, the law justices reasoned that 'the Indictment as laid under S.3(1) of the Treason and State Offences Act (TASOA), 1963 together with the overt acts was correct, proper and in conformity with the provisions of S.51 of the CPA, 1965 and Rules 3(4) and 3(5) thereof.' They stated that the overt acts laid in the count 'are no more than further particulars of the particulars of the offence charged and that they are in themselves not specific or distinct charges but merely further particulars.' The law justices relied heavily on the East African Court of Appeal decision in the Tanzanian case, *Mattaka & Others v The People.*[43]

In *Mattaka*, several persons had similarly been charged with treason under section 39 of the Penal Code of Tanzania. The Code made no provisions for the laying of overt acts in charging the offence of treason, but

---

[43] E.A.L.R. 627 (1963).

the prosecution followed the English practice of setting out the various overt acts in each count after having first set out the statement of offence. Although the laying of overt acts in a charge of treason had no provision in their Penal Code, the prosecution was deemed to have complied fully with the specific requirements for laying a charge in an indictment, as per section 135 of the Code[44] which requires the prosecution to set out a statement of the specific offence charged and then give such particulars as may be necessary for giving reasonable information as to the nature of the offence charged. Upon appeal against their convictions to the East African Court of Appeal, the Court did not question this procedure, which was, in their view, quite correct.[45]

ii) *Challenges against the indictment - Duplicity*

The second most crucial challenge against the indictment at trial and on appeal was the question of duplicity. The Appellants argued that the prosecution had charged several separate distinct offences under the single count of treason which, if correct, would be contrary to the charging rules in the CPA, 1965 and would render the count void. The Supreme Court explained the rule against duplicity thus: 'in law where two or more offences are charged in the same count in an indictment, the indictment is to that extent bad for duplicity.'[46] They explained further, 'the law against duplicity is to ensure the protection of the accused person, by not subjecting him to an unfair trial so that he knows exactly what case he has to answer. It also allows him to plead *autre fois convict*[47] or *autre fois acquit*[48] at a later date as the case may be.'

One limb of the argument against duplicity was that the prosecution had charged the Accused of 'preparing or endeavoring' to overthrow the Government of Sierra Leone under S. 3(1) of the TASOA, 1963, when in fact this amounts to separate and distinct offences under the section. They argue that by laying out the several overt acts in the particulars under the count, which in themselves show preparatory acts of endeavouring to overthrow the government, the prosecution had blended those acts with the act of

44 This provision is ipsissima verba with section 51 of Sierra Leone's Criminal Procedure Act, 1965.

45 *The State v Kaikai*, [1989] SLSC p.54-55.

46 *The State v Kaikai*, [1989] SLSC p.54-55.

47 This term translates to 'previously convicted.' It is a defendant's plea stating that they have already been tried for and convicted of the same crime they are now being charged with. Like 'autrefois acquit,' a successful 'autrefois convict' plea prevents a second prosecution for the same offence.

48 This is a French term that translates to 'previously acquitted.' It is a defendant's plea stating that they have already been tried for and acquitted of the same crime they are now being charged with. If this plea is successful, it bars any further proceedings on the indictment.

'preparing' charged in the statement of offence, thereby making the count duplicitous.

In dealing with this argument, the Judges first laid out the basis for establishing duplicity in a count in an indictment. They stated, 'duplicity in a count is a matter of form, not of evidence called in support of the count. To ascertain whether a count is bad for duplicity, one must examine the statement and particulars of the offence. If an examination shows that two or more offences have been charged therein, then the count is bad for duplicity.'[49]

The Appellants had relied on the Sierra Leone treason case, *David Lansana & 11 Others v Regina*,[50] where the Court of Appeal set aside the conviction because the counts were bad for duplicity. The Appellants, in that case, were charged with 'preparing' or 'endeavouring' to overthrow the Government of Sierra Leone under, amongst others, Count 3(1) of the Treason and State Offences Act (TASOA), 1963.

However, the Supreme Court reasoned that this was not the position in the instant case. The contention that the various overt acts laid in the indictment make Count One bad for duplicity was, in their view, 'insupportable in law and wholly untenable.' The various overt acts were laid not as substantive offences but as further particulars of the particulars of the offence of the one and only count of treason in the indictment. The Law Justices held that it was permissible to lay any number of overt acts in the same count of an indictment without making the count bad for duplicity.[51]

The Law Justices, in this same breadth, addressed an adjunct argument by the appellants that the Learned Trial Judge had misdirected the jury when he said that where several overt acts are laid in a count of an indictment and a judgement is given on a general verdict of guilty on that count, such judgement will be sustained, though some of the matters alleged as overt acts may be improperly so alleged, provided that the count contains allegations of overt acts that are sufficient or sufficiently laid. The Justices affirmed that in law, proof of one overt act would sustain the count provided that the overt act so proved is a sufficient overt act of the species of the treason count in the indictment.[52]

The third limb of duplicity argued by the appellants was that the count of treason charging 'preparing to overthrow the Government of Sierra Leone

49 *The State v Kaikai*, [1989] SLSC p.54-55.
50 *David Lansana & 11 Others v Regina*, (1970–71) A.L.R. (S.L.) 186.
51 *The State v Kaikai*, [1989] SLSC p.60.
52 *The State v Kaikai*, [1989] SLSC p.60.

by unlawful means' also included a conspiracy charge, which made the count duplicitous. According to the appellants, the several overt acts laid in the particulars introduced acts of preparation which amounted to a conspiracy or conspiracies to overthrow the Government of Sierra Leone by unlawful means. The Law Justices reasoned, as in the previous argument on duplicity, that whereas the count in the indictment charged the appellants with 'preparing to overthrow the Government of Sierra Leone by unlawful means' which is the forbidden act under the count, the overt acts provided evidence of conspiracy or conspiracies only but did not make the count duplicitous. Therefore, the evidence of an agreement made to overthrow the government by unlawful means, even though conspiratorial in nature, was to support the offence of preparing to overthrow under S. 3(1) of the Act. The Law Justices posited a line of authorities to support this position, including *Mulchay v The Queen*,[53] *Lansana & 11 Others v Regina*[54] and *R v. Greenfield.*[55] In *Greenfield*, it was held that the fact that the evidence disclosed other conspiracies did not make the count duplicitous.

iii) *Challenge against the admission of hearsay evidence*

Francis Minah and Haruna Vandy Jimmy, charged as the fifth and sixteenth Accused, respectively, became the fifth and twelfth Appellants in the Supreme Court. It was argued on their behalf that the Court of Appeal erred in dismissing their appeal against the wrongful admission of evidence against them at trial, which they alleged was hearsay. The evidence of DW 20, a District Officer called by the twelfth Appellant, was based on an intelligence report he received about meetings allegedly held at Nyannihun Village, Wonde Chiefdom, Bo District. The Appellants argued that the Court of Appeal erred in dismissing their appeal regarding the nature of the said evidence, the nature of the Learned Trial Judge's direction on it, and the wrongful basis on which the Learned Trial Judge admitted that evidence. They argued that the Learned Trial Judge misdirected himself in admitting the alleged hearsay evidence of DW 20. They argued that evidence should never have been given or admitted, considering its prejudicial effect on the minds of the jury.

It should be pointed out that this ground of appeal and the one to be dealt with next on an *alibi* defence rest on perhaps the strongest, if not the best, case

53 *Mulcahy v The Queen*, 1963 CanLII 1110 (SCC).

54 *David Lansana & 11 Others v Regina*, 186.

55 *R v Greenfield*, (1973) 3 All E.R. 1050.

that the prosecution had against Francis Minah on the charge of treason. It is based on overt acts three and four as formulated in the indictment, which are the only allegations of substance that implicate Minah directly in activities preparatory to the alleged coup.

To address the various strands of argument on hearsay, the Supreme Court Justices commenced their deliberation by first laying out the rule against hearsay as formulated by the Privy Council in *Subramanian v Public Prosecutor*,[56] which goes:

> 'Evidence of a statement made to a witness by a person who is not himself called as a witness may or may not be hearsay. It is hearsay and inadmissible when the object of the evidence is to establish the truth of what is contained in the statement. It is not hearsay and is admissible when it is proposed to establish by the evidence not the truth of the statement, but the fact that it was made. The fact that the statement was made, quite apart from its truth, is frequently relevant in considering the mental state and conduct thereafter of the witness or of some other person in whose presence the statement was made.'[57]

The prosecution alleged that on Sunday, 22 March 1987, the fifth and twelfth Appellants convened a meeting at Nyannihun, Wonde Chiefdom Bo District, where monies were collected in furtherance of a conspiracy to overthrow the Government of Sierra Leone by unlawful means. The prosecution called many witnesses who gave evidence establishing these facts. Both Appellants denied the allegation during their trial and produced alibi defences to show they were not present at the alleged meeting on this date. In addition, they both called witnesses to support their alibi. Unfortunately, DW 20, called by the twelfth Appellant, surprisingly testified that as a Senior District Officer in Bo District, he received intelligence reports from the area indicating that a meeting was held on this date at that location by the fifth and twelfth Appellants and that monies were collected on behalf of the Appellants. The fifth and twelfth Appellants argued that this evidence amounted to hearsay and should not have been admitted in the first place.

---

56 *Subramanian v Public Prosecutor,* [1965] 1 W.L.R. 965.

57 *The State v Kaikai,* [1989] SLSC p.80.

In his summing up at the end of the trial in the High Court, the Learned Trial Judge directed the jury to consider this evidence in considering their verdict, and if satisfied as to its credibility, they should use it in determining the verdict they will give against the fifth and twelfth Appellants. Both Accused deemed this summing up to the jury a misdirection. To them, not only had evidence that offended the hearsay rule been wrongly admitted, the direction on that evidence to the jury, to take it into consideration and give a verdict on it against them if considered credible, was equally wrong and unfair, in that evidence was prejudicial to the jury and would lead to an unsafe verdict.

However, the Law Justices in the Supreme Court reasoned that the fact that evidence is wrongly admitted does not make the verdict necessarily unsafe unless it can be shown that the evidence has influenced the jury's verdict. Before assessing the prejudice caused by wrongful admission of the alleged hearsay evidence to determine whether it affected the substantial justice of the trial, the Justices first considered the nature and effect of the other evidence on this issue that was adduced at trial. Barring the evidence of DW 20 for a moment, they considered whether there was other evidence before the jury for their consideration in assessing the guilt or otherwise of the Appellants. It turned out that several other witnesses had testified for both sides on this issue, whose evidence was before the jury for consideration and that was not in controversy. The Justices noted that some of the witnesses called to support the allegation by the prosecution were, in fact, very emphatic in their assertions, particularly their identification of the Appellants. On the other hand, the Appellants had called witnesses to support their alibi, that there were neither at Nyannihun on Sunday, 22 March 1987, nor took part in any transactions there.

The Justices took the view on a preliminary consideration that the Learned Trial Judge had, in summing up, properly directed the jury on the issue of the burden of proof. He had 'carefully and repeatedly explained to them'[58] the burden and standard of proof in criminal proceedings and the jury had heard the witnesses and watched their demeanor and their credibility before coming to a verdict. In the Learned Justice's view, therefore, even barring the evidence of DW 20, there was other evidence to be left to the jury for their consideration on the right direction in determining the guilt or otherwise of the Appellants. They were of the view that the jury would

[58] *The State v Kaikai*, [1989] SLSC p.84.

have arrived at the same verdict if the evidence complained of had not been admitted.

iv) *Alibi Defence*

As noted, the prosecution's most robust case against the fifth and twelfth Appellants rested on the allegations contained in overt acts 3 and 4 in the indictment, as formulated. Therefore, not only did the Appellants vigorously challenge the admission of the prosecution's evidence implicating them in the acts alleged, and against evidence of this being left to the jury for their consideration, they also produced an *alibi* defence each to negate the allegation that they had both attended a meeting in Nyannihun on 22 March 1987 where monies were collected in furtherance of the conspiracy to overthrow the Government of Sierra Leone by unlawful means. The Appellants contended that it was highly improbable, if not impossible, based on the evidence both for the prosecution and the defence, for them to have been together in Nyannihun Village at the time alleged. As produced in the Supreme Court's Judgement, the *alibi* for each goes thus:

> 'In his evidence at his trial, the 12th Appellant Haruna Vandy-Jimmy recalled the morning of Saturday 21st March 1987 in Bo. He left Bo that day and travelled to Freetown, arriving there at 4 p.m. He proceeded to 44 Wellington Road, Kissy Mess Mess, where he met P.W. 36 Anthony Kallon. He did not go out until the morning hours of the 22nd when he travelled to Freetown to attend Parliament on Monday 23rd March 1987. In short, he was not at Nyannihun on Sunday 22nd March and could not have done what the prosecution alleged he did.
>
> The 5th Appellant in his evidence stated that at 12.30 p.m. on Friday 20th March 1987 he and his party left Freetown for Bo, arriving there by 4 p.m. They had lunch in Bo at one Lansana Kallon's residence, and took off at 4.45 p.m. for Pujehun arriving there at 7 p.m.
>
> On Saturday 21st March 1987 he held a meeting at Yoni from 11 a.m.-1.40 p.m. On Sunday 22nd March 1987 after seeing into accommodation, he left Pujehun for Bo at 12.30 p.m. arriving there at 3 p.m. They had lunch at Lansana Kallon's

residence and the party left for Freetown at about 4 p.m. arriving in Freetown at 7.15 p.m.'[59]

The prosecution called several witnesses not only to prove that meetings were held in Nyannihun on the date in question but also to show that the Appellants participated in those meetings and that monies were collected in furtherance of a conspiracy to overthrow the Government of Sierra Leone by unlawful means. The Appellants also called witnesses who adduced evidence refuting the evidence of prosecution witnesses. Although the Appellants were not legally bound to do so, they called witnesses to support their *alibi* defences.

On behalf of the twelfth Appellant, it was contended that his alleged presence at Nyannihun must have been a case of mistaken identity, but this theory appeared not to have been developed further than just a mere statement. The Learned Trial Judge in the High Court had considered the whole evidence adduced by both the prosecution and the defence, including the respective alibi defences and dealt with the several burdens and standards of proof. The Supreme Court noted that there was no evidence of any misdirection on the part of the Learned Trial Judge in his summing-up to the jury, which could have amounted to a shifting of the burden of proof from the prosecution to the Appellants in respect of their respective alibi defences. In their verdict, the jury chose not to believe the alibi defence of the fifth and twelfth Appellants, and they believed the prosecution's case instead.[60]

The Justices of the Supreme Court did not see a reason to disagree with the Court of Appeal's dismissal of this ground of appeal and by that decision, Minah's fate was sealed.

v) *Alleged Misdirection to the Jury regarding Exhibit JJJJ*

It was argued on behalf of fifth Appellant Francis Minah that Exh. JJJJ, an unsworn statement of the first Appellant GMT Kaikai, did not constitute evidence against him and it was a fundamental misdirection of the Learned Trial Judge when he directed the jury that Exh. JJJJ could be used against fifth Appellant. It was further submitted that the Learned Trial Judge had a legal duty to inform the jury that Exh. JJJJ was not evidence against the fifth Appellant.[61]

---

59 *The State v Kaikai*, [1989] SLSC p. 85-86.

60 *The State v Kaikai*, [1989] SLSC p. 85-86.

61 *The State v Kaikai*, [1989] SLSC p. 90.

Exhibit JJJJ was an unsworn statement made by the first Appellant to the police in which he said certain things implicating the fifth Appellant in the alleged conspiracy to overthrow the Government of Sierra Leone by unlawful means. It contained evidence of conversations between himself, the fifth Appellant and one Jamil Sahid Mohamed in the latter's downstairs sitting room. The first Appellant went on to testify under oath in his defence at trial and 'gave extracts here and there' only of his previous unsworn statement, leaving out details about the conversations that implicated the fifth Appellant.

On behalf of the fifth Appellant, it was argued, in relation to this testimony at trial, that the first Appellant had 'retracted' those portions of his unsworn statement. Such retraction appeared not to have been expressly done by the first Appellant as the Supreme Court Justices stated they could not find any statement in the court records where he expressly retracted those portions of his unsworn statement.

In addressing this issue, the Supreme Court Justices considered that under the rules of evidence statements made by one accused person either to the police or to others, whether in the presence or absence of a co-accused in the course of or in pursuance of a joint criminal enterprise to which the co-accused is a party are not generally regarded as evidence against a co-accused, unless the co-accused expressly or by implication adopts the statements.[62] They also reasoned that it was the duty of the judge in a jury trial to impress on the jury that the statement of the accused person not made on oath in the course of the trial is not evidence against a co-accused and must be entirely disregarded.[63] They relied mainly on the dicta of Lord Goddard, Lord Chief Justice, for the latter principle.[64]

But the Justices noted that, like the first Appellant, the fifth Appellant had also made a voluntary cautioned statement Exh. HHHH and had elected to give evidence on oath from the witness box where he challenged portions of Exh. JJJJ, specifically areas where his name was mentioned. The fifth Appellant also denied on oath the testimony of the first Appellant. Therefore, in the judges' view, it became a question of whether it was correct and proper in the circumstance for the Learned Trial Judge to leave these matters to the jury. Presiding Judge Kutubu CJ had no reservations in his mind that the

62 *R v Rudd* [1948] 32 Cr. App R. 138.

63 *R v Gunewardene* [1951] 35 Or. App. R. 80.

64 In *The State v Kaikai,* [1989] SLSC p. 90, it was stated that 'If no separate trial is ordered, it is the duty of the Judge to impress on the jury that the statement of the one prisoner not made on oath in the course of the trial is not evidence against the other and must be entirely disregarded.'

Learned Trial Judge had acted correctly in leaving this to the jury. Like in the Court of Appeal, therefore, he dismissed this ground of appeal of the fifth Appellant.

However, Warne JSC, in his separate concurring Judgement, sticking to the fundamental principle in *Rudd* and *Gunewardene,* unequivocally struck down the Learned Trial Judge's statement as a misdirection. He cited, in particular, the following comments from the Trial Judge's summing up to the jury about the first Appellant's testimony:

> 'Why did he leave these out when testifying?
>
> What then is the inference you can draw from that behaviour, gentlemen of the jury?'

Warne JSC's position did not provide much solace to the fifth Appellant. In his much wider reasoning on the issue of misdirection to the jury, he stated, quite rightly, that not all cases of misdirection would or should lead to a conviction on that count being quashed.[65] He considered a long line of authorities in support of his view stating in particular that if the misdirection to the jury was on the law, it could lead to a conviction founded upon it being quashed, but not if it is a misdirection on questions of facts.[66]

vi) *Random musings on 'the facts, the evidence and the law'*

Thus, ended Francis Minah's several grounds of appeal against his conviction, each struck down by the Supreme Court with what seemed like precision-targeted arguments supported by relevant case law. Was this then an overwhelmingly strong case against Minah to which he had a weak defence that could not stand, a slam dunk for the prosecution? Or was it a case of not having had a solid legal team to represent him? Or were there underlying issues of irregularity affecting the fairness of the process that should have been addressed in the pre-trial phase to ensure a fairer outcome – selection of the trial judge, selection of the jury, the conduct of the investigations, disclosure, etc.?

None of these questions will seem to provide a definitive answer to the allegation of unfairness against Minah, nor would they be considered valid

---

65 *Mc Innes v HMA* (2010) UKSC 7; Fraser v HMA (2011) UKSC 24, per Hope LJ; Abdul Rahim v King-Emperor (1946) 48 BOMLR 473.

66 *The State v Kaikai,* [1989] SLSC p. 120-130.

factors that affected the outcome of the trial. For a start, the fact that the prosecution has an unassailable case against an accused is often something the Defence can do hardly much about, except perhaps to ensure that due process is followed throughout the proceedings.

Regarding the quality of representation, there is no question that Minah had a studded team that included some of the country's finest legal minds of the day. Any possible suggestion, therefore, of ineffective assistance of Counsel would have no place in this matrix. The high level of legal representation demonstrated by Counsel during the appeals is something Warne JSC specifically commented on in his Concurring Judgement in the Supreme Court. He stated:

> 'Much work and effort have been exerted by both sides in presenting their arguments to this court, indeed great scholarship has been displayed as well. As a result, I wish to congratulate Counsel both for the Appellants and the State/ Respondent for such dedication to duty in the interests of their respective clients.'

This highlights the argument about possible underlying issues during the pre-trial phase that should have been addressed earlier to ensure a fairer outcome. Even though matters to do with police investigations, interviewing of the accused and collection of evidence, the assignment of a trial judge, the selection of the jury, or disclosure may be quasi-administrative activities, they envision a role, however minimal, for defence counsel to raise a voice, offer advice to the client, or object to the irregularity of a procedure, in protecting their client's interest. Beyond this, Counsel could also raise complaints about the irregularity of the process, including the court's composition or the legality of the investigation procedure, in interlocutory motions before or during the trial or in closing submissions. In the writer's review of materials available for this work, nowhere was it found that Minah's Defence was at any time dissatisfied with the regularity of the process generally or over issues preparatory to the trial, including the court's composition.

However, it should be highlighted that there were often real concerns about the judge's impartiality in the courtroom. In an interview with a member of Minah's defence team still available,[67] instances were cited regarding the trial judge's attitude that, in small ways, questioned the fairness of the proceedings.

[67] Notes on file with the writer.

These included routinely ruling against the defence teams collectively in their first 17 objections taken, all of which bordered on issues of irregularity.

Another concern bordered on the over-reliance on the Judge's handwritten notes as the sole authoritative record of the proceedings, amidst the possibilities of human error in such a marathon trial, especially in the summing–up to the jury, which ran for four days. While the public media was allowed to record the proceedings in court and broadcast it in daily news outlets nationally, the Judge completely frowned at the idea that a defence counsel was doing his verbatim recording as an *aide memoire*. Whether any of these factors substantially affected the fairness of the process and should have been raised, is in the writer's view doubtful.

Perhaps also worth throwing in these musings is the view held by some that Minah ought not to have been indicted in the first place, given the weight of the evidence adduced in support of the case against him. As will be demonstrated, this argument is drawn both from a legal and non-legal perspective. It is intended at this stage to focus only on the legal arguments that support this position, noting that this was not in and of itself an argument canvassed on Minah's behalf, save that it could have formed the basis of the general submission on appeal, 'that the verdict is unreasonable or cannot be supported having regard to the evidence.'[68] One implication of this submission was of course the insufficiency of the evidence generally adduced to meet the gravity of the offence charged. But before getting lost in this omnibus analysis, the question implicit in the main position canvassed should be addressed, which is, 'Was Minah wrongly charged?' Being 'wrongly charged' could mean the prosecutor charging under the wrong statutory provision, but its import could be much more one of malice, such as the prosecutor acting capriciously or maliciously by preferring a charge not supported by the evidence. No Prosecutor worth their salt, it is submitted, would tread down such a treacherous path, let alone in this case, where the Learned Attorney General of the Republic was heading this all-important prosecution.

Those possibilities being so far-fetched, the only other circumstance that this question gives inference to is the issue of discharge of the legal burden by the prosecution. If the view that Minah should never have been charged equates to asserting that the evidence adduced at trial was insufficient to ground the serious offence of treason, then it is by implication stating that the prosecution did not discharge the legal burden of proving the case against

---

68 *The State v Kaikai*, [1989] SLSC p.103.

Minah beyond a reasonable doubt. This view fundamentally challenges the verdict of the jury, a verdict which neither the Court of Appeal nor the Supreme Court, in their separate and collective wisdom, felt warranted any disturbance.

Within the realm of speculation, certain matters about the trial could be questioned to satisfy our curiosity. Matters that could have impacted the fairness of the process more positively if managed differently. For instance, given the crucial nature of the evidence about the meeting in Nyannihun, it is surprising that the defence did not call Minah's driver or any member of his security detail to testify on his behalf. Their evidence would have been crucial for his alibi defence as Minah could not have gone anywhere without them. Was this failure to call them an oversight or intimidation?

vii) *Did the various issues raised amount to a miscarriage of justice?*

It is important at this stage to remind ourselves of the scope of the task at hand, which is to determine whether there was unfairness against Francis Minah in his trial for treason, and if established, to determine whether such unfairness was so substantial that it rises to the level of a miscarriage of justice. As noted, the task is beset with challenges, some of which have already been highlighted. The fact that this analysis is being undertaken on the strength of the Supreme Court Judgement only and based on their analysis of the issues narrows the prism through which the defence case and their arguments could be seen. Also worth pointing out is that the judgement which is the subject of this exercise is a jury verdict, which, while providing plenty of opportunity to raise challenges against the Trial Judge's management of the proceedings, including in particular his summing-up, also inherently limits the chances of a higher court overturning that verdict, having regard to the standard of injustice that must be shown for it to be overturned. Warne JSC cited this standard from Section 58(2) of the Courts Act No.31 of 1965, as amended by Act No.3 of 1976, thus:

> 'On an appeal against conviction the Court of Appeal, notwithstanding that they are of the opinion that the point raised in the appeal might be decided in favour of the appellant, may (a) either dismiss the appeal, or (b) order the appellant to be retried by a court of competent jurisdiction, *if they consider that no substantial miscarriage of justice has actually occurred.*' (Emphasis added).

Therefore, despite the dismissal of all of Minah's grounds of appeal, it is worth commenting on one legal issue that, in the minds of many, continues to raise doubt. This relates to the admissibility of the evidence of DW 20, which many legal minds agree was hearsay. A former member of the prosecution team, then a junior state counsel, recounted how at the end of proceedings on the day of DW 20's testimony, Counsel on both sides came out of court in rare agreement that the evidence admitted which implicated Minah was hearsay.[69] However, it should be recalled that on appeal, the Supreme Court, without striking it out as inadmissible hearsay evidence, reasoned that even without it, there was other evidence on the issue before the court that could be left with the jury, which was sufficiently cogent and dispositive of Minah's guilt. Some still believe that the admissibility of that evidence prejudiced the jury's minds and tainted the case against Minah. They argue that this unfairness substantially amounted to a miscarriage of justice.

Aside from the admissibility issue, there was also the question of the reliability of the evidence given by PW 20 regarding the meeting at Nyannihun. Given that this evidence was based on intelligence reports received by the witness, it raises questions about how the information was sourced, its accuracy and ultimately its reliability. It would have been unsafe to rely on this evidence to find a conviction without corroboration.

7. Theories of a Political Witch-hunt and Vendetta

Various theories have been advanced, mostly non-legal, to try and provide a motive or meaning for Minah's alleged involvement in a coup. Most of these theories question the rationale behind Minah, a sitting First Vice President, being involved in a coup with his minion GMT Kaikai against his government, perhaps only to have ended up remaining vice president had the coup succeeded.

It is essential not to overlook Minah's personality as a politician as we examine these theories. The wider literature about Minah's political life paints the picture of a shrewd and ambitious politician whose penchant for violence and ruthlessness against his opponents knew no bounds.[70] His flaunting ambition for power became his undoing and, eventually his demise. Many

---

69 Interview with former State Counsel in *The State v Kaikai*, [1989] SLSC on 10th October 2022 - Notes on file with the writer.

70 Cocorioko SL Newspaper, "Why all the fuss."

Sierra Leoneans espouse beliefs which deeply subscribe to the theory of divine justice. In this sense, despite their criticism of the lack of fairness of his trial, there is a widely held view rightly or wrongly, that nemesis caught up with Minah and he was served just desserts in the way he met his demise.[71]

Even the staunchest critics of Minah's trial have had to wrestle foremost with his conflicted political personality. Musa could not help but acknowledge this. He wrote: 'In Pujehun, Minah used his political power with iron pertinacity with the APC warrant to purge political opposition. He indulged in an atrocious freak of abuse of power and authority, whenever the whim possessed him because the APC rifles seconded him.' Thus 'throughout his unhallowed political history, he was in public contempt in the nation and especially in his home district of Pujehun.'[72]

However, the limited nature of Minah's alleged role in this enterprise is worth clarifying. In his opening statement at the trial, lead Prosecutor, Attorney-General Abdulai Conteh, gave the impression of Minah being in control of Kaikai from the backstage when he stated that Minah had used Kaikai 'to remove his political chestnuts from the fire.'[73] The evidence in court, however, pointed in a different direction. Not only was Kaikai the mastermind and coup leader, he also acted with a clear intention of taking the country's leadership. An excerpt from his proposed speech on a successful takeover, Exhibit ZZZZQ, which was played in court, states:

> 'The soldiers are not at war with each other or with the police, *and in my capacity as your new leader,* I take this opportunity to warn all members of the SSD Unit in the country and those soldiers resisting and fighting for the cause of the deposed government and some remaining senior officers still hiding, to lay down their arms and surrender themselves peacefully for the good of this our country.' (Emphasis added).

Nevertheless, the theory that political power play may have had a strong hand behind Minah's downfall appears to find validity on the basis that he, a south-easterner and traditionally SLPP, being a relative newcomer to the APC

---

71 'During his heydays, he was arguably the most powerful south-easterner. He was second vice president and acted as first vice president on numerous occasions. He came very close to becoming president, but his insatiable thirst for power destroyed him in the end just like the cockroach that craves for palm-oil and decides to go into the palm-oil bottle, only to seal its own fate.'

72 Sierra Leone Live, "Was Francis M. Minah Guilty? Part II.

73 Sierra Leone Live, "Was Francis M. Minah Guilty? Part II.

party, had suddenly outshined older members to catch the eye of President Siaka Stevens, who until his retirement in 1985 had appointed Minah to many high profile ministerial positions including Attorney General and Minister of Justice. Minah was also highly favoured by President Momoh, who upon succeeding Stevens, appointed him to the position of First Vice President and Attorney General and Minister of Justice. To say, therefore, that such a rise within the party ranks created rivalries with older members will be an understatement. Therefore, the suggestions deriving from this theory are that Minah's alleged implication in a coup arose from a coup in itself, contrived outside the courtroom to bring about his political downfall.

Berewa writes:

> 'Minah's meteoric rise in the APC hierarchy resulted in a lot of jealousy against him, especially as he was a newcomer to the party from the SLPP and a southerner ... The desire to put a halt to this rise was strong among senior and long-standing members of the party... The decision to charge Minister [Minah] had been spearheaded by the Inspector-General of Police, Bambay Kamara.'[74]

Berewa explained that President Momoh 'faced a very personal challenge' when Minah was implicated in the coup, given that 'there had developed a bond of friendship between Minah and him.' But Momoh 'did not have the courage to question' Bambay's decision to charge Minah, as Bambay was just one of those powerful figures within the party.[75]

But John Musa who also strongly argues the political theory as contributory towards Minah's implication in a coup, excludes President Momoh from the mix and puts him above the fray. He dismissed 'rumours' that President Momoh had a hand in this and that Minah, who had 'constitutionally' cleared the way for Momoh to become President, was 'no longer in his good graces.' Musa argues, 'Had Minah been at odds with President Momoh, the President could easily have dismissed him.'[76] This reasoning, it is submitted, makes a lot more sense.

Instead, Musa focussed his theory on the rivalry between Minah and Abdulai Conteh, who succeeded Minah as Attorney General and Minister

---

[74] Berewa, A New Perspective, p. 84.

[75] Berewa, A New Perspective, p. 84.

[76] Cocorioko SL Newspaper, "Why all the fuss" Part I.

of Justice and became the lead state prosecutor in the treason trial. Musa writes, 'The conjecture of a Minah-Conteh fight for the soul of the APC is a more cogent speculation than a Minah-Momoh struggle.' He cites the rivalry between the two since their days as Siaka Stevens' 'Small Boys,' whom he equally favoured, until the question of selecting Steven's successor led to Conteh being side-lined for opposing Steven's unconstitutional methods while Minah became more favoured for championing that cause, a cause that saw a hand-picked Momoh succeeding Stevens. Minah, who had held several high-profile ministerial positions under Stevens, eventually became First Vice President under Momoh, while Conteh, an erstwhile Attorney General and Minister of Justice himself as well as one-time foreign minister, lost his position under Stevens and was an outsider even in Momoh's new government.

Thus, when Minah was implicated in the coup and removed from office, Conteh was appointed the Attorney General and Minister of Justice. Musa argues that Conteh should have exercised discretion not to lead the prosecution team in the courtroom and should have instead left this task in the hands of other senior and competent lawyers in his department. That he made this choice was to cash in on an opportunity to settle old scores, to 'harangue' and 'persecute' Minah, and pursue something of a personal vendetta. Conteh was, therefore, not free from suspicion of 'political bias' as a prosecutor, especially given the 'tenuous evidence' advanced at trial to convict Minah.[77]

On this theme, the TRC, for its part, stated in its Final Report that:

> 'Minah was almost certainly a victim of a political vendetta within the APC, but a compromised judiciary was not likely to acquit him of treason in a climate where political favours mattered more than legal justifications.'[78]

None of these political theories, it is submitted, provide the factual evidence necessary to establish the unfairness complained of against Minah. To be accorded any amount of validity or significance, the facts in issue must be ascertainable and justiciable in answer to the charge of treason in the courtroom. At best, they provide only a motive for why anyone would have disliked Minah and their desire to bring about his downfall, perhaps influenced strongly by a fit of pent-up anger towards the government of the day.

---

[77] Cocorioko SL Newspaper, "Why all the fuss."

[78] Sierra Leone Truth and Reconciliation Commission, Final Report, 95.

8. Improbability of the Charge: Could Minah Have Been Involved in the Act of Treason?

Critics have frequently commented on the improbability of Minah being involved in a coup. These comments no doubt highlight one facet of the argument about unfairness surrounding Minah's indictment, trial and conviction. Some of this is already referenced in an earlier part of this work. Different interpretations can be given to the concept of improbability, which seems to epitomise most of the comments criticising Minah's trial. These can range from downright disbelief - as in incredibly irrational - to the use of vague and unsubstantiated assertions to challenge the fairness of the process.

Thus, even in the courtroom, Minah's lawyers attempted to bolster their legal arguments with logical reasoning that raised the improbability of Minah being involved in a coup with GMT Kaikai, in effect questioning the existence of a motive for his alleged conduct. After Exhibit ZZZZQ was played in court, lead defence counsel Solomon Berewa reportedly asked whether Minah would have been 'crazy' to serve as vice president under Kaikai if the coup had succeeded.[79] Berthan Macaulay Snr., the lead appellate counsel, questioned the notion of Minah joining Kaikai in any conspiracy to overthrow the Government when it was clear from the coup speech that Kaikai was acting alone in his quest for illegal power and authority.[80]

Musa, a leading critic,[81] without providing any evidence to substantiate his views, wrote:

> 'It is my contention that Minah was wrongly charged and the Trial Court, the Court of Appeal and the Supreme Court erred in or deliberately conjoined in the alleged conspiracy to juridically murder an innocent man. Courts invariably err and judges act politically especially in treason trial where the evidence is often picayune.'

He stretched his theory even further to cover the defence and the jury by stating:

> 'Many criminal suspects are wrongly charged and invariably found guilty because defence lawyers are incompetent. Or

---

79 Cocorioko SL Newspaper, "Why all the fuss" Part III.
80 Cocorioko SL Newspaper, "Why all the fuss" Part III.
81 Cocorioko SL Newspaper, "Why all the fuss" Part III.

> the jury returned the wrong verdict because they did not understand the facts they were called to resolved.'

Similarly, these are non-justiciable issues that would earn Minah no merits in a quest for justice against any alleged unfairness. They are only strong expressions of personal feelings about his innocence that add no real value in any legal proceedings.

9. Tenuous Evidence: is the Legal Burden Discharged?

A variant of the argument about 'improbability' in Minah's case relates to the evidence. Much has been said about how tenuous the evidence adduced was, implying that it was so weak that it was improbable that Minah or anyone could be convicted on a charge of treason on it. Berewa recalls, as Defence Counsel, his comments on the case to former President Stevens thus: 'I proffered my opinion that the allegations were flimsy and preposterous and that it was unlikely that a reasonable jury would convict Minah on those charges.' The 'hollowness' in Garvas Betts' interview with the New York Times was no doubt in reference to the lack of transparent evidence to connect Minah to the charge of treason, or perhaps the lack of any tangible evidence.

These are obvious allusions to the view that the prosecution had not met the legal burden or was unable to prove the charge of treason against Minah beyond all reasonable doubt on the strength of the evidence adduced. That said, I submit that the verdict of guilty returned by the jury should have been overturned on appeal if this were true, even on the omnibus submission that the verdict was against the weight of the evidence against Minah, but it was not. It should be remembered that the jury was the ultimate trier of facts in this case and absent any evidence pointing to a substantial miscarriage of justice, no higher court or reviewing body would interfere with their verdict, unless it can be shown that no reasonable jury on a proper direction would have returned such a verdict.

10. Was There a Miscarriage of Justice?

Determining whether there was a miscarriage of justice against Francis Minah is an arduous but not impossible task. It is not a tightrope walk but an act that still requires tact, skill, knowledge, and experience in criminal law and procedure. The first question to ponder is whether this is a legal issue to be decided in a court of law or left in the court of public opinion, given the deafening cry from the public.

Opening up an avenue for redress after the exhaustion of the normal legal process has to be guided by ascertainable and justiciable principles. Whereas the clamour for justice from the public cannot be dismissed out of hand, any basis for seeking redress in these circumstances should be required to meet specific standards, including any supporting reasons being put through an ascertainable process. Therefore, it helps to appreciate that the principles and standards must be legal and acceptable. If the public's complaint/grievance does not measure to those standards, it fails the qualifying test.

Most legal systems that avail the remedy of judicial review provide only limited or restricted access. A certain threshold must be met regarding the seriousness of the wrong complained of. Post-appeal review processes are often based on a showing that a miscarriage has occurred or is likely to occur from the execution of a judgement unless the court takes into account some new evidence that was not available at trial and would lead to a different outcome. However, the legal issues raised in Minah's case that would potentially enable him to take advantage of such a remedy, assuming it was available in Sierra Leone, do not point to the omission of evidence that has become available after the trial. Instead, they point to different issues. Therefore, a remedy by way of a review might be challenging to grant based on these standards. But does that mean Minah has not suffered an injustice?

Francis Minah may have suffered an injustice in his trial, but does it amount to a miscarriage, and if so, how is it remediable? The admission of what everyone agreed was hearsay evidence may have prejudiced the jury into returning a guilty verdict against him on such a critical piece of evidence. The Supreme Court's position that excluding the evidence of DW 20 would still have led the jury to arrive at this same verdict is not, in the writer's view, sufficient to address the legal issue of the prohibition on such evidence being left with the jury, for the simple reason that it will have the effect of prejudicing their minds. Furthermore, the direction of the Learned Trial Judge on the treatment of that piece of evidence by the jury even compounded the problem. In effect, a verdict was reached against Minah that may have been influenced wrongly. It is submitted therefore that the guilty verdict against Minah should have been overturned on appeal and, at the very least, a retrial ordered pursuant to Section 58 (2) (b) of the Court's Act 1965.

11. Conclusion

Technically speaking, any legal process involving a fresh examination of adjudicated facts after a final judgement has been rendered in a case amounts to a review. It could be a review of the judgement, sentence, or procedure that produced that judgement. This extraordinary measure afforded to the parties after the exhaustion of the normal legal process is intended to prevent any blatant injustice or a miscarriage of justice. Some legal systems make provision for this exceptional measure by prescribing certain requirements within the country's justice system, for example, in the constitution, court rules, or other statutory provision. Whether or not such express provision exists, it behooves every state in the present age to be ready, willing and able to open up a process of review after any final judgement if it is shown that that judgement will result in a miscarriage of justice if executed. In other words, an innocent person(s) may stand wrongfully convicted, owing to any number of reasons, including, that certain piece(s) of evidence that could have led to a just and fairer outcome was not put before the trier of facts, or perhaps a grossly unjust procedure was used which deprived the convicted person(s) of certain fundamental due process rights, e.g., not affording the accused their internationally recognized fair trial rights.

Thus, the standard expected to enable a party to avail themselves of this extraordinary measure varies from country to country. While some legal systems have express provisions, others make this possible on an *ad hoc* basis, following previous practice or precedent. In Ghana[82] and South Africa,[83] there are provisions specifically designed to address situations where a review is necessary to avoid a miscarriage of justice after appellate rights to the highest courts have been exhausted. Specific procedures are embedded in these provisions to ensure that an affected party seeking this measure of redress meets a certain threshold or qualifying test for the review.

In countries where post-appeal measures for addressing wrongful convictions exist, the requirement or qualifying criteria are strict, often limited to the production of new material, information or fact only, which was not available at trial, and more importantly, that its use if available, would have led to a different outcome - an acquittal or exoneration on one or more

[82] The Constitution of Ghana, 1992, art. 133 in conjunction with Supreme Court Rules 1996, rules 54 (a) and 56 (1). See also *Republic v High Court*, General Jurisdiction, Accra, (J7 18 of 2019) [2020] GHASC 9 (14 January 2020).

[83] South Africa Criminal Procedure Act, 51 of 1977, sec. 327.

counts or absolutely. These are generally the applicable standards at national as well as international criminal justice systems. In South Africa, where the provision exists by virtue of Section 327 of its Criminal Procedure Act, the Constitutional Court, which is the highest court in the country, has held that 'the procedure in Section 327 of the CPA is not an appeal.'[84] The same court added that Section 327 is 'geared at preventing an injustice'[85] and the section 'applies after the appeal processes are spent and permanently closed. The Section 327 procedure is also not a substitute for an appeal. It is a process beyond the appeal stage that is meant to be the final net to avoid a grave injustice.'[86]

In Sierra Leone, the provision in Section 122(2) of the 1991 Constitution which empowers the Supreme Court, the country's highest judicial body, to 'depart from a previous decision when it appears right to do so'[87] to avoid being fettered in its decision-making powers, could potentially capacitate the court to address miscarriages in some way. However, this provision is not explicitly intended or designed to serve as an avenue for judicial or post-appeal review in the sense envisioned in the provisions of other jurisdictions. One of its limitations in this sense is that it makes no provision for a person in such need to approach the court and invoke this aspect of its jurisdiction.

A good starting point in strengthening Sierra Leone's judicial system with the creation of an avenue for judicial review could be to look at the review provisions of the Residual Special Court for Sierra Leone (RSCSL) as a template for drafting its judicial review law. Rule 120 of the RSCSL Rules of Procedure and Evidence reads:[88]

> 'Rule 120 – Request for Review
>
> (A) Where, following a final judgement, a new fact has been discovered which was not known to the moving party

[84] Jamil Ddamulira Mujuzi, "The Trial of Civilians Before Courts Martial in Uganda: Analysing the Jurisprudence of Ugandan Courts in the Light of the Drafting History of Articles 129(1)(d) and 120(a) of the Constitution," Potchefstroom Electronic Law Journal 25 (2022). The case of Liesching and Others v S. and Another 2017 (4) B.C.L.R. 454 (C.C.); 2017 (2) S.A.C.R. 193 (C.C.), para. 59 was cited.

[85] *Liesching and Others v S. and Another*, para. 59.

[86] Liesching and Others v S. and Another, para. 59. See also *Chidi v Minister of Justice*, 1992 (4) S.A. 110 (A.D.), para. 10, where the Court held that Section 327 is applicable where the case has 'effectively and finally been concluded.'

[87] The Constitution of Sierra Leone, Act No. 6 of 1991, S. 122 (2).

[88] Rules of Procedure and Evidence of the Special Court for Sierra Leone, accessed on 31 December 2024 http://www.rscsl.org/Documents/RSCSL-Rules.pdf.

at the time of the proceedings before the Trial Chamber or Appeals Chamber of the Special Court or Residual Special Court, and which could have been a decisive factor in reaching the decision, the convicted person, or the Prosecutor may submit an application for a review of the judgement.

(B) An application for review shall be submitted to the President.

(C) Any response to an application for review shall be filed within forty days of the filing of the application.

(D) Any reply shall be filed within fifteen days after the filing of the response.'

POWER, POLITICS AND THE CONSTITUTION - THE CASE OF ALHAJI SAMUEL SAMSUMANA VS. THE ATTORNEY GENERAL & MINISTER OF JUSTICE AND VICTOR BOCKARIE FOH

VICTOR IDRISSA LANSANA, Esq.

1. Introduction

Sierra Leone's constitutional and political landscape has long been shaped by tensions between executive power, judicial independence, and the rule of law, with the controversial dismissal of Vice President Alhaji Samuel Sam-Sumana in 2015 serving as a pivotal case study. This chapter examines the legal battle that ensued following Sam-Sumana's sacking by President Ernest Bai Koroma, a decision that sparked a constitutional crisis and raised profound questions about the balance of power in democracy. The narrative follows the events surrounding Sam-Sumana's removal as Vice President of Sierra Leone on March 17, 2015, due to allegations of seeking asylum at the U.S. Embassy and his expulsion from the All Peoples' Congress (APC) party. It details the subsequent legal battles in the Supreme Court of Sierra Leone and the ECOWAS Community Court of Justice. Through a critical analysis of the Supreme Court's unanimous ruling by Justices Valesius V. Thomas, N.C. Browne-Marke, F.F. Roberts, V.M. Solomon, and the late P.O. Hamilton, as well as the contrasting ECOWAS Court verdict, this chapter unveils the legal reasoning, constitutional implications, and broader societal repercussions of this landmark case.

Sierra Leone's governance frameworks have historically been fraught with discriminatory and exclusionary practices. The 1991 Constitution, Act No. 6, marked a significant shift from the one-party state established under the 1978 Constitution, introducing multi-party politics and a single vice-presidency elected alongside the President, thereby limiting the President's discretion to dismiss the Vice President at will. Under the 1978 Constitution, the President could appoint and remove two vice presidents from among elected parliamentarians, a power that facilitated executive dominance. In contrast, the Constitution stipulate that the Vice President, as a directly elected official, can only be removed through parliamentary impeachment for misconduct or incapacity, ensuring checks on executive authority.[1] The Sam-Sumana case tested these constitutional safeguards, with President Koroma's reliance on section 40(1)'s 'supreme executive authority'[2] and section 41(b)'s requirement of political party membership[3] to justify the dismissal raising critical questions about the interpretation of presidential powers. The Supreme Court's decision to uphold the sacking, arguing that Sam-Sumana's expulsion from the APC created a vacancy in the vice-presidency, highlighted a troubling expansion of executive influence over elected offices, as noted in contemporary analyses.

The judiciary's role in this case underscores broader systemic challenges. The Supreme Court's ruling, delivered on 9 September 2015, was met with public outcry and accusations of political bias, with critics, including the Sierra Leone People's Party (SLPP) and the Sierra Leone Bar Association, deeming it unconstitutional. The ECOWAS Court's 2017 ruling, which found the dismissal to be a violation of Sam-Sumana's rights to a fair hearing and political participation under the African Charter on Human and Peoples' Rights, further exposed the Supreme Court's failure to uphold constitutional principles. This chapter critically evaluates the legal reasoning of both courts,

---

1 Sections 50 and 51 of the Constitution of Sierra Leone, 1991, establish procedures for addressing the President's incapacity or misconduct. Section 50 allows the Cabinet to initiate an investigation into the President's mental or physical capacity by notifying the Speaker, who appoints a Board of at least five medical practitioners to assess and report on the President's ability to perform constitutional duties. If the Board finds the President incapable, the Speaker certifies this, the President ceases to hold office, and a vacancy is declared, with parliamentary review required within strict timelines. Section 51 enables Parliament to investigate allegations of constitutional violations or gross misconduct if half its members submit a motion. A two-thirds vote triggers a Tribunal, chaired by a Supreme Court Justice, to probe the allegations within three months. If substantiated, Parliament may remove the President by a two-thirds vote, creating a vacancy.

2 The provision states that '(T)here shall be a President of the Republic of Sierra Leone who shall be Head of State, the supreme executive authority of the Republic and the Commander-in-Chief of the Armed Forces.'

3 No person shall be qualified for election as President ......unless he is a member of a political party.

exploring how the Supreme Court's deference to executive authority, as seen in earlier cases like those of John Akar and Kandeh Yumkella, perpetuates systemic inequities and undermines public trust in the judiciary.

Historically, Sierra Leone's governance evolved from pre-colonial chieftaincy systems, where a chief led as first among equals, to British colonial rule, which established a governor-general and prime minister under the British Monarch. The 1961 Independence Constitution marked the transition to leadership, with Sir Milton Margai as the first Prime Minister, followed by Siaka Stevens' presidency after the 1971 declaration of a Republic. Stevens' subsequent establishment of a one-party state in 1978 consolidated executive power, a legacy that lingers in modern constitutional disputes. The 1991 Constitution sought to restore democratic checks, but its implementation was delayed by military rule from 1992 to 1996, during which the National Provisional Ruling Council (NPRC) suspended constitutional governance.[4] The Sam-Sumana case, occurring nearly two decades after the Constitution's full operationalisation in 1996, reveals persistent tensions between democratic ideals and executive overreach, compounded by societal prejudices against marginalised groups, as discussed in earlier chapters on citizenship.

This chapter unravels the layers of the Sam-Sumana case, offering a comprehensive analysis of the Supreme Court's and ECOWAS Court's decisions and their implications for the constitutional and political landscape. It situates the case within the broader context of the book's exploration of judicial independence, access to justice, and systemic discrimination, drawing parallels with historical cases like Francis Minah's and contemporary citizenship disputes. This chapter examines the interplay of power, politics, and constitutional interpretation, advocates for reforms, such as strengthening judicial independence, amending ambiguous constitutional provisions, and enhancing public education on civic rights, to ensure that the judiciary upholds the rule of law and fosters an inclusive democracy.

2. The Removal of Sam Sumana

---

4 Jimmy D. Kandeh, "Transition Without Rupture: Sierra Leone's Transfer Election of 1996," African Studies Review 41, no. 2 (1998) p. 91-111. See also Truth and Reconciliation Commission of Sierra Leone, Witness to Truth: Report of the Truth and Reconciliation Commission, vol. 2, chap. 2 (Freetown: Truth and Reconciliation Commission, 2004), http://www.sierraleonetrc.org/index.php/view-the-final-report/download-table-of-contents.

Former President Koroma came into office in September 2007. He had chosen Alhaji Samuel Samsumana at their party's convention as his running mate, both of whom ran on the same ballot pursuant to the 1991 Constitution. Ernest Bai Koroma was the Chairman and Leader of the All Peoples' Congress (APC) throughout his tenure in office as President. Sam Sumana was said to be a successful businessman with significant financial resources. He was again selected to run with the President in 2012 elections, and they were re-elected. However, in a letter dated 6th March 2015, the APC Party expelled Samuel Sam Sumana from the party, while he was still serving as the Vice President of the Republic. This triggered the removal of the Vice President from Office by the President. By letter from the office of the President dated 17th March 2015, the President informed the public thus:

> 'And whereas Alhaji Samuel Sam Sumana is no longer a member of a political party in Sierra Leone and therefore does not have the continuous requirement to hold office as vice President of the Republic of Sierra Leone, provided for in Section 41(b) of the Constitution of Sierra Leone Act No. 6 of 1991, I hereby relieve Alhaji Samuel Sam Sumana of the duties and from the Office of Vice President of Sierra Leone with immediate effect, pursuant to my supreme executive authority as President of the Republic of Sierra Leone as enshrined in Section 40(1) of the said Constitution of Sierra Leone.'[5]

The Vice President, Sam Sumana, by way of a first step, responded to the action of the President by a statement dated 18th day of March 2015 in which he stated,

> 'That the President has absolutely no power to "relieve me of the duties of Vice-President" in any part of the Constitution, Act No. 6 of 1991.'

Like any other member of the APC Party, Sam Sumana had a thirty (30) days window to appeal to the party against his expulsion from the party. However, the President subsequently appointed Victor Bockarie Foh, the then Ambassador to the People's Republic of China and former Secretary General of the APC, Vice President of the Republic of Sierra Leone. Sumana

---

[5] Office of the President of Sierra Leone, "Press Release," accessed August 28, 2025, https://www.critiqueecho.com/office-of-the-president-press-release/.

challenged his removal in court, in what was to be a long-drawn legal battle in the Supreme Court of Sierra Leone and the Economic Community of West African States (ECOWAS) Court in Abuja, Nigeria.

3. The Case Before the Supreme Court

An Originating Notice of Motion dated 20th March 2015 referenced as S. C. 4/2015 filed in the Supreme Court, the Plaintiff, Alhaji Samuel Sam-Sumana, urged the Court through his lawyers to declare the action of the President in relieving him of his office and duties as 'unconstitutional, null and void and of no effect.'[6] The Attorney General and Minister of Justice and Victor Bockarie Foh were cited as defendants, as the President is immune from civil and criminal litigations while he occupies office, pursuant to section 48(4) of the Constitution of Sierra Leone.[7] The Attorney-General and Minister of Justice is the Principal Legal Adviser to the Government.[8] Although the Supreme Court held that the Attorney General and Minister of Justice was wrongly made a party to the action, it also held that the reliefs sought by the Plaintiff were merely declaratory in nature and not those that would incur sanctions or liability if the Court were to hold in favour of the Plaintiff. So, the Court allowed the matter to proceed as filed.

What then was before the Court for determination? There were two questions put before the Court, followed by a request for certain reliefs:

> '(a) Whether the Constitution of Sierra Leone empowers the PRESIDENT to relieve the Vice-President of his office and duties in any way other than by the procedure set out in sections 50 and 51 of the said Constitution?
>
> (b) Whether the Supreme executive authority of the President mentioned in Section 40(1) of the Constitution of Sierra Leone includes the power to relieve the Vice President of his Office and duties other than by the procedure set out in Sections 50 and 51 of the said Constitution?
>
> If the Answer to the questions is NO, then the Plaintiff will

---

6 *Alhaji Samuel Sam-Sumana v The Attorney-General & Minster of Justice & Others,* (SC 4 of 2015) [2015] SLSC 1205 (5 May 2015), accessed on 20th July 2025 https://sierralii.gov.sl/akn/sl/judgment/slsc/2015/1205/eng@2015-05-05.

7 The Constitution of Sierra Leone, Act No. 6 of 1991.

8 Constitution of Sierra Leone, S. 64.

seek the following further reliefs:

> For a declaration that the Public Notice announcing that the Vice-President had been relieved of his duties and office (Exhibit A herein) is unconstitutional, null and void, and of no effect.
>
> For a declaration that the appointment of Victor Bockarie Foh as Vice-President of Sierra Leone is also unconstitutional, null and void, and of no effect.
>
> For an Injunction restraining the said Victor Bockarie Foh from acting in the Office of Vice-President of Sierra Leone, pending the hearing and determination of this action.
>
> For a declaration that the elected Vice-President of Sierra Leone (the Plaintiff herein) remains in Office as Vice-President thereof unless and until removed from Office as required by Section 50 and 51 of the Constitution of Sierra Leone.'

The plaintiff's counsel, Mr. M. Fofanah, argued that section 41(b)'s party membership requirement applies only at candidacy, not throughout the term, and that only Parliament could remove the Vice President. The defendants, represented by Mr. Macaulay, countered that section 127[9] was misapplied, advocating a purposive interpretation of sections 41(b) and 54(5).[10]

---

[9] Constitution of Sierra Leone, S. 127 provides as follows – '(1) A person who alleges that an enactment or anything contained in or done under the authority of that or any other enactment is inconsistent with or is in contravention of a provision of this Constitution, may at any time bring an action in the Supreme Court for a declaration to that effect. (2) The Supreme Court shall, for the purposes of a declaration under subsection (1), make such orders and give such directions as it may consider appropriate for giving effect to, or enabling effect to be given to, the declaration so made. (3) Any person to whom an order or direction is addressed under subsection (1) by the Supreme Court shall duly obey and carry out the terms of the order or direction. (4) Failure to obey or to carry out the terms of an order or direction made or given under subsection (1) shall constitute a crime under this Constitution.' This section establishes the framework for constitutional challenges in the Supreme Court. It allows any person to bring an action claiming that a law or action authorized by law contravenes or is inconsistent with the Constitution, seeking a judicial declaration to that effect. The Supreme Court is empowered to issue orders or directions to enforce or facilitate such declarations. These orders must be obeyed by those to whom they are directed, and failure to comply constitutes a criminal offense under the Constitution.

[10] Constitution of Sierra Leone, S. 54(5) provides as follows, 'Whenever the office of the Vice-President is vacant, or the Vice-President dies, resigns, retires or is removed from office, the President shall

4. The Supreme Court Decision

On 9 September 2015, five Supreme Court justices, Acting Chief Justice Valesius V. Thomas, Hon. Justice N.C. Browne-Marke, Hon. Justice E.F. Roberts, Hon. Justice V.M. Solomon, and the late Hon. Justice P.O. Hamilton, delivered unanimous judgements upholding President Ernest Bai Koroma's authority to dismiss Vice President Alhaji Samuel Sam-Sumana.

The Court addressed two central questions raised by the plaintiff, first, whether the 1991 Constitution grants the President power to relieve the Vice President of office outside the impeachment procedures outlined in sections 50 and 51 and second, whether the 'supreme executive authority' vested in the President under section 40(1) includes such power.

The Court's rulings, grounded in a purposive interpretation of the Constitution, affirmed the President's action, citing Sam-Sumana's expulsion from the All Peoples' Congress (APC) as creating a vacancy under sections 41(b) and 54(5). This section critically examines each justice's reasoning, highlighting the legal and constitutional implications of their decisions and their broader impact on Sierra Leone's judiciary and democratic framework.

The Supreme Court, in a unanimous decision delivered on 9 September 2015, rejected the plaintiff's claim. Each of the five justices, Acting Chief Justice Valesius Thomas, Justice Nicholas Browne-Marke, Justice Eku Roberts, Justice Vivian M.M. Solomon, and Justice Patrick Omolade Hamilton, authored separate concurring judgments, agreeing on the outcome but offering distinct reasoning.

Acting Chief Justice Valesius Thomas delivered the leading judgment, articulating a clear and purposive interpretation of the 1991 Constitution. He noted that on a purposive and holistic interpretation of the Sierra Leone Constitution, membership of a political party under section 41(b) is a continuous qualification for holding the office of Vice-President, extending beyond the time of election and throughout the tenure. Thomas, Acting CJ noted that the loss of such membership, e.g., through expulsion creates a vacancy in the office under section 55, which is not exhaustive and is modified by sections 54(2)(b), 41, and 54(5). He opined that this vacancy falls outside the removal procedures for incapacity or misconduct in sections 50 and 51,

appoint a person qualified to be elected as a Member of Parliament to the office of Vice-President with effect from the date of such vacancy, death, resignation, retirement or removal.'

which do not apply pointing out that

> 'In my opinion therefore, both sections 50 and 51 of the Constitution are inapplicable in resolving the issue before the Court. The situation that the Plaintiff found himself is not one of the circumstances for removal from office dealt with in those two sections of the Constitution. Losing one's membership of a political party is neither mental/ physical incapacity (section 50) nor is it a 'violation' of the Constitution or a gross misconduct in the performance of the functions of his office.'

Instead, the President, as the supreme executive authority under sections 40(1) and 53(1) and (4), has the inherent power to relieve the Vice-President of his duties and office in such circumstances, and to appoint a replacement, without violating the Constitution. He concluded that the President's action in this case was therefore constitutional, rendering the plaintiff's claims for declarations and injunctions untenable. He stated that

> 'When read holistically, these provisions inform me that the President is the highest executive authority in Sierra Leone and his executive powers are only limited by the Constitution... I hold that there is no provision in the Constitution which curtails the powers and duties of the President in the exercise of the executive authority of Sierra Leone in respect of the vacancy in the office of Vice President that arose when the Plaintiff lost one of the qualifying requirements for his office.'[11]

Justice Nicholas Browne-Marke offered a complementary perspective, focusing on the automatic constitutional consequence of the Vice-President's loss of party membership. He also adopted a purposive and holistic interpretation of the Constitution and agreed that membership of a political party under section 41(b) is a continuous qualification for holding the office of Vice-President, not limited to the election period but extending throughout the tenure. The expulsion of the Vice-President from his political party creates a vacancy in the office under section 55, which is not exhaustive and arises outside the removal procedures for incapacity or misconduct in sections 50

---

11 *Alhaji Samuel Sam-Sumana v The Attorney-General,* [2015] SLSC p. 22-23.

and 51. He noted

> 'When all of these Constitutional provisions are considered together and not in isolation, it will become quite clear that the circumstances in which the office of Vice President might become vacant are not dealt with exhaustively in Section 55... I am of the view that the purposive rule of interpretation is in accordance with good sense and that Section 41(b) of the Constitution should be interpreted in that way: that continued membership of a political party was a requirement of a Vice President's continued stay in office; and that a Vice President could be removed from office in those circumstances.'[12]

In such circumstances, the President, exercising supreme executive authority under sections 40(1) and 53, has the power to relieve the Vice-President of his duties and appoint a replacement, as this aligns with the legislative intent to ensure political party affiliation for executive officeholders. The President's action was constitutional, and the Nigerian case of Atiku Abubakarr is distinguishable due to differences in constitutional provisions and interpretive approaches. He concluded that

> 'In the premises, my answer to the questions posed by the Plaintiff, are as follows: (a) The Constitution does empower the President to relieve the Vice President of his office and duties where he has ceased to be a member of a political party. The provisions in Sections 50 and 51 of the Constitution are unconnected with the exercise of this power. (b) The Supreme Executive Power of the President mentioned in Section 40(1) of the Constitution empowers the President to relieve the Vice President of his office and duties in a situation where the Vice President has ceased to be a member of a political party.'[13]

Justice Eku Roberts adopted a similar stance, emphasizing the clarity and

---

12 *Alhaji Samuel Sam-Sumana v The Attorney-General,* [2015] SLSC p. 50-51.

13 *Alhaji Samuel Sam-Sumana v The Attorney-General,* [2015] SLSC p. 58.

continuous nature of the party membership requirement under Section 41(b). He stated

> 'Having applied the various principles I have come to the considered conclusion that the provision in section 41 including section 41 (b) is continuous. In other words the Vice President must be a member of a political party when he is being designated as a running mate to the President and should continue to be a member of a political party so long as he is in office as Vice President.'[14]

Roberts JSC clarified that the plaintiff's expulsion from his party created a vacancy in the office under section 55, which is not exhaustive and must be read impliedly with section 41(b) to avoid absurdity or unworkable results. This vacancy does not constitute a violation of the Constitution or gross misconduct, rendering sections 50 and 51 inapplicable, as they require deliberate acts or incapacity. The President, as supreme executive authority under section 40(1), has the power to relieve the Vice-President of his duties upon such a vacancy and to appoint a replacement under section 54(5), without acting unconstitutionally. Section 127 is inapplicable, as no enactment is challenged; the action is properly under section 124 for interpretation. The Nigerian Atiku Abubakar case is distinguished due to textual differences, interpretative approaches, and non-binding nature. The questions are answered affirmatively, and the reliefs are refused.

> 'I have carefully read the decision in the Atiku Abubakarr Case. However I have observed some differences in relation to the present case in terms of a) the text or wording of the respective (corresponding) legislative provisions sought to be interpreted or construed, b) the reasons or circumstances creating the alleged vacancy c) the guidelines for interpretation used in arriving at the decision d) the two Constitutions are certainly not identical. Let me conclude my consideration of the Atiku Abubakarr case by reference to the case of Charles Francis Margai –v- Solomon Ekuma
>
> Berewa & Ors SC 2/2007 unreported in which the Hon.

[14] *Alhaji Samuel Sam-Sumana v The Attorney-General,* [2015] SLSC p. 71-72.

Justice U.H. Tejan-Jalloh, CJ had this to say:

> 'Furthermore it must be remembered that no two Constitutions are the same, hence their interpretations must to that extent also differ and in interpreting the provisions of our National Constitution I have and I must not put any gloss or interpretation from another Constitution or statute. I remind myself also that similar provisions in other Constitutions or statutes are only of persuasive effect and in no way binding on our Courts.' I therefore do not find it appropriate or useful to adopt the decision in the Atiku Abubakarr case.'[15]

Justice Vivian M.M. Solomon adopted a formalist approach, grounding her *ratio decidendi* in the strict wording of the Constitution. She held that the President's action was not a removal but a recognition of the Vice-President's automatic disqualification due to the loss of political party membership under Section 41(b), which operates as a constitutional fact without requiring further confirmation. She noted

> 'The President being the Guardian of the Constitution as provided in Section 40(3) also imposes a duty of watchfulness on him and not only the duty or power to execute the laws... In the circumstances therefore, the intention of the legislature can be implied if it is not expressly provided for. And all provisions dealing with the Executive and Executive Power are to be considered in the interpretation of the phrase 'Supreme Executive Authority'. The President therefore by his Supreme Executive Authority pursuant to the Constitution has the power to relieve the plaintiff from his office.'[16]

She partially adopted Justice Akintan's reasoning from *Atiku* on executive powers emphasizing a 'single executive' vested in the President, akin to American/Nigerian models, to support the President›s authority under section 40(1) pointing out that

---

15 *Alhaji Samuel Sam-Sumana v The Attorney-General,* [2015] SLSC p. 78.

16 *Alhaji Samuel Sam-Sumana v The Attorney-General,* [2015] SLSC p. 105.

> 'Though I do not find it applicable, I do adopt a part of the reasoning of Justice Sunday Akinola Akintan relating to the Executive Powers of the President... 'The Nigerian Constitution, like the American presidential system, envisages single executive for which the President is the head and in whom the executive powers are vested.'... The power and authority to execute the laws is therefore the quintessential executive power. As seen in other parts, the drafters of the 1991 Constitution clearly understood and intended Supreme Executive Authority to be the power to execute the laws.'

Justice Patrick Omolade Hamilton concluded the panel's judgments, aligning with his colleagues in viewing the Vice-President's expulsion from the APC as fatal to his tenure. He noted that

> 'In my opinion Section 41(b) of the Constitution is continuous in that the Vice-President must be a member of a Political party that is a running mate or co pilot of the President at election and must continue to be a member of a Political Party whilst he is Vice-President. I have held on this view since to hold otherwise would create an absurd position between the President and the Vice-President which is not the intended intention of Parliament in drafting the Constitution of 1991.'[17]

He further went on to state

> 'What happened when the Vice-President ceases to possess his membership of a Political Party as contained in Section 41(b) of the Constitution in which it must be continuous. In my opinion wherein he is expelled from the party a vacancy is automatically created although not contained in Section 55 but can be implied and this is a situation which in my opinion a vacancy can be created.'[18]

---

17 *Alhaji Samuel Sam-Sumana v The Attorney-General,* [2015] SLSC p. 122.
18 *Alhaji Samuel Sam-Sumana v The Attorney-General,* [2015] SLSC p. 124.

Adding further that

> 'In my opinion Exh. A. did not remove the Plaintiff from office. All what Exh. A did was that the President was informing the entire populace at large that there is now a vacancy in the Office of the Vice-President. Parliament could not have done so as there is no express provision in the Constitution where a vacancy occurs in the Office of Vice-President following an expulsion from a Political Party as occurred in this case.'[19]

Hamilton rejected the need for parliamentary involvement, asserting,

> 'Parliament could not have done so as there is no express provision in the Constitution where a vacancy occurs in the Office of Vice-President following an expulsion from a Political Party as occurred in this case.'[20]

He also emphasized the judiciary's role in upholding the Constitution's effectiveness, stating,

> 'The Supreme Court in exercising its jurisdiction pursuant to Section 124 of the Constitution the Court ought to interpret or construe any enactment of the Constitutional provision to determine its legal meaning in such a way as would have been the clear intention of Parliament. It is the duty of the Supreme Court to arrive at the concise legal meaning of any enactment this is before it for interpretation.'[21]

The five justices, despite their distinct emphases, converged on several critical principles that unified their rulings. They unanimously agreed that Section 41(b) of the 1991 Constitution imposes a continuous requirement of political party membership for the Vice-President, extending beyond candidacy to the duration of the officeholder's tenure. The Plaintiff's expulsion from the APC was thus seen as an automatic disqualification, triggering a vacancy under Section 55 without necessitating the impeachment processes outlined in Sections 50 or 51 for incapacity or misconduct. The President's action in relieving the Vice-President was consistently viewed as a declaratory

---

19 *Alhaji Samuel Sam-Sumana v The Attorney-General,* [2015] SLSC p. 125.
20 *Alhaji Samuel Sam-Sumana v The Attorney-General,* [2015] SLSC p. 125.
21 *Alhaji Samuel Sam-Sumana v The Attorney-General,* [2015] SLSC p. 119.

act, recognizing a constitutional fact rather than effecting a disciplinary removal, and was authorized under his supreme executive authority[22] and the power to appoint a new Vice-President under Section 54(5). The justices also agreed that the Court's role was limited to interpreting the Constitution, not reviewing the APC's internal disciplinary process, and that parliamentary involvement was unnecessary for disqualifications under Section 41(b).

This consensus distinguished the case from the Nigerian precedent of *Attorney-General of the Federation v Alhaji Atiku Abubakar* (2007), cited by the Plaintiff, due to differences in constitutional frameworks and the absence of an impeachment requirement for disqualification in Sierra Leone. Collectively, the judgments affirmed the centrality of party affiliation in Sierra Leone's democratic system, upholding the President's authority to act on constitutional disqualifications and reinforcing the rule of law through a purposive and context-sensitive interpretation of the Constitution.

5. Dissecting The Sam Sumana Supreme Court Verdict

While the first question posed by the Plaintiff for a determination by the Court was inaccurate, I strongly disagree that the President can remove his Vice President under the Constitution for whatever reason, not even just for the loss of membership in a political party. The Supreme Court justices collectively erred in law to have returned such judgement for the reasons canvassed below.

First, they failed to consider the 'mischief rule' that the drafters of the 1991 Constitution intended to remedy. The 1991 Constitution emanated from the 1978 One-Party Constitution. In the latter, Vice Presidents were appointed by the President after elections. They did not have to run alongside the President as it obtains in the 1991 Constitution. This was to reduce some of the powers of the President, who had the vice presidents at his whims and caprices and could sack them at will. With the 1991 Constitution, procedures are clearly set out to relieve the Vice President pursuant to sections 50 and 51 so that the drafters of the 1991 Constitution considered that the Vice President can be removed from office in the case of mental or physical incapacity or misconduct. Section 55 of the 1991 Constitution clearly sets out situations where vacancy is deemed to occur in the office of the Vice President. In addition to sections 50 and 51, those situations include:

22 Constitution of Sierra Leone, S.40.

- expiration of the term of office of the President
- resignation
- retirement
- death of the Vice President
- and upon the assumption of office by the Vice President to the office of the President under subsection (4) of section 49.

Therefore, there should be no other means or source of removal or creating a vacancy in the office of the Vice President except by way of a constitutional amendment, which is not the domain of the Judiciary but Parliament. Anything other than that is a travesty of justice. While the Supreme Court's determination in the Sam-Sumana case carries the weight of legal authority, its expansive interpretation of presidential power undermines constitutional safeguards and represents a misstep in upholding the principles of justice and democratic accountability. The Court created a dangerous approach to constitutional interpretation by imputing words into the Constitution and creating a new form of removal of an elected Vice President. Even if the Supreme Court thought that the provisions for a vacancy in the office of the Vice President, as in the office of the President, are not exhaustive, it is the role of Parliament and not the Court to cure such inadequacy. Judges who are not elected representatives should be slow to make laws since such laws do not undergo any scrutiny.

The purposive rule of interpretation that the Supreme Court heavily relied on may have been misapplied. The Court limited its inference to the text of the Constitution and looked no further. It failed to look at the generality of the context of the office of the Vice President, which includes the 1978 One-Party Constitution, the Report of the 1978 National Constitutional Review Commission, the Hansard of Parliament, the 1995 APC Party Constitution and the then leadership of the APC Party. All these would have informed the Court to uphold the justice of this matter if a holistic approach of this nature had been adopted in the instant case.

Second, the failure of the Court to establish the legality or lack thereof and the reason surrounding the expulsion of the Vice President by his party executive, of which the President was the Chairman and Leader, is a fatal error that transformed justice into a plaything in the hands of the Executive. The Supreme Court remarked thus, 'Whether or not he ought to have been expelled from the Party is not an issue before the Court.' With the latitude of the jurisdiction of the Supreme Court, one only wonders what legal impediment could have stood in the way of that Court inquiring into the expulsion and the procedures that must be followed in expelling such a member who is not just an ordinary member but whose membership has a deep-rooted relationship with the Constitution and the entire governance architecture as a Vice President. Political parties are a creation of the Constitution[23] and are registered pursuant to the Political Parties Registration Act, 2002.[24]

Section 35 (2) of the Constitution states that 'the internal organization of a political party shall conform to democratic principles, and its aims, objectives, purposes and programmes shall not contravene, or be inconsistent with, any provisions of this Constitution.' It is, therefore, a fundamental error by the Court to have reasoned that they could not inquire into the Vice President's expulsion from his political party because it was not an issue for determination before them. The Supreme Court itself admitted that the Vice President did no wrong, neither did he resign from his party. According to the acting Chief Justice, '(H)e did not resign from the party so that losing his membership was not his voluntary act…It cannot be said that he 'committed' any act.'[25] Any reasonable person should think that this is more the reason why the Court ought not to have returned an adverse ruling against the Vice President.

Third, the Court did not give due regard to public interest consideration. The Sam Sumana case attracted massive public attention and condemnation as it had to do with the office of the Vice President. Many civil society groups like the Center for Accountability and Rule of Law (CARL), the Renaissance Movement, Campaign for Good Governance (CGG), Native Consortium and Research Center, to name but few, put out press statements condemning the act of relieving the Vice President of his office and duties and declaring such an act by the President as unconstitutional. Similarly, distinguished legal practitioners wrote articles expressing their views and condemning the action of the President to relieve his Vice President.[26]

---

23 Constitution of Sierra Leone, S. 35 (1) provides 'Subject to the provisions of this section, political parties may be established to participate in shaping the political will of the people, to disseminate information on political ideas4 and social and economic programmes of a national character4 and to sponsor candidates for Presidential, Parliamentary or local Government elections.'

24 The Political Parties Act, 2002, Act No. 3 of 2002, https://aceproject.org/ero-en/regions/africa/SL/sierra-leone-the-political-parties-act-2002/view.

25 See the Judgement of Acting Chief Justice V.V. Thomas at p. 21. https://sierralii.gov.sl/akn/sl/judgement/slsc/2015/1203/eng@2015-09-09.

26 Sierra Leone Telegraph, "Sierra Leonean US-based lawyer Alieu Iscandri says expulsion

One such is the erudite and experienced Dr. Abdulai O. Conteh, former Vice President, Attorney-General and Minister of Justice, and at the time, a serving Justice of Appeal of the Court of Appeal of the Commonwealth of The Bahamas. In an open letter to the President, Ernest Bai Koroma, dated 19th March 2015, Conteh wrote thus, 'In short, Your Excellency, neither you nor the Vice President can lawfully be removed from office except as provided for in sections 50 and 51 of the Constitution.'[27]

Dr. Conteh played a pivotal role as a member of the National Constitutional Review Commission, established by the late President Joseph Saidu Momoh, tasked with examining and reformulating the 1978 One-Party Constitution. Under the leadership of the late Dr. Peter Tucker, this Commission conducted extensive consultations nationwide and subsequently submitted its comprehensive report to the President.[28] Notably, the Committee, recognizing the need for reform, proposed a crucial amendment to render the office of the Vice President elective, mirroring the process for the President, rather than an appointive position.[29]

This significant recommendation, aimed at rectifying the flaws of the previous system, was duly embraced by the government and subsequently incorporated into the 1991 Constitution. Dr. Conteh, an integral member of this reformative team, actively contributed to identifying and addressing the underlying issues of the One-Party Constitution. In their deliberations, it is regrettable that the Supreme Court Justices overlooked the valuable insights and reforms proposed by this expert Committee, missing an opportunity to consider the historical context and intentions behind the constitutional amendments.

---

of vice president is unlawful," March 19, 2015, accessed on 22 August 2024, https://www.thesierraleonetelegraph.com/sierra-leonean-us-based-lawyer-alieu-iscandri-says-expulsion-of-vice-president-is-unlawful/.

27 Sierra Leone Telegraph, "International lawyer Dr. Abdulai Conteh says President Koroma's sacking of vice president is illegal," March 19, 2015, accessed on 22nd August 2024, https://www.thesierraleonetelegraph.com/international-lawyer-dr-abdulai-conteh-says-president-koromas-sacking-of-vice-president-is-illegal/.

28 Peter L. Tucker, Report of the Constitutional Review Commission (Freetown, Sierra Leone, 2008), accessed on 22nd August 2024, https://www.parliament.gov.sl/uploads/other_resources/3-%20Dr%20Peter%20Tucker%20Report%202008.pdf.

29 Tucker, Constitutional Review Commission.

6. A Comprehensive Analysis of the ECOWAS Court's Landmark Verdict

Being dissatisfied with the decision of the supreme court, Sumana lodged a petition with the ECOWAS Court. The case before the ECOWAS Court unraveled a complex web of constitutional and human rights issues, with the former Vice-President of Sierra Leone seeking redress for his alleged unconstitutional removal.

The ECOWAS Court grappled with jurisdictional complexities arising from Sumana's expulsion from his political party, the APC, and subsequent removal from office by the President. The Court asserted its authority based on the violation of human rights under regional and international instruments. However, the Supreme Court's refusal to investigate the expulsion created a jurisdictional gap, leaving a critical aspect unexamined. The Court recognized the potential conflict of interest in the President acting as both the 'player and referee.' Sumana's expulsion from the APC was presided over by the President, who was also the APC's Chairman, raising concerns about impartiality. The Latin maxim, 'nemo judex impropria causa sua,' encapsulated the essence of this predicament, prompting the ECOWAS Court to highlight the need for an inquiry into the expulsion for a more holistic understanding.

The Defendant raised concerns about an abuse of procedure, citing a refusal to submit to the Court's jurisdiction. While addressing this, the Court reiterated its duty to verify jurisdiction and emphasized its commitment to delivering true justice, even in the absence of a defense. This stance showcased the Court's dedication to upholding fairness and justice, irrespective of procedural challenges.

The ECOWAS Court emphasized the right to a fair trial, echoing international human rights standards. It underscored the necessity of exhausting domestic remedies, particularly the appeal process, before seeking international adjudication. The Court's analysis highlighted the interconnectedness of fair trial rights and due process, reinforcing the importance of procedural safeguards.

The Court delved into the constitutional framework surrounding Sumana's expulsion, emphasizing the right of appeal provided within the APC's Constitution. The meticulous examination of timelines and the applicant's filing of an appeal on the same day as his dismissal underscored the Court's commitment to scrutinizing legal processes.

The ECOWAS Court's final verdict addressed each aspect of Sumana's claims. Reparations rooted in national law were deemed beyond its jurisdiction, reflecting respect for national sovereignty. The declaration of the President's act as premature and violative of Sumana's right to a fair trial underscored the Court's commitment to upholding human rights.

The ECOWAS Court's landmark ruling in *Samuel Sam-Sumana v Republic of Sierra Leone*[30] represents a pivotal moment in West African jurisprudence, affirming the court's role in upholding human rights and constitutional principles amidst complex jurisdictional and procedural challenges. The court found that the dismissal of Vice President Alhaji Samuel Sam-Sumana by President Ernest Bai Koroma on 17 March 2015 violated Article 7(1)(a) of the African Charter on Human and Peoples' Rights, which guarantees the right to have one's cause heard by competent national organs. Specifically, the court determined that the President's unilateral action, prompted by Sam-Sumana's expulsion from the All People's Congress (APC) and unverified allegations of seeking asylum at the US Embassy, lacked due process, as Sam-Sumana was denied the opportunity to appeal his party expulsion within the 30-day period stipulated by Article 8(i) of the 1995 APC Party Constitution. The ECOWAS Court ruled that the President's decision was premature, violating Sam-Sumana's right to a fair hearing, and ordered Sierra Leone to pay him all salaries, allowances, and entitlements due from the date of his unlawful dismissal until the end of his constitutional term.

The ECOWAS Court's comprehensive analysis exposed a critical conflict of interest, encapsulated in the Latin maxim *nemo judex in propria causa* (no one should be a judge in their own case). As both the President of Sierra Leone and the Chairman and Leader of the APC, Koroma acted as both 'player and referee' in orchestrating Sam-Sumana's expulsion and subsequent dismissal, bypassing the constitutional impeachment procedures outlined in sections 50 and 51 of the 1991 Constitution. The court noted that an inquiry into the reasons for Sam-Sumana's expulsion, potentially related to gross misconduct or mental/physical incapacity, should have been conducted by Parliament, not the President, to ensure accountability and fairness. The Supreme Court of Sierra Leone, in its 2015 ruling, dismissed the relevance of investigating the expulsion, claiming it was not before them for determination, a stance the ECOWAS Court critiqued as undermining due process. This judicial omission

[30] *Samuel Sam-Sumana v Republic of Sierra Leone*, ECW/CCJ/APP/38/16; ECW/CCJ/JUD/19/17, https://caselaw.ihrda.org/en/entity/4ykzlqlzqt3.

reflects broader systemic vulnerabilities in Sierra Leone's judiciary, where executive influence often overshadows constitutional safeguards.

7. Conclusion

It becomes evident that the ramifications of this miscarriage of justice are far-reaching and will cast a long shadow over the Judiciary and those involved in the unanimous decision that granted the President seemingly unchecked powers to relieve his Vice under the Constitution.

The heart of the matter lies in the questionable maneuvering within the political realm, where the President, wearing the dual hats of party Chairman and national leader, orchestrated the removal of the Vice President. This stratagem, however, defied the constitutional provisions outlined in sections 55, 50, and 51. These sections explicitly outline the circumstances under which the office of the Vice President becomes vacant and the lawful procedures for filling such vacancies.

The expulsion of the Vice President from his political party without due process, a hearing, or the opportunity to exhaust the appeals process, as mandated by the APC Party 1995 Constitution, is a constitutional calamity. The failure to distinguish between expulsion and voluntary loss of membership, coupled with the Supreme Court's assertion that party membership is a continuous requirement under section 41 of the Constitution, further compounds this legal quagmire.

This singular instance emerges as a constitutional crisis of substantial magnitude, reminiscent of the tumultuous post-war period since 2002. The decision overlooked due process and neglected the intricate constitutional provisions that govern the tenure and removal of the Vice President. The implications of this decision echo beyond the courtroom, raising concerns about the integrity of the Judiciary and its role in safeguarding constitutional principles.

This miscarriage of justice underscores the persistent challenges faced by the Judiciary in Sierra Leone, despite the strides made since the end of the eleven years of civil war. It serves as a stark reminder that to truly contribute to the country's healing and progress and judicial authorities must steadfastly strive to redeem the Judiciary from the shackles of such constitutional calamities. The Truth and Reconciliation Commission Report's assertion that miscarriages of justice contributed to the brutal civil war resonates strongly, emphasizing the urgent need for ongoing efforts to fortify the Judiciary against the recurrence of such grievous errors. Only through a vigilant commitment to upholding justice and constitutional principles can the Judiciary regain the trust and confidence of the nation it serves.

FREE SPEECH AND JUDICIAL INDEPENDENCE: LESSONS FROM THE PAUL DUMBAR AND MICHAEL MANSARAY CASES

CONRAD LISK

1. Introduction

The interplay between freedom of expression and judicial independence lies at the heart of any democratic society. In Sierra Leone, this delicate balance has been tested repeatedly, most notably in the legal controversies surrounding the cases of Reverend Paul Dumbar and Michael Mansaray. These cases, though separated by decades, reflect enduring challenges in reconciling public order legislation with constitutional rights, particularly the right to free speech.

This chapter critically examines the legal dynamics of these two landmark cases, focusing on how the judiciary navigated the complex intersection of political sensitivities and legal principles. Reverend Dumbar's case,[1] set against the backdrop of Sierra Leone's transition from a constitutional monarchy to a republic, highlights the judiciary's response to politically charged prosecutions under the Public Order Act of 1965.[2]

Similarly, the prosecution of Michael Mansaray in the digital age underscores the evolving nature of free speech challenges, with new technologies introducing additional dimensions to existing legal tensions.

---

1 *Dumbar v S.*, [1972] SLCA 1279 (15 February 1972), accessed on 2nd April 2025 https://sierralii.gov.sl/akn/sl/judgment/slca/1972/1279/eng@1972-02-15.

2 The Public Order Act, 1965, Act No. 46 of 1965, accessed on 2nd April 2025 https://www.sierra-leone.org/Laws/1965-46s.pdf.

This chapter explores what these cases mean for judicial independence and freedom of expression in Sierra Leone by analysing judicial reasoning, procedure, and socio-political context. Framed by history and law, the discussion underscores the tensions that persist and the reforms that could follow.

2. Historical Context

On 15 January 1971, a public meeting took place at the Koidu Community Centre, attended by Sierra Leone's Lands, Prime Minister, Siaka Stevens, and Reverend Paul Dumbar, a clergyman and Sierra Leone People's Party (SLPP) politician. An incident occurred during the gathering, prompting a police investigation. On 19 January 1971, at 10:10 a.m., police arrested Reverend Dumbar and brought him before a magistrate. No record specifies whether the arrest was by warrant or otherwise, suggesting potential violations of sections 4 to 15 of Part 1 of the Criminal Procedure Act 1965. Despite these irregularities, Reverend Dumbar submitted to the court's jurisdiction, and his defence did not challenge the arrest's legality. This case, set against the All People's Congress (APC) government's political tensions, reflects the judicial irregularities and political interference critiqued by the Truth and Reconciliation Commission[3] underscoring issues of arbitrary justice that persist in Sierra Leone's judiciary.

On 19 January 1971, Reverend Dumbar was charged in the magistrate's court under section 3(1) of the Public Order Act 1965 with using threatening and abusive language intended to provoke a breach of the peace. The charge stated:

> 'That you, the Reverend Paul Dumbar, on 15th January 1971, made use of threatening and abusive language with intent to provoke any person or others to commit a breach of the peace, contrary to s.3(1) of the Public Order Act, 1965.'[4]

Reverend Dumbar pleaded not guilty, stating, 'I am not aware of this charge because I do not remember that I insulted anybody on 15th January 1971, anywhere. This is all and true.' The prosecution relied on two witnesses:

[3] Truth and Reconciliation Commission of Sierra Leone, Witness to Truth: Report of the Truth and Reconciliation Commission, vol. 1 (Freetown: Truth and Reconciliation Commission, 2004), 27.

[4] The Public Order Act, S. 3(i).

the arresting police officer, who took Dumbar's statement but was not confirmed present at the scene, and the Minister of Information, who claimed Dumbar's words caused a commotion requiring security intervention.

Reverend Dumbar testified that he was invited by the Senior District Officer, believing the meeting was a public event. However, it turned political, with a government minister leading partisan chants. When Dumbar attempted to address the Minister, the Resident Minister rebuffed him, prompting an apology. Subsequently, APC supporters attacked him. His counsel submitted a no-case argument, citing insufficient evidence, but the magistrate overruled it. The defence rested without further addresses, and on the following day, the magistrate found Dumbar guilty, sentencing him to two months' imprisonment. This swift conviction, amid questionable arrest procedures, highlights the article's theme of judicial bias and parallels modern non-assignment issues.

Following an investigation by the arresting police officer and the recording of the statement, the appellant was summarily presented before the magistrate. Although the case had to be momentarily adjourned at 1 p.m., the appellant was granted bail, and the trial recommenced ten minutes later. Regrettably, there is no evidence on record detailing the circumstances of the appellant's arrest, whether by warrant or other means. Despite potential irregularities, the appellant submitted to the jurisdiction, and the defence did not contest this action, despite its seemingly arbitrary and unlawful nature, given the provisions of ss.4 to 15 of Part 1 of the Criminal Procedure Act, 1965.[5]

3. The Appeal to the High Court

The Appeal to the High Court, Reverend Paul Dumbar, a clergyman and SLPP politician, appealed his conviction under section 3(1) of the Public Order Act 1965, seeking exoneration during Sierra Leone's transition from a constitutional monarchy to a republic on 19 April 1971, which centralized executive power in the presidency. On 25 May 1971, after serving approximately 40 days, Dumbar filed his appeal, initially on two grounds, later amended to five, with the fifth abandoned. The four grounds argued before the High Court were:

---

5 The Criminal Procedure Acts, 1965, Act No. 32 of 1965, https://www.sierra-leone.org/Laws/1965-32.pdf.

(a) The charge upon which the learned trial magistrate convicted the appellant was bad for duplicity in that it charged two separate offences in one count.

(b) The charge upon which the learned trial magistrate convicted the appellant was bad for uncertainty and vagueness.

(c) The learned trial magistrate was wrong in law in finding the appellant guilty of the offence charged.

(d)The verdict was unreasonable or could not be supported having regard to the evidence.

In his appeal, Reverend Dumbar contended that the charge was uncertain and vague. He challenged the use of the words 'any or other person' in the charge, asserting confusion and prejudice. The asserted that the charge was duplicitous, contending that it accused him of two separate offenses in a single count. The third ground highlighted a legal error in the magistrate's finding of guilt, and the fourth questioned the reasonableness of the verdict in the light of the evidence presented. Additionally, he argued the circumstances of his words were neither threatening nor insulting.

The State argued that Reverend Dumbar, by not objecting to the charge during the trial, acknowledged the case against him. They asserted that the words '*I am sorry for Sierra Leone*' implied insult towards the Minister and government, intending to provoke a breach of the peace.

The learned judge in the High Court considered arguments on the various grounds put forth. The learned judge, Tejan, J., who heard the appeal, reviewed the evidence before the magistrate and considered the criticisms against the latter's judgment, then finally disallowed the appeal hence upholding the trial magistrate's decision. The learned judge confirmed both the conviction and the sentence. In his judgment, Tejan, J. noted as follows:

> 'However, the appellant was charged for an offence under the Public Order Act, 1965. In the case of *Ward v Holman*[6] the defendant was charged under s.5 of the English Public Order Act, 1936.

6 *Ward v Holman*, [1964] 2 Q.B. 850.

> The section enacts that-'Any person who in any public place or at any public meeting uses threatening, abusive or insulting words or behaviour with intent to provoke a breach of the peace or whereby a breach of the peace is likely to be occasioned, shall be guilty of an offence.' This provision is similar to the provision of the Public Order Act, 1965.'

Section 3 of the Public Order Act, 1965 under which the appellant was charged reads:

> 'Any person who-
> (i) makes use of any threatening, abusive, insulting or obscene language, gesture, or behaviour, or says or sings any insulting or offensive song or ballad, or makes any noise with intent to provoke any other person to commit a breach of the peace; ... shall, on conviction, be liable to a fine, not exceeding twenty leones or imprisonment for a period not exceeding three months or both.'

Tejan, J. in his judgment quoted this extract from the judgment of the learned trial magistrate:

> 'The accused is a politician of long-standing experience and a clergyman. In both capacities he is constantly in contact with the public and I am satisfied that a reasonable man in his position would expect the public at the meeting to react with some degree of hostility to his behaviour.'

The legal issues surrounding Reverend Dumbar's arrest and conviction reflect a complex mix of events, conflicting narratives, and legal arguments. The case highlights the tension between protecting freedom of expression and enforcing restrictions under public order laws.

4. Judicial Decision and Rationale of the Court of Appeal

Undeterred by the High Court's decision, Reverend Dumbar appealed to the Court of Appeal, introducing nuanced arguments regarding the perceived similarity between Sierra Leone's Public Order Act 1965 and England's Public Order Act 1936. The appeal panel, consisting of Forster JSC, Cornelius Harding JA, and Percy Davies JA, delivered their judgement on February 15, 1972.

The grounds of appeal were originally three, but by leave of the Court amended to four grounds as follows:

1. The learned trial judge[7] was wrong in law in holding that the charge against the appellant was not bad for duplicity.
2. The learned trial judge was wrong in law in holding that the charge against the appellant was not bad for uncertainty and/or
3. The learned trial judge was wrong in law in holding that s.3(i) of the Public Order Act, 1965 was similar to s.5 of the English Public Order Act, 1936.
4. The verdict was unreasonable, unwarranted and such as could not be supported having regard to the evidence.

Forster JSC scrutinized the facts, expressing concern over arbitrary and unlawful arrest procedures. Despite acknowledging flaws in the charge's wording, he affirmed its adequacy. Cornelius Harding JA swiftly dismissed certain grounds, emphasizing procedural form over substance. Percy Davies JA, while concurring, drew an analogy between Reverend Dumbar's words and potential insults to judicial independence, providing a unique perspective on the case.

The Court of Appeal's decisions merit critical evaluation. The analogy drawn by Percy Davies JA raises questions about the perceived offense in criticizing government leaders and the potential implications for freedom of expression. The political context, marked by historical tensions between opposition and ruling parties, adds complexity to the interpretation of Reverend Dumbar's words.

5. Critical Analysis of the Judgement of Justice Forster, JSC

The judgement of Justice Forster, JSC, in the appeal of Reverend Dumbar under section 3(i) of the Public Order Act 1965 provides a comprehensive legal analysis, emphasising procedural fairness, the clarity of charges, and the sufficiency of evidence. However, it also raises critical questions about the broader implications of judicial interpretation and the balance between public order and individual rights.

---

[7] As a matter of correction, the learned judge was not the trial judge, the original case having been heard by a magistrate, and thence to the High Court on appeal.

Justice Forster's reasoning reflects a strict adherence to the legal principle that mens rea, or the intent to provoke a breach of the peace, is a crucial element of the charged offence. He emphasised that the magistrate's findings on the accused's intent were sufficiently supported by evidence, particularly the inflammatory nature of the appellant's remarks within the charged political atmosphere.

While this focus aligns with established principles of criminal liability, it arguably underplays the broader context of the case, including the appellant's position as a clergyman and politician attempting to participate in public discourse.

Forster's reliance on the English Criminal Justice Act 1967 to justify inferences about intent further underscores the centrality of mental state in his reasoning. However, this comparative approach risks imposing external jurisprudential standards without fully accounting for the socio-political dynamics of Sierra Leone.

The judgement carefully dismisses challenges to the procedural aspects of the case, including the charge's alleged duplicity and vagueness. Forster rejected the claim that the charge was ambiguous, noting that the appellant had understood the allegations against him and was not prejudiced in his defence.

This finding reflects a pragmatic view, prioritising substance over form. However, it raises questions about whether such leniency in procedural matters could inadvertently lower the threshold for legal precision in criminal charges.

Forster's assertion that the appellant did not object to the form of the charge during the trial effectively shifts responsibility onto the defence, reinforcing the principle that failure to raise objections constitutes a waiver. This approach upholds procedural fairness but could be critiqued for overlooking the power imbalance between the state and the accused in politically charged cases.

Justice Forster upheld the magistrate's evaluation of the evidence, particularly the testimony of prosecution witnesses. He concluded that the appellant's conduct was reasonably interpreted as insulting and intended to provoke a breach of the peace.

Notably, Forster concurred with the magistrate's reasoning that the appellant, as a seasoned politician and cleric, should have anticipated the public reaction to his remarks. This reliance on the appellant's social position to infer intent introduces a moral dimension to the legal analysis, suggesting an expectation of heightened responsibility for public figures.

However, this reasoning could be critiqued for being overly subjective. It risks conflating the appellant's personal identity with his legal culpability, potentially undermining the neutrality required in assessing criminal intent.

Justice Forster briefly acknowledged the absence of an appeal against the imposed sentence but did not engage in a substantive evaluation of its appropriateness. The two-month custodial sentence, while within the statutory limits, appears disproportionate given the non-violent nature of the offence.

A deeper examination of the sentence's proportionality would have strengthened the judgement, particularly in light of the potential chilling effect such punitive measures might have on free speech in politically sensitive contexts.

Forster's judgement reflects a judicial approach that prioritises legal clarity and evidentiary sufficiency over broader considerations of constitutional freedoms and procedural precision. His reasoning reinforces the importance of public order in a nascent republic but raises concerns about the potential for state overreach in regulating political expression.

The dismissal of the appeal on all grounds underscores the judiciary's commitment to upholding legislative intent but also invites scrutiny regarding the role of courts in safeguarding individual rights against the backdrop of political tensions.

Justice Forster's judgement is a meticulous exercise in legal reasoning, affirming the magistrate's decision through a structured analysis of the appellant's arguments. However, the emphasis on intent and procedural fairness, while legally sound, overlooks critical opportunities to address the broader implications for freedom of speech and judicial independence. The judgement underscores the judiciary's role in maintaining public order but leaves unresolved questions about the boundaries of state power in curtailing political expression by relying on pragmatic interpretations of procedural challenges and deference to legislative intent. The decision, therefore, serves as a pivotal case in understanding the delicate balance between individual rights and societal stability in Sierra Leone's evolving legal landscape.

6. Post-Dumbar Legal Developments

Sierra Leone underwent significant transformations in the five decades following the Dumbar judgement, marked by political shifts, civil unrest, and legal reforms. The aftermath of the Dumbar judgement saw a consolidation of power under a one-party constitution in 1978,[8] with President Stevens's All People's Congress (APC) emerging as the sole recognized party. This political landscape, where government ministers enjoyed relative immunity from opposition criticism, persisted for years, shaping the dynamics of governance.

Tragically, the nation plunged into a devastating civil war in 1991, lasting until 2002. During the period from 1992 to 1996, Sierra Leone experienced military rule, adding another layer of complexity to its political history. The year 1996 witnessed the return of multi-party elections, leading to the victory of the Sierra Leone People's Party (SLPP) under President Ahmad Tejan Kabbah. However, the war persisted, culminating in Tejan Kabbah's temporary ousting by a military junta. Reverend Dumbar, who had assumed the role of SLPP Chairman, met a poignant end in March 1998, succumbing to a rebel attack at Yardu village in Kono District at the age of eighty-six. Posthumously, he was honoured as an Officer of the Order of the Rokel.

The political landscape further evolved with a transition back to a dominant two-party system. In 2007, Ernest Bai Koroma, the candidate of the APC, was elected president, serving until 2018. Succession brought President Julius Maada Bio of the SLPP into office as the incumbent. President Bio, in alignment with his manifesto commitment, declared his intention to repeal the defamatory and seditious libel laws embedded in the Public Order Act of 1965. Subsequently, Sierra Leone's Parliament, two years later, took a significant step by repealing Part V of the Public Order Act.[9] This part contained the contentious defamatory and seditious libel provisions, long criticized for stifling dissent during the preceding five decades.[10]

While the repeal of these laws marked a positive development for advocates of free expression, concerns arose the following year with a legal case reminiscent of Reverend Dumbar's prosecution. The echoes of the past raised questions about the enduring challenges to free speech and the need for ongoing vigilance in protecting democratic values in Sierra Leone. The nation's legal landscape continued to evolve, shaped by its historical context and the ongoing pursuit of a more just and inclusive society.

---

8 Constitution of Sierra Leone.

9 IFEX, "Sierra Leone's parliament repeals criminal libel law that threatens free speech," November 1, 2020, accessed on 2nd April 2025 https://ifex.org/sierra-leones-parliament-repeals-criminal-libel-law-that-threatens-free-speech/.

10 ARTICLE 19, "Sierra Leone: Decriminalisation of Defamation," November 2, 2020, accessed on 2nd April 2025 https://www.article19.org/resources/sierra-leone-decriminalisation-of-defamation/.

7. The Case of Michael Mansaray - A Comprehensive Analysis

Michael Mansaray, a youth leader of the opposition APC party in Sierra Leone, found himself at the center of a legal maelstrom that exposed the challenges to free speech and the evolving legal landscape in the aftermath of the Dumbar case. The intricate details of his case, spanning from the alleged abduction to the legal proceedings that followed, illuminate the complex interplay between politics, law, and technological advancements.

In April 2021, Mansaray filmed a video in front of the Bo Mini Stadium, praising former President Ernest Bai Koroma and criticizing the incumbent President Bio. The video, posted on WhatsApp, went viral, sparking a sequence of events that underscored the vulnerability of individuals expressing dissenting political views.

Mansaray's subsequent abduction, allegedly by supporters of the ruling SLPP, revealed a disturbing trend of suppressing opposition voices. A video emerged showing him unclothed and verbally abused in a vehicle, raising concerns about his well-being.[11] The circumstances of his detention, orchestrated by individuals identified as governing party activists, highlighted the blurred lines between political allegiance and law enforcement.

The legal backdrop against which Mansaray's case unfolded was characterized by a technological leap since the Dumbar case. The proliferation of internet access and mobile phones facilitated the dissemination of information, often through platforms like Facebook and WhatsApp. The absence of specific legislation addressing cyber offences led to the introduction of the Cybersecurity and Crime Act in 2021,[12] which was yet to be passed when Mansaray made his video.

The legal vacuum became apparent when the police, unable to charge Mansaray under repealed laws like 'seditious words,' resorted to a questionable drug possession charge. The seizure of painkiller tablets, notably the 'Relief' medication, became the focal point of the prosecution. Critics argued that the medication did not fall under prohibited or restricted drugs, questioning the basis of the charges.

---

[11] The Makoni Times - Sierra Leone, "Michael Mansaray is in hiding from the ruthless SLPP kamajors," Facebook video, December 30, 2021, accessed 2nd April 2025, https://www.facebook.com/watch/?v=1326209611149050.

[12] The Cybersecurity and Crime Act, 2021, Act No. 12 of 2021, accessed 2nd April 2025, https://www.parliament.gov.sl/uploads/acts/THE%20CYBERSECURITY%20AND%20CRIME%20ACT,%202021%20-%20%2025TH%20NOVEMBER,%202021.pdf.

The court proceedings unfolded with Mansaray initially remanded in custody, later pleading not guilty. The defence presented evidence of his unlawful detention by forest guards and governing party supporters, but the legal arguments did not delve into free speech considerations. The trial magistrate, seemingly viewing Mansaray's initial detention as a submission to the court's jurisdiction, eventually found him guilty and sentenced him to eight months in custody.

The legality of the sentence imposed on Mansaray under the National Drugs Control Act 2008 was fiercely contested, as the Act prescribes a minimum five-year custodial sentence for offences under its provisions. However, the court invoked section 14, a unique provision that permits the suspension of the whole or part of a penalty for a first-time offender, provided it serves the interests of justice and aligns with the broader public interest.[13] This section allows the court to impose terms and conditions to prevent reoffending, marking a significant departure from standard sentencing practices. The decision to suspend the custodial sentence sparked significant controversy, with sections of the press alleging political motivations behind his prosecution, suggesting that the case was an attempt to suppress freedom of expression.

Reports suggesting threats against the regional police chief, if Mansaray was released added a layer of political pressure on the case. The absence of a clear legal basis for the search at Mansaray's home further fueled suspicions of politically motivated actions. His release in November, after serving two-thirds of his sentence, raised questions about the legality and motivations behind his imprisonment.[14]

The parallels with Reverend Dumbar's case were evident - both opposition figures, attacked by government supporters and faced criminal charges under unconventional laws. Yet, differences emerged, such as the clarity of events leading to Mansaray's arrest and the absence of charges like seditious words due to legislative changes.

The post-Mansaray legal landscape witnessed the introduction of the Cybersecurity and Crime Act in 2021. The Act, introduced to combat

---

13 National Drug Control Act 2008, Act No. 10 of 2008, S. 14, https://www.sierra-leone.org/Laws/2008-10.pdf.

14 Sylvia Olayinka Blyden, "Opposition APC Youth Michael Magba Mansaray Unlawfully Spends 45th Day in Custody," Sierra Leone Telegraph, June 12, 2021, 2nd August 2025, https://www.thesierraleonetelegraph.com/opposition-apc-youth-michael-magba-mansaray-unlawfully-spends-45th-day-in-custody/comment-page-1/.

cybercrimes like online fraud and cyberbullying, has been applied in high-profile cases that highlight tensions between cybersecurity and political free expression. Notably, musician Alhaji Amadu Bah (LAJ) was arrested in 2022 for threatening a journalist on Facebook,[15] reality TV star Hawa Hunt faced charges in 2024 for criticizing President Julius Maada Bio and First Lady Fatima Maada Bio,[16] with charges later dropped in March 2025, and student Mohamed Kabia was charged in 2023 for defamatory WhatsApp messages about a politician.[17] These cases underscore the act's broad enforcement but also raise concerns about its potential to suppress dissent, as it remains untested against Sierra Leone's constitutional free speech protections, prompting calls for greater transparency and legal scrutiny. [18]

8. Implications of Repealing Sections of the Public Order Act

Sierra Leone marked a significant milestone on July 23, 2020, as Parliament repealed sections of the Public Order Act of 1965.[19] This legislative move, celebrated by various segments of society, marked a commendable step toward fostering freedom of speech and the right to free expression in the country. However, the implications of this repeal extend beyond the domestic legal landscape, intertwining with international human rights standards and the evolving role of Sierra Leone within the ECOWAS community.

In understanding the ramifications of the repealed sections, it is essential to consider the ECOWAS Court's decision in the Federation of African Journalists and the Republic of Gambia case.[20] This case, originating from The Gambia, highlighted the violations of human rights, particularly freedom of expression, through the enforcement of laws criminalizing free speech.

---

15 Media Foundation for West Africa (MFWA), "Sierra Leone: Popular rapper spews threats, insult against Journalist," Media Foundation for West Africa, December 28, 2021, accessed on 2nd April 2025 https://mfwa.org/sierra-leone-popular-rapper-spews-threats-insult-against-journalist/.

16 Amnesty International, "Sierra Leone: Authorities must release and guarantee fair trial for TV personality detained under accusations of insulting the President and First Lady," Amnesty International, January 30, 2025, 2nd April 2025, https://www.amnesty.org/en/latest/news/2025/01/sierra-leone-fair-trial-hawa-hunt/.

17 Concord Times newspaper, June 18, 2025.

18 Humphrina Pearce and Francis Turay, "The State of Cyber-Bullying in Sierra Leone: Where Is the Law?," Sierra Leone Legal Information Institute, December 8, 2023, https://sierralii.gov.sl/articles/2023-12-08/Humphrina/the-state-of-cyber-bullying-in-sierra-leone-where-is-the-law.

19 The Public Order Act.

20 *Federation of African Journalists and Others v The Gambia*, Judgment, ECW/CCJ/JUD/04/18 (2018), accessed on 2nd April 2025 https://caselaw.ihrda.org/entity/w9z5b6xfwy?-file=16137402186609stg9st25rg.pdf.

The ECOWAS Court's directive in this judgement was clear, it directed the Gambian government, the Defendants, to repeal or amend the laws that violated international human rights standards. The Court deemed the criminal laws on libel, sedition, and false news as 'obvious' and 'gross' violations of the right to freedom of expression. This judgement served as a precedent with direct implications for Sierra Leone, a member of the ECOWAS Court, under the Revised ECOWAS Treaty.

Sierra Leone, by repealing the relevant sections of the Public Order Act, has taken a significant step in aligning its national laws with the ECOWAS Court's decisions. According to Article 5(2) of the Revised ECOWAS Treaty, each member state is obligated to incorporate such legislative and statutory texts into its national legislation. This incorporation ensures the direct applicability and effect of ECOWAS Court decisions on national laws.

The repealed Public Order Act, therefore, acts as a conduit for Sierra Leone to adopt the legal standing of decriminalizing libel laws. This aligns with the ECOWAS Court's directive and reinforces the commitment to international human rights principles, as Sierra Leone brings its domestic laws in harmony with the ECOWAS Revised Treaty.

The implications of this repeal resonate beyond legal technicalities. It signifies a profound shift in Sierra Leone's commitment to freedom of expression and access to information. The criminal defamation and seditious libel provisions, which have stifled the media and led to self-censorship, are now eradicated. This move reinforces the fundamental rights enshrined under Section 25 of the 1991 Constitution,[21] echoing the sentiments of the ECOWAS Court.

Sierra Leone has not only embraced a more progressive legal framework by responding to the ECOWAS Court's directive but has also positioned itself as a champion of democratic values and human rights. The repeal serves as a beacon for journalists, free speech advocates, and the general public, assuring them that the government acknowledges the indispensability of these rights in a democratic society.

The international community, including organizations like ARTICLE 19 and the International Federation of Journalists (IFJ), has lauded Sierra Leone's decision. The repeal of criminal libel laws is hailed as a victory for freedom of expression and press freedom. Such recognition further underscores Sierra

---

21 Constitution of Sierra Leone.

Leone's commitment to democratic principles and aligning its legal framework with international standards.

The repeal of sections of the Public Order Act is not merely a legal amendment but a transformative step toward upholding democratic values, fortifying freedom of expression, and aligning with the evolving human rights landscape in the ECOWAS region. Sierra Leone's journey toward a more progressive legal framework stands as an exemplar for nations grappling with similar challenges to freedom of expression.

9. Judicial Independence and Free Speech - Lessons from Dumbar and Mansaray

The legal narratives of Reverend Dumbar's case and the more recent ordeal of Michael Mansaray unveil intricate layers that not only delve into freedom of expression but also cast a critical spotlight on the state of judicial independence in Sierra Leone. Analyzing these cases illuminates the challenges and concerns surrounding the autonomy of the judiciary and its intersecting dynamics with the broader canvas of freedom of expression.

The very foundation of judicial independence, a cornerstone of any democratic society, was tested in both Dumbar and Mansaray cases. Reverend Dumbar's arrest and subsequent legal proceedings occurred at a time when Sierra Leone was navigating the complexities of political transition. The allegations of interference or influence in the judicial process, although not explicitly proven, hinted at a fragility in the autonomy of the judiciary. Fast forward to Mansaray's case, and a troubling pattern emerges. The questionable legal basis for his arrest, subsequent charges, and the swift sentencing without robust scrutiny of the legal parameters underscore potential pressures on the judiciary.

The appointment and removal of chief justices and judges, particularly in politically charged environments, become focal points of concern.[22] The specter of undue influence, whether direct or indirect, poses a threat to the impartiality and autonomy that judicial independence demands. The judiciary's ability to act as a check on executive power and safeguard individual rights is contingent upon its freedom from external pressures.

---

[22] Jan Van Zyl Smit, The Appointment, Tenure and Removal of Judges under Commonwealth Principles: A Compendium and Analysis of Best Practice (London: British Institute of International and Comparative Law, 2015), https://www.biicl.org/documents/689_bingham_centre_compendium.pdf.

Judicial independence is intrinsically linked to the protection and preservation of fundamental rights, including freedom of expression. In both Dumbar and Mansaray cases, the individuals faced legal consequences for expressing dissenting views against the government. The judiciary's role in upholding the right to freedom of expression is pivotal, as it acts as the ultimate arbiter in determining the constitutionality of laws and actions that may impede this fundamental right.

However, when judicial independence is compromised, the enforcement and interpretation of laws affecting freedom of expression become susceptible to political considerations. In Mansaray's case, the seemingly arbitrary application of drug possession charges, which critics argue were a pretext to stifle political dissent, showcases the vulnerabilities in the judicial system. The judiciary's role in scrutinizing laws for conformity with constitutional principles becomes imperative to prevent the misuse of legal mechanisms to suppress dissenting voices.

The intersection of judicial independence challenges and freedom of expression issues is evident in the perceived politicization of legal proceedings. The judiciary, as the guardian of fundamental rights, must act independently to ensure that laws affecting freedom of expression are applied impartially. In both cases, concerns were raised about the potential influence of political actors on legal processes. This influence, whether direct or indirect, can compromise the judiciary's ability to safeguard constitutional rights, leading to a chilling effect on freedom of expression.[23]

Moreover, the absence of robust legal mechanisms to address cyber offenses, as seen in Mansaray's case, reflects a broader challenge. The judiciary's capacity to adapt to evolving legal landscapes, especially in the age of technology, is crucial. Delays or gaps in updating legal frameworks may inadvertently infringe on freedom of expression, as seen in Mansaray's case where the absence of specific cyber offense laws left room for potential misuse of existing statutes.

To fortify judicial independence and its intersection with freedom of expression, several recommendations emerge. Strengthening legal frameworks

---

[23] Dirk Neuburger et al., "The Need for Independent Judges and a Free Press in a Democracy," UNODC Doha Declaration Global Programme, May 3, 2021, https://www.unodc.org/dohadeclaration/en/news/2021/05/the-need-for-independent-judges-and-a-free-press-in-a-democracy.html and Margaret Satterthwaite, Report of the Special Rapporteur on the independence of judges and lawyers: Safeguarding the independence of judicial systems in the face of contemporary challenges to democracy (A/HRC/56/62), United Nations Human Rights Council, 2024, https://docs.un.org/en/A/HRC/56/62.

to address contemporary challenges, such as cyber offences, is paramount. Regular judicial training on evolving legal landscapes ensures judges are well-equipped to navigate complexities.

Additionally, transparent processes for judicial appointments, security of tenure, and safeguards against external pressures are pivotal. Creating mechanisms for oversight and accountability within the judiciary, without compromising its independence, fosters public trust and confidence in the legal system.

10. Conclusion

The trajectory of free speech in Sierra Leone, as illuminated by the pivotal cases of Dumbar and Mansaray, mirrors a complex interplay between political dynamics and legal frameworks. Despite the repeal of Part V of the Public Order Act, ostensibly a stride towards greater freedom of expression,[24] the emergence of the Cybersecurity and Crime Act has posed new challenges to the landscape of free speech, particularly in online political discourse.

The political landscape, characterized by the alternating reign of the two main parties, reflects a recurring pattern of stifling dissent, where those in power leverage the criminal law to curb critical voices, perpetuating a cycle that mere legal amendments cannot unshackle. The metamorphosis of legislation, from the repealed Public Order Act to the Cybersecurity and Crime Act, highlights the adaptability of mechanisms to stifle expression, particularly in the evolving online sphere.

The cases of *Dumbar* and *Mansaray* cast a spotlight on the intricate balance between judicial independence and freedom of expression. In the face of political pressures and the ever-evolving landscape of communication technologies, a resilient, independent judiciary emerges as the linchpin for upholding democratic values. Judicial independence, fortified by an unwavering commitment to impartiality and justice, becomes the safeguard against encroachments on fundamental rights.

However, the journey towards a society where free speech is not merely a legal provision, but a palpable reality necessitates more than legal amendments.

---

24 ARTICLE 19, "Sierra Leone: Repeal of criminal defamation and seditious libel law a victory for freedom of expression," ARTICLE 19, July 25, 2020, https://www.article19.org/resources/sierra-leone-repeal-of-criminal-defamation-and-seditious-libel-law-a-victory-for-freedom-of-expression/ and Philip Ishmail, "A Viewpoint on the Amended Public Order Act 1965," Politico SL, August 12, 2020, https://politicosl.com/articles/viewpoint-amended-public-order-act-1965.

It demands a seismic shift in Sierra Leone's political culture, a paradigm where those in power view critical speech as an opportunity for dialogue rather than a threat to be suppressed. The delicate equilibrium between the judiciary's autonomy and the imperative to preserve freedom of expression underscores the profound challenges faced by Sierra Leone.

As the nation grapples with these challenges, the imperative remains clear – fostering a political culture where robust, independent institutions, particularly the judiciary, serve as guardians of democratic values. Addressing concerns related to judicial independence becomes not just a legal necessity but a cornerstone for a society where the echoes of free speech resonate undeterred, underpinned by an unwavering commitment to justice, fairness, and the preservation of fundamental rights.

THE WELLINGTON STREET MURDER - COMPLICITY, COMMON PURPOSE AND MENS REA DEBATE

MILLICENT STRONGE

1. Introduction

The Wellington Street murder, as it was popularly known, was one of the most notorious cases in Sierra Leone in the 1970s. Having been born and raised on Wellington Street, I grew up hearing a mixture of facts, stories, and old wives' tales about the crime, which made the case particularly gripping for me. In the annals of Sierra Leonean jurisprudence, the Wellington Street murder, encapsulated in the landmark judgment of *John and Four Others v The State* ('*John* Case'),[1] stands as a striking example of the complexities and dilemmas that shape judicial decision-making.

In the decade before the John case, Sierra Leone jurisprudence examined the criminal law on degrees of complicity, focusing on modes of participation such as 'accessory before the fact,' 'aiding and abetting,' and incitement.[2] The *John* case is significant for addressing accessorial liability in criminal law, a complex and unresolved area in Sierra Leone's jurisprudence. It examines the mental element required for an accessory before the fact, specifically whether they must intentionally desire the crime's commission or if mere foresight of the crime, without intent, suffices to establish guilt for a collateral crime committed by accomplices under the doctrine of common purpose. These cases clarified the definitions and elements required to establish liability for each mode of participation in a crime. In *Kargbo v R*,[3] the Sierra Leone Court

1 *John and four others v The State,* 1972-73 ALR S.L. 441.

2 *R v Bob Jones* 1967-68 ALR S. L. 237.

3 *Kargbo v R* 1967-68 ALR S.L.146.

of Appeal determined that for a defendant to be found as an accessory before the fact to a crime, they 'must be absent' at the time of the commission of that crime. These cases clarified the definitions and elements required to establish liability for each mode of participation in a crime.

This chapter will discuss the mental element of accessorial liability within the doctrine of common purpose, an area for which well-established principles of law on the surface are adrift. With reference to cases from common law jurisdictions, this article argues firstly that based on existing common law cases at the time of the John case, not all the defendants should have been convicted of murder. It also seeks to show that the doctrine of common purpose pursuant to which the defendants in the John case were convicted was and remains an uncertain area of law.

2. The Facts

The brief facts of the case, as related in the ruling of the Court of Appeal,[4] are that during the very early hours of 27 June 1973, the was breaking and entering into the Travellers Lodge situated at Wellington Street, Freetown. On hearing the intruders, the deceased, Mr. Vidal Theophilus King, an elderly man about 70 years old, who was the proprietor of the said lodge, left his room on the first floor to investigate. He was seized and pinned down onto the floor in the parlour.

Meanwhile, his son Reginald, aged about ten years, who was with him in the room, had taken cover underneath a bed. Two intruders entered the bedroom and lifted the mattress from the bed under which he was hiding, whereupon he was forced to give himself up. He was told to come out from under the bed, and when he did, he was asked to show them where his father kept his money. He was told that if he refused, he would be killed. One of the two men carried a knife which he placed at Reginald's back. The safe where the deceased kept his money was accordingly shown to them, and after they had helped themselves to whatever amount that was in the safe, the boy was forced to go with them from room to room on the first floor of the house where they stole yet another amount of money comprising 10 and 5 cent coins, an Omega wristwatch, a radio tape recorder and a camera all belonging to the deceased, Mr. Vidal Theophilus King.

---

4 *John and four others v The State.*

The deceased, Mr. Vidal Theophilus King, was kept pinned down to the floor by a third man. The electric lights were on, and Reginald stated that he could clearly see who the three men were. He said that he implored them not to kill him or his father. He identified the third appellant, Sillah Kamara, as the person pinning his father to the floor and the fourth and fifth appellants, Moses Demby and Michael Danielson, as the two men who burst into the room and who led him around from room to room at knifepoint. After they had collected all they wanted, they told the boy to open the door leading to the steps, and when this had been done, they told him to go back into the bedroom. They then tied up the hands and feet of the deceased and bound his head, face, and neck with a pair of underpants, after which they left the house.

After they had departed, the little boy came from the bedroom to where his father lay, and he shook him, trying to wake him up, but he got no response. He thereupon ran downstairs and called the servant, one Baimba Dumbuya, who came up with him, followed by the first appellant, Sylvanus Balogun John, who at the time was a lodger at the house. The deceased was found dead. A pathologist was called to the scene soon afterwards and pronounced the deceased dead; subsequent examination revealed the cause of death as asphyxia. Undoubtedly, death directly resulted from the attack on the deceased when the intruders broke into his house.

The case was initially heard in the High Court of Sierra Leone. The five defendants, namely, Sylvanus Balogun John, Johnny Grant, Silla Kamara, Moses Demby, and Michael Danielson, were charged with murder[5] and robbery with aggravation.[6]

The Jury in the High Court was directed by the learned trial Judge as follows:

> 'Has the prosecution shown each of the accused to be of sound memory and discretion; that the act of one of them acting in concert with the others and in pursuance of a common design or the acts of all of them together caused the death of another human being; that such act was unlawful; that such act was accompanied by malice. ... If you find that there was no malice in the killing but that it occurred purely as an accident and cannot be divorced from the robbery, you

---

5 Offences Against the Persons Act 1861, S. 1.

6 Larceny Act, 1916, S. 23, as amended by Imperial Statutes (Criminal Law) Adoption (Amendment) Act 1971, S. 2.

> will return a verdict of not guilty of murder. If you find that of all the accused, there is an actor - perpetrator of the fact, and that the common purpose or design of all the accused went to the extent of either express or implied understanding that if anybody sought to prevent them from carrying their purpose into effect he would be dealt with by violent means, it is murder in all of the accused. If you find that the act went beyond the common purpose and that his act was with malice, it is murder only in such an act.[7]'

On the count of robbery with aggravation, the jury was directed that the prosecution had to prove independently of the charge of murder that all the accused 'acting in concert, feloniously and forcibly took from the person or in the presence of Vidal Theophilus King, against his will, property of any value, by violence or putting him in fear.'[8]

On 31 August 1973, all the accused were found guilty, convicted, and sentenced to death[9] in respect of the murder charge. The sentence in respect of aggravated burglary was held in abeyance. They appealed, and their appeals were dismissed.

The second defendant/appellant, Jonny Grant ('Grant'), the subject of this chapter, was found guilty of the charges as an accessory before the fact.[10] He had assisted the 3rd, 4th, and 5th defendants by driving them to the crime scene. He was neither present during the crime, nor did he remain near the crime scene.

Grant and his co-accused have been said to have been part of the rebellious youth culture in Freetown in the 1970s,[11] whereby lack of job opportunities and the means to acquire necessary skills led to drop-outs prone to criminal behaviour, petty theft, and drug abuse.[12] While some of these youths were politically conscious of what was happening in society and very critical, some were only interested in the good life, acquiring a taste for the latest fashion

---

7 *John and four others v The State* p. 446.

8 *John and four others v The State* p. 446.

9 The charge of murder carried a mandatory death sentence at the time of this case.

10 One who, though not physically present during the commission of a felony, procures, counsels, or assists in its preparation. See Archbold Criminal Pleading, Evidence and Practice (London: Sweet & Maxwell, 1966), para. 1500.

11 See political context paragraph 5 below.

12 Ibrahim Abdullah, "Where Did We Go Wrong?': The Youth Question and The Nation-State Project in Sierra Leone," (University of The Western Cape, 2015).

funded by petty theft at home or on the streets.[13] Grant was a working man, described as a 'gold tooth driver,' working at Road Transport Department while the car he used to drive the other defendants to the lodge is said to have been a 'Road Transport Mercedes Benz.'[14]

The question whether it was just for Grant to have been found guilty of murder and robbery with aggravation based on the doctrine of common purpose. He was convicted for assisting the principal defendants, believing they would not use violence, kill, or cause serious injury with intent. Alternatively, he could have been found guilty of manslaughter, which avoids the death penalty.

3. The Doctrine of Common Purpose

The doctrine of common purpose, sometimes referred to as joint enterprise, is a foundational component of criminal liability in common law jurisdictions such as Sierra Leone. It enables the law to hold individuals criminally accountable not only for their direct actions but also for the acts committed by others with whom they shared a criminal plan or understanding. When two or more individuals engage in a collective unlawful enterprise, the doctrine allows for each participant to be held liable for any offence committed by another party to the enterprise, provided that the offence was committed in furtherance of the shared objective.

This doctrine, deeply rooted in English common law, is recognized under Sierra Leonean law through Section 125 of the 1991 Constitution, which incorporates English common law, doctrines of equity, and statutes of general application as of 1 January 1880. In its basic formulation, the doctrine imposes liability for the principal offence that forms the crux of the common enterprise, such as assault, robbery, or treason, so long as the secondary participant knowingly assisted or encouraged the commission of that crime. It places emphasis not on individual action, but on collective intent and mutual participation in the criminal design.[15]

To establish liability under this doctrine, two primary elements must be proven: a conduct element and a mental element. The conduct element requires that the accused person contributed to the execution of the crime,

13 Abdullah, "Where Did We Go Wrong?

14 *John and four others v The State* p. 446.

15 *R. v Macklin*, (1838) 2 Lew. CC 225, 168 E.R. 1136

whether by planning, supplying resources, providing moral support, or facilitating its commission in any meaningful way. The mental element, or mens rea, necessitates proof that the accused intended to promote or assist in the execution of the principal crime, or at least foresaw that such a crime was part of the plan and willingly associated themselves with it.

One of the more complex aspects of this doctrine involves its extension to collateral or unintended crimes. If, during the execution of a joint criminal enterprise, a party to the enterprise commits an additional, unforeseen offence, the question arises whether the remaining participants should be held liable.[16] Sierra Leonean courts have generally followed the principle that if the secondary participant foresaw the risk of such a collateral offence occurring, that foresight might be sufficient to establish criminal liability. However, this approach remains controversial, as it arguably stretches the limits of criminal liability and risks attributing guilt in the absence of specific intent.

The Court of Appeal in the John Case[17] considered the common law as it related to degrees of complicity and accessories.[18] The main issues before them were:

a. Whether the appellants acted in furtherance of a 'common design.'
b. Was the common design a felony involving violence?
c. Was the act which caused the death in furtherance of the common design?

They concluded[19] that on a charge of murder against one or more accused whose common design extended to the express or implied understanding that violence would be used if anyone sought to prevent them from carrying out their purpose, all would be guilty.

The application of the doctrine in Sierra Leonean jurisprudence is exemplified in landmark cases such as *Kaikai & 13 Others v The State*,[20] where the Court of Appeal deliberated on the nature of a common design in the context of treason. The Court held that where a group conspires to commit a crime involving violence, and a fatality results from that violence, all those engaged in the conspiracy may be convicted of murder, even if they did not

---

16 Halsbury's Laws of England, 3rd ed., vol. 10, para. 1370

17 *John and four others v The State* p. 446.

18 Bankole Thompson, The Criminal Law of Sierra Leone (Lanham, MD: University Press of America, 1999), 45.

19 *John and four others v The State* p. 446.

20 *The State v Kai-Kai,* [1989] SLSC p. 7.

directly cause the death. However, where the purpose of the enterprise involved only an unlawful act without the intention of causing serious harm or death, the appropriate charge may be manslaughter. This distinction remains vital in evaluating the proportionality and fairness of liability under joint enterprise.

Another notable decision, *David Lasana & 11 Others v R*[21] highlighted procedural concerns surrounding the doctrine. The Court emphasized that charges must be clearly framed to reflect the degree and nature of each accused's participation. Vague or duplicative counts could obscure the application of the doctrine and result in unfair trials, particularly in politically sensitive prosecutions.

The jurisprudence of the Special Court for Sierra Leone (SCSL) further developed the doctrine through the international legal concept of Joint Criminal Enterprise (JCE), as seen in *Prosecutor v Charles Ghankay Taylor.*[22] This international framework allowed for liability based on participation in a common criminal plan, even where the accused did not commit or directly order specific crimes. The Court considered it sufficient that Taylor contributed to a common purpose that foreseeably resulted in war crimes or crimes against humanity. This interpretation of collective liability, though effective in addressing complex atrocities committed during the civil war, has raised concerns about the breadth and potential overreach of joint liability doctrines.

The practical application of common purpose in Sierra Leone has often intersected with political considerations. The Truth and Reconciliation Commission (TRC) Report criticized how the doctrine was used in treason trials to target political opponents and silence dissent. It noted that courts sometimes relaxed evidentiary standards and failed to adequately assess individual mens rea, thereby undermining the fairness of trials. The politicization of joint enterprise liability has eroded public trust in the judiciary and exposed the need for greater procedural safeguards.

Furthermore, unresolved issues regarding the mental element, particularly whether foresight alone is sufficient to convict an individual for a collateral crime, continue to complicate the legal landscape. Although English law, post-*R v Jogee*,[23] now requires positive intent rather than mere foresight for such liability, Sierra Leonean courts have yet to definitively adopt

---

21 *David Lansana & 11 Others v Regina*,186.

22 *Prosecutor v Charles Ghankay Taylor,* SCSL-03-01-T-1285, https://www.rscsl.org/Documents/Decisions/Taylor/1285/SCSL-03-01-T-1285.pdf.

23 *R. v Jogee*, [2016] UKSC 8.

this standard. The result is legal uncertainty, which can lead to overbroad applications of the doctrine, especially in cases involving mass arrests or politically charged accusations.

In light of these challenges, the doctrine of common purpose in Sierra Leone stands in need of refinement. Greater clarity from the judiciary on the requisite mental element, especially in cases involving extended liability, is essential to ensure that criminal responsibility is assigned fairly and accurately. Legislative reforms that narrow the scope of the doctrine or codify clearer standards for its application may also be warranted. Additionally, improved training for law enforcement and prosecutors on the proper use of the doctrine could help prevent its misuse in politically sensitive cases.

While the doctrine of common purpose remains an important legal tool in addressing group criminality, its application must be tempered by the principles of individual justice, procedural fairness, and constitutional protections. As Sierra Leone continues to rebuild its legal institutions and affirm its commitment to the rule of law, the doctrine must evolve to reflect a more nuanced understanding of shared liability and personal culpability.

4. Applying The Law to the Grant Case

Did Grant, in fact, have a common purpose with the rest of the defendants? Grant, in this case, while admitting to being part of a plan to steal, did not partake in any plan to use weapons or violence.[24] He was not present at the scene, so he could not have actively encouraged the use of violence. Therefore, the common purpose was to steal and not use violence or kill. There was no evidence that Grant knew the plan involved potentially a violent robbery. In his testimony, which went unchallenged,[25] he stated that the other four defendants/appellants had told him that the room which they intended to burgle was 'empty and would be open' and all that had to be done was 'to go in, collect the money and go away.' He was also nowhere near the scene of the crime, having stated in his defence that he only dropped off the 3rd, 4th, and 5th defendant and did not wait but drove off to the 'road transport department…so my side of the affair was over.'[26] He could not be said to have

24 *John and four others v The State* p. 449.

25 In *John and four others v The State* p. 450, the Court of Appeal acknowledged the difference of Grant's position, acknowledging his testimony and the fact that the trial Judge had failed to put Grant's defence to the jury.

26 *John and four others v The State* p. 450.

actively encouraged the other defendants. Apart from assisting in driving the other defendants to the lodge, he could not be said to have actively promoted the crime.

So why was he held liable for murder and robbery with aggravation under the principle of common purpose and not for a lesser crime of manslaughter, which, unlike murder or robbery with aggravation, manslaughter was not a capital offence[27] Must an accessory before the fact intend the crime the principal commits or is the foresight of the principal's commission of the crime alone sufficient?

The legal doctrine of common purpose, also referred to as a joint enterprise, has not been static. In fact, over the years, it has been unsatisfactory and uncertain[28] as to the elements necessary to impose liability on the secondary party for the acts of the principal, particularly in cases where the principal defendant(s) had allegedly gone beyond the scope of what was agreed.

Common law cases have varied in deciding the mental element necessary for liability to be imposed on an accomplice without agreement with the perpetrator(s).

In *R v Collison*,[29] D and his companion, P, went out with the common purpose of stealing apples. They were caught in the act by two-night guards. Without warning, P struck one of the night guards and caused him serious injury. Collison required an intention by P to commit the collateral crime, i.e., to strike one of the night watchmen. It was held that to make D a principal offender, the jury must be satisfied that when D and P went out, they had not only a common purpose to steal apples but also to use violence of a serious level to affect their escape should they be discovered while jointly stealing the apples. The Court held that if they only had a common purpose of stealing, and P's collateral crime was merely the result of the situation in which he found himself, without any previous agreement, D should not be liable for this collateral offence.

In *R v Grant and Gilbert*,[30] the defendants broke into a London hotel, bound and gagged the guards, and stole from the hotel. The guard died

---

[27] Sierra Leone has subsequently abolished the death penalty. See the Abolition of the Death Penalty Act No 6 of 2022 which amends section 23(1) of the Larceny Act 1916. The Abolition of the Death Penalty Act also repealed the death penalty for murder by amending section 1 of the Offences Against the Persons Act 1861.

[28] G.J. Virgo, "Joint Enterprise Is Dead: Long Live Accessorial Liability," Criminal Law Review [2012], 850.

[29] *R. v Collison*, (1831) 4 Car. & P. 565, at 827.

[30] *R. v Grant and Gilbert*, (1954) 38 Cr. App. Rep. 107.

of asphyxia. Both defendants blamed each other but were convicted and hanged. The court ruled that if several persons jointly commit a felony with a preconceived intent to use any degree of violence to overcome resistance, and death results, all are guilty of murder. This applies even if the felony, like larceny, does not inherently involve violence.

In a line of common law[31] cases, the English courts recognized that even where there was a joint intent to use weapons to overcome resistance or avoid arrest, the participants might not share an intent to cause death or really serious harm. If the principal had that intent and caused the death of another, he would be guilty of murder. Another party who lacked that intent but who took part in an attack that resulted in an unlawful death would be not guilty of murder but would be guilty of manslaughter unless the act which caused the death was so removed from what they had agreed as not to be regarded as a consequence of it.

In R *v Spraggett,*[32] a burglar's conviction for the killing by his co-accomplice was held not safe, where the trial judge wrongly directed that a common intention to commit burglary was the same as a common intention to commit violence. The appeal court stated that the jury had to be satisfied with the evidence that a preconceived intent existed to use violence.

Both the *Collison* and *Spraggett* cases were determined before the John case. On the other hand, the *Collison* and *R v Smith (Wesley)*[33] were considered by the Court in the John case. The Court of Appeal acknowledged that Grant's role differed, as he only knew of a plan to steal and merely drove his companions to the scene. Despite noting it was 'unfortunate' that the trial judge did not specifically address Grant's defense of simply dropping off his companions, the Court concluded that Grant, as an ordinary man, must have realized some violence would likely be used during the burglary.[34]

It would seem that the Court of Appeal in the John case chose the legal principle that placed individuals in peril of being convicted of a crime, not because they intended to commit it but because they merely foresaw an ordinary man would know that some sort of violence might be committed by someone else with whom they were engaged in a joint criminal enterprise.

---

31 *R. v Smith* (Wesley), [1963] 1 WLR 1200; *R. v Betty*, (1964) 48 Cr. App. R. 6; *R. v Anderson* and *R. v Morris*, [1966] 2 QB 110; *R. v Reid*, (1976) 62 Cr. App. R. 109.

32 *R. v Spraggett*, [1960] Crim. L.R. 840.

33 *R. v Smith (Wesley)*, 1202. Referred to on behalf of the 1st accused in the John Case.

34 *John and four others v The State* p. 441 per Cornelius Harding J A at p. 449.

Therefore, whereas the person causing death had to intend to kill or cause really serious injury, the secondary party was equally guilty, not because he shared that common purpose with the killer, but merely because he foresaw that death or severe injury might possibly occur.

Grant could have been convicted of manslaughter, and the reasoning in cases such as Collison should have applied at least to Grant. The acts of the principal defendants, i.e., the 3rd, 4th, and 5th defendants, were outside the scope of the common design to burgle an 'open empty room,'[35] and the use of violence resulting in the murder could not have been within the foresight, contemplation or intention of Grant nor could he have anticipated the circumstances that occurred at the scene.

In *Chang Wing-Siu v R*,[36] Sir Robin Cooke stated that there was no doubt that there existed a principle to the effect that a secondary offender is criminally liable for the acts of the primary offender of a type that the former foresees but does not necessarily intend. The mental element of foreseeability alone is sufficient to impose criminal liability on the secondary offender. The reasoning in Chang was on the same footing as that of the Court of Appeal in the John case.

Would a reasonable man have believed that it was more probable than not that a murder would result from a plan to steal from an open, empty room? It is submitted that the constructive liability placed on Grant was most disproportionate. The English courts recognized this unfairness in the most recent English case of *R v Jogee*.[37]

In the facts of the case, Jogee and Hirsi seemed to have been engaged in a 'common plan' of assault, during which Hirsi committed a more serious 'collateral' offence (murder) against a man named Fyfe. Jogee had been vocally encouraging the principal while he murdered a former police officer. Jogee was also held liable for the murder since, according to the trial judge, it could be reasonably inferred that, before carrying out the common plan, Jogee had foreseen the possibility, not just the likelihood, that Hirsi might murder. Despite such foresight, Jogee had continued with the common plan.

The UK Supreme Court disagreed with the trial judge. It restricted the scope of the rules on common purpose by overruling Chang Wing Siu and

35 *John and four others v The State* p. 441.

36 *Chang Wing-Siu v R.*, [1985] A. C. 168, at 175.

37 *R. v Jogee*, [2016] UKSC 8. The ruling was delivered jointly with the Judicial Committee of the Privy Council, which was considering an appeal from Jamaica, *Ruddock v The Queen*, [2016] UKPC 7.

holding that complicity liability requires nothing less than intention and that foresight of the target crime is not enough; also, that complicity liability requires actual assistance or encouragement, and that association has no real part in the common law.

The Court stated that where -

> 'a person is a party to a violent attack on another, without an intent to assist in the causing of death or really serious harm, but the violence escalates and results in death, he will not be guilty of murder but guilty of manslaughter. So also, if he participates by encouragement or assistance in any other unlawful act which all sober and reasonable people would realize carries the risk of some harm (not necessarily serious) to another, and death in fact results ...'[38]

The Court also found that the foresight principle introduced in *Chan Wing-Siu* was based on an 'incomplete, and in some respects erroneous, reading of the previous case law.'[39] According to *R v Jogee*, for an accessory to be liable for a target crime that the principal perpetrator has committed, it has to be proved that accessory provided actual assistance or encouragement to the principal perpetrator's commission of that crime, that accessory intended to do the act of assisting or encouraging, and that he intends that the principle perpetrator will commit the requisite actus reus of that collateral crime with the requisite mens rea.

The Court in *Jogee* approved the principles in *R v Smith (Wesley)* that if a person is a party to a violent attack on another, without intent to assist in the causing of death or really serious harm, but the principal perpetrator escalates the violence which results in death, the accessory is guilty of manslaughter instead of murder. As noted above, the Court of Appeal dismissed this principle in *R v Smith (Wesley)* in the John Case. Where it had been applied, Grant should have could have only been liable for manslaughter.

Therefore, in line with *Jogee*, it must have been proved by the prosecution in the John case that Grant, apart from assisting with his driving the other defendants to the scene, foresaw and intended the other defendants to use violence and kill the lodge proprietor which it is submitted the evidence did not show.

---

38 *R. v Jogee*, [2016] UKSC 8, para 96.

39 *R. v Jogee*, [2016] UKSC 8, para 79-80.

It has been suggested[40] that the most likely explanation for the development of the law of common purpose is that it was a way to avoid four procedural limitations for accessories to misdemeanours:

- that an accessory could not be tried until a principal had been convicted.
- an accessory could not be liable for more than the principal.
- some offences left uncertain whether an accessory could be responsible for the full punishment of a principal and
- the evidence of a party to an offence could not be admitted against other parties without corroboration.

Since an accessory might escape justice because of these procedural rules, Russell on Crime explained, 'to obviate this mischief the judges by degrees adopted a different rule, and at length, it became settled law that all those who are present aiding and abetting when a felony is committed are principals in the second degree.'[41]

In addition, the felony murder [42]rule applied that an intention to commit a felony where death resulted would generate liability for murder. The rule originated in the ancient doctrine of strict liability in crime and placed constructive liability on Grant. The issue with this is that such liability does not require the mens rea of Grant to correspond with the harmful consequences of his actions.[43]

The *Jogee* case establishes an intention to commit a crime as the real basis of liability for all involved in an offence. So, in the case of Grant, nothing short of an intention that the other defendants would use violence, and proof of that intention, would have been sufficient to convict Grant of murder and robbery with aggravation in the *John* case.

---

[40] Matthew Dyson, "Principals without Distinction," Criminal Law Review, 2018, 296, accessed on 20 August 2025 https://ora.ox.ac.uk/objects/uuid:eb5394ca-c169-4df2-b1ee-5ef7c4850d68/files/mce0ef1576a3c8c3faaf45554c01a21d4.

[41] William Oldnall Russell, A Treatise on Crimes, and Indictable Misdemeanors, vol. 1 (London: J. Butterworth, 1819).

[42] Abolished in England by Homicide Act 1957, S 1.

[43] Bo Wang, "Participation in Crimes: An End to Derivative Complicity Liability?" (Paper, Law Press, China, 2018), 5, SSRN, https://ssrn.com/abstract=3452492.

5. The Political Context

The John case occurred in the early 1970s and came six years after the murder of Louis Farmer.[44] The trial ended just before another murder known as the Mammy Yoko Street Murder, which occurred in 1974. The verdict in the *John* case can also be considered considering the aggregate mood and opinions of the political society in Sierra Leone at the time of the murder. Sierra Leone was recovering from the coups and countercoups in 1967 and 1968 and political unrest afterwards.

The 1970s in Sierra Leone were said to have been full of violence, mass roundups, and State-sponsored imprisonments under repeated State of emergency with one traumatic event after another.[45]

Young men became 'prone to criminal behaviour, petty theft, drugs, drunkenness, and anti-social tendencies. Some had special skills but no jobs, and they drifted in and out of the numerous potes in the urban centres.[46] The money came from petty theft, at home and on the street, and gambling.'[47] An atmosphere of instability and violence existed then, and burglary and robbery with aggravation became more frequent.

The then-president, Siaka Stevens, emphasized the need to 'clamp down on such unbridled threats to citizens in their own God-given country.'[48]

The public was horrified by the murder of an older man and the horrific ordeal of the boy. Public opinion may have pushed for the conviction of all the defendants in the John case as a deterrent to others, leading to all involved in the crime suffering the ultimate penalty – irrespective of what their part was.

Journalists around then could recall President Siaka Stevens's address to the press at State House in which he expressed great fear and alarm at the circumstances surrounding the *John* case. A visibly shaken and worried Siaka

---

44 *Walker v R.*, 1964-1966 ALR S.L. 144.

45 Jusu Sheriff, Yasmin post on "Sierra Leone Nostalgia Experience" group on Facebook, August 30, 2019. https://www.facebook.com/yasmin.jususheriff.7.

46 Ibrahim Abdullah, "Bush Path to Destruction: The Origin and Character of the Revolutionary United Front/Sierra Leone," The Journal of Modern African Studies 36, no. 2 (1998): 205, https://doi.org/10.1017/S0022278X98002766.

47 Abdullah, "Where Did We Go Wrong?

48 Truth and Reconciliation Commission of Sierra Leone, Witness to Truth: Report of the Truth and Reconciliation Commission, vol. 2, chap. 2 (Freetown: Truth and Reconciliation Commission, 2004), http://www.sierraleonetrc.org/index.php/view-the-final-report/download-table-of-contents. See also Jimmy D. Kandeh, "Politicization of Ethnic Identities in Sierra Leone," African Studies Review 35, no. 1 (1992): 85, https://doi.org/10.2307/524446.

Stevens promised his government would ensure the matter was thoroughly investigated and perpetrators brought to justice.[49]

Did this political stance and public uproar have any influence on the judges' reasoning regarding Grant? So that they were prepared to stretch the law away from existing and argued precedents such as the Collison and Spraggett cases? It would seem so.

Unfortunately, Grant received the death sentence[50] and was executed[51] Grant was no saint as he was prepared to assist in a burglary. He was arguably unjustly executed for offences of which he may not have been guilty. The evidence was insufficient to support his conviction when the law on accessorial liability is correctly applied.

President Siaka Stevens believed that a well-publicized trial followed by the execution of those involved at the Pademba Road maximum security prison would send a no-nonsense message about the then Government's stance on crime.

Following the case, Parliament amended the Criminal Procedure Act 1965[52] to provide that defendants sentenced to death for robbery with aggravation would be executed by shooting in public rather than hanging in private.[53]

6. The Ebb and Flow of the Doctrine of Common Purpose

The law of degrees of complicity in Sierra Leone, England, Wales, and other commonwealth countries remains inconstant. In Australia, for example, the High Court in these three cases, namely, *Miller*, *Presley*, *and Smith* (*'Miller'*)[54] refused to follow the *Jogee case*.

In the *Miller case*, the appellants and a man named Betts were convicted of murder, following a trial in the Supreme Court of South Australia. There was evidence that the four were involved in an altercation in which Betts stabbed the deceased Clifford Hall fatally. The appellants in *Miller* were granted leave

---

49 Kandeh, "Politicization of Ethnic Identities," 88.

50 Abdullah, "Where Did We Go Wrong?

51 Doubts existed as to whether the executions were carried out. Those doubts led to the Government displaying the hung bodies of the perpetrators of the Mammy Yoko Murder – Amadi, Abadi, Sierra Express Media 10th August 2021.

52 Criminal Procedure (Amendment) No. 3 Act, 1973, Act No. 25 of 1973, S. 1.

53 The perpetrators of the Mammy Yoko Murder where to be the first to face a firing squad, under the new legislation – WE YONE Newspaper May 12, 1974. They were however hung by the gallows - WE YONE Newspaper Friday December 6, 1974.

54 *Miller v R.*; *Smith v R.*; *Presley v DPP* (SA), [2016] HCA 30.

to argue that consistent with the *Jogee case*, the decision of the High Court in *McAuliffe v R*[55] should be reopened and overruled.

The *McAuliffe* case represents the Australian common law's foundation of directly basing liability in participating in a joint criminal enterprise with the necessary foresight, whether such foresight is unilateral, shared, agreed to, or not.[56]

In that case, three youths decided to go to a park to bash someone. One went with a hammer and another with a stick. Two of the youths were experienced in kickboxing. At the park, the two attacked a man standing near the top of a high cliff. They kicked him and beat him with a stick. The other youth then kicked the man in the chest, which caused him to fall into a puddle of rocks 3-5 metres from the cliff's edge.

The Trial Judge separately directed the jury in relation to common purpose in the case of each of the defendants. Those directions by the trial judge conveyed to the jury that, even if the common purpose of the three youths did not embrace the intentional infliction of grievous bodily harm, there was sufficient intent on the part of either appellant for murder if he contemplated the intentional infliction of grievous bodily harm by one of the other participants as a possible incident in the carrying out of their joint enterprise and continued to participate in that enterprise.

On appeal, the Court upheld the convictions, finding that a party to a joint criminal enterprise who foresees but does not agree to the commission of the incidental crime in the course of carrying out the agreement and who, with that awareness, continues to participate in the enterprise is liable for the incidental offence.[57]

After consideration of the history and basis of the doctrine, the majority of the Court in Miller held that the law in Australia should remain as stated in *McAuliffe*.[58]

In the case of *Chan Kam Shing*,[59] the appellant was a member of the triads. Following an order from his boss to 'chop' members of a rival organization, he went searching for victims. When fellow gang members found some of their

---

55 *McAuliffe v R*., (1995) 183 CLR 108.

56 Belinda Rigg, "Joint Criminal Enterprise," Criminal CPD Australia, March 7, 2017, 1, accessed on 4tj April 2025, https://criminalcpd.net.au/wp-content/uploads/2016/09/jointcriminalenterprise1.pdf.

57 John and four others v. The State para 115-118.

58 It was held in McAuliffe that the person who was not directly involved in the extra act need only have 'foresight' of the possibility' that it would occur.

59 *HKSAR v Chan Kam Shi*ng [2016] HKCFA 8.

rivals, he went to join in their attack. The victim was fatally injured before the appellant arrived at the scene. No evidence had been put forward that the appellant was present during the attack on the deceased or that he had caused injury or death of the deceased. The appellant's conviction for murder was based on his participation in the joint enterprise to 'chop' their rivals. The Court noted that his involvement constituted encouragement to other members of his gang.

The Court of Appeal dismissed the defendant's appeal. He then appealed to the Hong Kong Court of Final Appeal, raising the legal question: Should the doctrine of joint enterprise, as established in *Chan Wing-Siu v R*[60] and *Sze Kwan Lung v HKSAR*[61] continue to apply in Hong Kong, given the rulings in *R v Jogee*[62] and *R v Ruddock*?[63]

The Court of Appeal dismissed his appeal, and the defendant took his case to the Hong Kong Court of Final Appeal on the following question of law: - 'What is the law of Hong Kong regarding the doctrine of joint enterprise namely should *Chan Wing Siu v R*[64] and *Sze Kwan Lung v HKSAR*[65] continue to be applied in the light of *R v Jogee and R v Ruddock*.'[66]

In dismissing the Appeal, the Court of Final Appeal held that the doctrine of joint enterprise should continue to be applied in Hong Kong. Ribeiro PJ[67] identified three principal reasons for this:

a. 'That secondary parties to a joint criminal enterprise deserve 'to be regarded as gravely culpable.[68]

b. That abolition of the joint enterprise doctrine would 'deprive the law of a valuable principle for dealing with dynamic situations involving evidential and situational uncertainties which traditional accessorial liability rules are ill-adapted to addressing.[69]

c. Jogee's introduction of the concept of 'conditional intent'... gives rise to significant conceptual and practical problems.' [70]

---

60 *Chan Wing-Siu v R.*, [1985] 1 AC 168.

61 *Sze Kwan Lung v HKSAR*, (2004) 7 HKCFAR 475.

62 *R. v Jogee*, [2016] UKSC 8

63 *Ruddock v The Queen*, [2016] UKPC 7, https://www.jcpc.uk/cases/jcpc-2015-0020.

64 *Chan Wing-Siu v R.*, 17.

65 *Sze Kwan Lung v HKSAR*, 480.

66 *HKSAR v Chan Kam Shing*, [2016] HKCFA 8.

67 *HKSAR v Chan Kam Shing*, [2016] HKCFA p. 97-98.

68 *R. v Jogee*, [2016] UKSC p. 65.

69 *R. v Jogee*, [2016] UKSC p. 71.

70 *R. v Jogee*, [2016] UKSC p. 58.

The *Jogee* case was not adopted, and the joint criminal enterprise doctrine expounded in *Chan Wing Siu* case[71] continues to apply in Hong Kong.

7. Conclusion

One of the enduring utilities of accessory liability lies in its capacity to secure a conviction for a defendant even when the precise mode of participation, whether as a principal or an accomplice, cannot be definitively established. Under the doctrine of common purpose, a participant in a criminal venture can be found guilty of the principal offence, regardless of whether the evidence supports their direct execution of the act or merely their facilitation or encouragement of it. This flexibility has made accessory liability a pragmatic prosecutorial tool, especially in complex cases involving multiple actors, where lines of responsibility are blurred or evidentiary gaps exist.

However, the application of the doctrine in Sierra Leonean courts has revealed a jurisprudence that is unsettled and inconsistent. The law of common purpose appears to ebb and flow, shaped as much by evolving judicial attitudes and shifting political climates as by the stability of precedent. This fluctuation raises profound concerns about legal certainty, proportionality of culpability, and the retrospective application of criminal standards. It is often the case that new judicial pronouncements in this area are treated as having always represented the law, a position that undermines the fundamental legal principle of *nullum crimen sine lege* (no crime without law).

Given the malleable nature of this doctrine and its susceptibility to overreach, there is a compelling argument that the rules governing accessory and secondary liability should no longer be left to the common law alone. Rather, Parliament should consider codifying the doctrine through a comprehensive statutory framework that explicitly delineates the circumstances under which a secondary party may be convicted as a principal. Such legislation should carefully balance the *actus reus*, the external conduct, and the *mens rea*, the mental intent, of the accused, ensuring that neither element is disproportionately emphasized to the detriment of fairness and justice. Without such balance, there is a danger that courts will continue to impose principal liability on peripheral actors whose culpability may be significantly less than that of the main perpetrators.

---

71 *Chan Wing-Siu v R.*, 17.

This tension is illustrated in the landmark *Wellington Street murder case*, adjudicated in *John and Four Others v The State*. This case remains a poignant reminder of the doctrinal and moral complexities that surface in criminal adjudication involving joint criminal enterprises. The judgment encapsulates the difficulties faced by the courts in parsing degrees of complicity, weighing accessorial liability, and applying the elusive contours of the doctrine of common purpose. The decisions rendered in this case underscore how deeply intertwined judicial determinations are with broader socio-political undercurrents.

In the *John* case, the legal system found itself at the intersection of legal principle and societal expectation, where the court's role in administering justice clashed with the opacity of collective criminal intent. The treatment of the second accused, Jonny Grant, exemplifies the dangers of doctrinal overreach. Despite the ambiguity surrounding his specific role in the alleged offence, the court's reasoning reflected an expansive reading of common purpose liability, one that threatened to blur the line between active participation and passive association. The case laid bare the risk of attributing criminal liability based on proximity, presence, or group affiliation, rather than on demonstrable individual intent or action.

The implications of this judicial narrative are not limited to the courtroom; they reverberate through the nation's broader justice system, particularly in its ongoing struggle to ensure fair trials amidst political turbulence. The *John* decision mirrors a pattern in Sierra Leone's legal history in which courts, sometimes under pressure from political actors or public sentiment, have deployed the doctrine of common purpose in ways that risk miscarriages of justice. The Truth and Reconciliation Commission (TRC) was not silent on this matter. It warned that political interference in prosecutions and the judiciary's occasional failure to uphold due process principles had eroded public trust in the legal system.

To prevent further erosion, a renewed commitment to judicial independence must be coupled with a doctrinal recalibration. Codifying the doctrine of common purpose would provide the judiciary with a statutory compass, reducing ambiguity and ensuring that liability is grounded in clear, prospective legal rules rather than the shifting interpretations of common law precedent. Such a statute could delineate different thresholds of intent required for primary versus secondary liability and could include provisions to prevent the retroactive application of expanded liability rules. Importantly, it would also guide prosecutors and defence counsel alike, fostering consistency and transparency in the administration of justice.

The broader narrative of this book, contextualized by the legal odyssey of the *John* case, calls for an honest reckoning with the past and a forward-looking vision for the future. The principle of accessorial liability must evolve within a framework that is as committed to accountability as it is to fairness. As Sierra Leone continues to emerge from the shadows of political instability and institutional weakness, the judiciary's capacity to dispense impartial justice will be tested again and again.

This is why a clear and deliberate legal structure governing the doctrine of common purpose is not merely advisable, it is essential. It would serve to limit the arbitrary extension of criminal liability and reaffirm the judiciary's role as a bulwark against injustice. Ultimately, in the crucible of legal decision-making, the Sierra Leonean judiciary must strive to be not only a repository of law but also a guardian of liberty, ensuring that justice is not sacrificed on the altar of expediency or public pressure.

BEYOND BIRTHRIGHT - INTERROGATING SIERRA LEONE'S CITIZENSHIP JURISPRUDENCE IN AKAR AND YUMKELLA CASES

RONALD GIDWANI

1. Introduction

This chapter identifies the current and old laws governing citizenship in Sierra Leone, describing their history and the revisions made to date. It explains how, before independence, the law created two classes of citizens, those born in Sierra Leone and those who acquired citizenship. Many writers have described this as discriminatory, especially in politics, where people faced unequal treatment based on skin colour, names, or family background. The cases of the *State v Akar, David Fornah v Alhaji Dr. Kandeh Kolleh Yumkella*[1] and others provide a clear explanation of the citizenship laws in Sierra Leone and their discriminatory nature.

The chapter examines several statutes, journals, articles and decided authorities on citizenship, together with some international frameworks on the subject, including regional African instruments. From those frameworks, it could be clearly seen that most of these human rights instruments address issues of nationality, committing member states to handle issues of citizenship with a human rights lens.

---

1 *David Fornah v Alhaji Kandeh Yumkella and others,* Supt. Ct. Case No. 2/2018, Judgment delivered on September 3, 2021, https://www.judiciary.gov.sl/wp-content/uploads/2021/09/DAVID-FORNAH-VS-ALHAJI-DR-KANDEH-KOLLEH-YUMKELLA-SUPREME-COURT-JUDGEMENT-BY-HON.-JUSTICE-SENGU-KOROMA-1.pdf.

In Sierra Leone, citizenship can be obtained in a variety of ways, including through birth, descent, naturalisation, honorary membership, etc.[2] It can also be lost within the confines of the existing law. However, many controversies have arisen due to these laws, including which categories of citizens can acquire certain rights over others, which this chapter addresses. The chapter further identifies landmark cases in the superior courts in Sierra Leone and England that concluded that our laws were discriminatory in view of international standards.

2. The Concept of Citizenship

Citizenship relates to a legal relationship between the individual and the State.[3] Most people are legal citizens of one nation-state, though some may hold citizenship in multiple nation-states. Being a citizen entails certain responsibilities in terms of what the state expects of individuals under its jurisdiction. Citizens thus fulfil certain obligations to their state in exchange for protecting their vital interests and rights. However, the concept of citizenship encompasses considerably more nuances than legal citizenship.[4] Citizenship is not just a legal status granting rights and duties in a country; it also reflects an individual's connection to a community they can actively shape and influence.[5]

Article 15 of the Universal Declaration of Human Rights[6] recognises the right to a nationality, the right to change one's nationality, and the right not to be deprived of one's nationality.[7] This right is confirmed in other regional human rights instruments, including the African Charter on the Rights and

---

[2] Citizenship Act 1973, no 4 of 1973 https://citizenshiprightsafrica.org/wp-content/uploads/2016/01/Sierra_Leone_Citizenship_Act_24-May-73.pdf.

[3] Benedikt von Rütte, "An Individual Right: Realizing the Right to Citizenship," in The Human Right to Citizenship: Situating the Right to Citizenship within International and Regional Human Rights Law and Daniel Weinstock, "Citizenship," in The Stanford Encyclopedia of Philosophy, ed. Edward N. Zalta, Fall 2021 ed. (Stanford, CA: Stanford University, 2021), https://plato.stanford.edu/archives/fall2021/entries/citizenship/.

[4] Seyla Benhabib, The Rights of Others, Aliens, Residents, and Citizens (Cambridge: Cambridge University Press, 2007); Linda Bosniak, The Citizen and the Alien: Dilemmas of Contemporary Membership (Princeton, NJ: Princeton University Press, 2006), and T. Alexander Aleinikoff and Douglas Klusmeyer, eds., Citizenship Today: Global Perspectives and Practices(Washington, D.C.: Carnegie Endowment for International Peace, 2001).

[5] Von Rütte, "Individual Right," p. 339.

[6] Universal Declaration of Human Rights, G.A. Res. 217A (III), U.N. Doc. A/810 (Dec. 10, 1948), art.15 , https://www.un.org/en/about-us/universal-declaration-of-human-rights.

[7] Universal Declaration of Human Rights, art. 15.

Welfare of the Child (ACRWC)[8] and the European Convention on Nationality of the Council of Europe (1997).[9]

Citizenship laws in Sierra Leone are provided in the Constitution and several statutes.[10] Numerous citizenship laws have been amended and repealed many times, yet it is still contended that the current laws are discriminatory. The laws prohibit a substantial number of Sierra Leoneans by birth from acquiring automatic citizenship. In the case of dual citizenship, it is most contestable when an individual seeks public office. The idea that many countries worldwide, including Sierra Leone, prevent some category of its citizens from holding key jobs by questioning their loyalty is of grave concern. Outside the political arena, they usually face fewer obstacles.

3. Definition

There is no embracing definition of the term citizenship. It is seen as a legal status of an individual in a state incorporated in the Constitution and/or statute. 'Citizenship' is a term often used to indicate the legal relationship to the state of an individual, which defines the legal bond between the state and the individual that confers rights and responsibilities as a result of such status.[11] This includes the right to live, work, and pay taxes in that nation in exchange for the state's protection and security.[12] In the case of *Herriott v City of Seattle,*[13] 'Citizens' are defined as, 'members of a political community who, in their associated capacity, have established or submitted themselves to the

8 African Charter on the Rights and Welfare of the Child, adopted July 1990, OAU Doc. CAB/LEG/24.9/49 (1990), art. 6, https://www.acerwc.africa/sites/default/files/2022-06/African%20Charter%20on%20the%20Rights%20and%20Welfare%20of%20the%20Child_ENG_5.pdf.

9 Council of Europe, Citizenship and Participation: Manual for Human Right and Young People (Strasbourg: Council of Europe Publishing, 2021), https://www.coe.int/en/web/compass/citizenship-and-participation.

10 Constitution of Sierra Leone, S. 64., S. 27 (4) (c) and 173, http://www.sierra-leone.org/Laws/constitution1991.pdf. See also Bronwen Manby, Citizenship Law in Africa: A Comparative Study, 3rd ed. (New York: Open Society Foundations, 2016), 55, https://www.opensocietyfoundations.org/publications/citizenship-law-africa-comparative-study.

11 In Von Rütte, "Individual Right," it is noted that citizenship is commonly defined as the legal bond between an individual and a state, which grants the person a specific status that comes with both rights and responsibilities., notes that this traditional view sees citizenship as a 'privilege granted on a discretionary basis.'

12 T. H. Marshall, "Citizenship and Social Class" (1950), in Citizenship and Social Class, by T. H. Marshall and Tom Bottomore (London: Pluto Press, 1992), 9.

13 *Herriott v City of Seattle*, 500 P.2d 101, 81 Wn.2d 48 (Wash. 1972).

dominion of a government for the promotion of the general welfare and the protection of their individual as well as collective rights.'[14]

Consequently, citizenship is the concept of belonging to a nation or a sovereign state. In the majority of countries, citizens have the additional right to hold dual or multiple citizenship, allowing them to belong to more than one nation or sovereign state.

4. Evolution of Citizenship Laws

Sierra Leone citizenship has a long history, not unconnected to the coming of religious people and settlers from different parts of the world. Like other African countries, Sierra Leone has experienced inward migration and settler communities from Islamic scholars, traders and warrior invaders. These groups were mainly from West and North Africa and Sudan. There were also traders and businesspeople from Asia, such as the Indians, Lebanese and Syrians, who migrated to Sierra Leone to settle and trade, setting up a new community of different races and cultures.

The country also experienced inward migration from slave traders, Christian missionaries and British colonial conquest. Britain founded Freetown as a resettlement site for freed slaves after the abolition of the Atlantic slave trade in the latter part of the 18th century. Therefore, Sierra Leone's socio-political reality constituted settler communities of 'strangers' or 'incomers' of freed slaves, African, Asian and European traders, Christians, Muslims and colonialists.[15]

After the Berlin conference of 1884-1885, the British administration in the Western Area of Freetown expanded from the existing 'Colony' to establish a 'protectorate' in the rural regions. This colonial appropriation of territory and governance of the hinterland is another important political context that shapes the evolution of citizenship in Sierra Leone. By extending to the Protectorate, rural populations were transformed into British Protected Persons (BPPs), whilst those in the Colony, including freed slaves, were British subjects.[16] Until 1948, the status of a British subject was the highest

---

14 Black's Law Dictionary with Pronunciations, 6th ed., s.v. (St. Paul, MN: West Group, 1991).

15 Amadu Wurie Khan, "Country Report on Citizenship Laws in Sierra Leone" (paper, European University, 2021), 5, https://cadmus.eui.eu/bitstream/handle/1814/71023/RSCAS_GLOBALCIT_CR_2021_11.pdf?sequence=1&isAllowed=y.

16 In colonial Sierra Leone, British subjects (primarily residents of the Colony, such as Freetown, including freed slaves and Krios) held full nationality status with direct allegiance to the British Crown, granting them rights like British passports, consular protection, and access to British

in British law and one shared with persons of British ancestry in the United Kingdom.

Before independence, Sierra Leone's citizenship laws were based on the British Nationality Act of 1948. The Act established the status of 'citizen of the UK and Colonies' (CUKC) to replace the previous status of 'British subject,' with effect from 1 January 1949. The CUKC status was extended to persons in the Sierra Leone Colony, including the Krios, who had been 'British subjects,' whilst those in the Protectorate remained British Protected. Additionally, CUKCs had free movement throughout the British Empire, whilst the movement of non-Europeans, including Asians and people of African descent, was restricted.[17]

By bestowing British citizenship on former colonised British subjects, the 1948 British Nationality Act (BNA) was a political attempt by a crumbling British colonial administration to facilitate a Commonwealth citizenship framework under a pan-British post-independence realm. The Act created the umbrella status of 'British subjects' for the citizens of what was referred to as 'independent Commonwealth countries,' which included the citizens of the 'dominions' and former colonies as they gained independence from Britain.[18] BPPs, the term used to designate persons born in the Protectorate who were not CUKCs, had restricted rights and were considered to be 'aliens' in British law, barred from challenging state Acts in courts, who were rather 'subjects' of local rulers or chieftains in the protected states.

Sierra Leone's 1961 Independence Constitution, like other West African colonies, modeled its citizenship laws on those of its colonizer, Great Britain, except for Liberia, which, despite U.S. influence in its 1956 and 1973 citizenship laws, was never fully colonized. Pre-independence, Sierra Leone's nationality laws followed the British Nationality Act 1948, unchanged until

courts, akin to UK citizens. In contrast, British Protected Persons (BPPs, mainly rural populations in the Protectorate) were nationals of protected territories under British indirect rule, owing allegiance to local rulers (e.g., chiefs) rather than the Crown directly; they had limited rights, were treated as aliens in British law for purposes like entry to the UK, and lacked automatic nationality or full legal protections, reflecting the distinction between annexed colonies and nominally sovereign protectorates. George E. Brooks, Landlords and Strangers: Ecology, Society, and Trade in Western Africa, 1000–1630 (Boulder, CO: Westview Press, 1993); Annie Wilkinson and James Fairhead, "Comparison of Social Resistance to Ebola Response in Sierra Leone and Guinea Suggests Explanations Lie in Political Configurations Not Culture," Critical Public Health 27, no. 1 (2016): 5, https://doi.org/10.1080/09581596.2016.1252034.

17 Bronwen Manby, Citizenship in Africa: The Law of Belonging (London: Hart Publishing, 2018).

18 Laurie Fransman, Adrian Berry, and Alison Harvey, "Sierra Leone," in Fransman's British Nationality Law, 3rd ed. (London: Bloomsbury Professional, 2011), 500.

independence, when the Sierra Leone (Constitution) Order in Council 1961 established its first citizenship regime.[19]

For those born before independence, the Constitution stated that: 'Every person who, having been born in the former Colony or Protectorate of Sierra Leone, was on the twenty-sixth day of April 1961, a citizen of the United Kingdom and Colonies or a British protected person shall become a citizen of Sierra Leone on the twenty-seventh day of April 1961: Provided that a person shall not become a citizen of Sierra Leone by virtue of this subsection if neither of his parents nor any of his grandparents was born in the former Colony or Protectorate of Sierra Leone.'[20] These transitional provisions, therefore, gave automatic citizenship to those persons born in the country before independence who were CUKCs or BPPs, if a parent or grandparent was also born there.

Persons born outside Sierra Leone whose fathers became citizens at independence were automatically granted citizenship. Those who did not qualify for automatic citizenship, such as women married to citizens under transitional rules, individuals born in Sierra Leone with parents or grandparents born abroad, and other Citizens of the United Kingdom and Colonies (CUKCs) or British Protected Persons (BPPs) ordinarily resident in Sierra Leone, could register as citizens.[21] Others meeting specific conditions could apply for naturalization as citizens.

In respect of those born after independence, the 1961 Independence Constitution extended a *ius soli* right to citizenship to all those born in the country, except for children of a father who was a diplomat of another country or an enemy alien, unless their mother was a citizen. Citizenship by descent or *ius sanguinis* was extended to persons born outside the country if the father was a citizen at the time of birth, albeit limited to one generation.[22] In short, there was a defined path to acquiring Sierra Leone citizenship both at independence and thereafter, through birth in the country, descent, registration, naturalisation and marriage.[23]

Within a year of independence, Sierra Leone citizenship laws were amended to reflect the nationalistic bent of post-independence politics to

---

19 Khan, "Country Report," 8.

20 The Sierra Leone (Constitution) Order in Council 1961, S. 1, https://citizenshiprightsafrica.org/wp-content/uploads/2021/04/Sierra-Leone-Independence-Constitution-1961.pdf.

21 Aaron Hale and Fredline M'Cormack-Hale, "Statelessness, Nationality, and Citizenship in Sierra Leone," Journal of Global South Studies 35, no. 2 (2018): 320.

22 Hale and M'Cormack-Hale, "Statelessness, Nationality, and Citizenship," p. 331.

23 Manby, Citizenship in Africa.

restrict the citizenship right of 'non- negro' Sierra Leoneans, particularly those of Indian, Lebanese and Syrian ancestry, to seek elected office. Under the first elected post-independent government of Prime Minister Sir Milton Margai of the Sierra Leone's People Party (SLPP), Parliament used its majority to amend the 1961 Constitution retroactively to thwart the efforts of John Akar, a prominent and politically astute Sierra Leonean Lebanese, to contest elected office in the Sierra Leonean House of Parliament.[24] Though John Akar's mother was Sierra Leonean and of 'negro-African descent' like many others born in Sierra Leone, the new law defined a 'person of Negro African descent' by ancestry as a person whose father and paternal grandfather were Negroes of African origin.

The significant amendments to Sierra Leone's citizenship laws were

- The removal of transitional provisions of the Constitution providing for non-discretionary registration of those excluded from the automatic acquisition of citizenship for lack of a parent or grandparent born in the country. [25]
- The introduction of 'negro African descent' and its retroactive application as a requirement for the right to automatic citizenship at independence and those born in the territory after independence.[26]
- The lifting of the restriction of *ius soli* citizenship for a person of 'negro African descent' whose father held diplomatic status or was an enemy alien.[27]
- The stripping off of Sierra Leone citizenship from persons not of 'negro African descent' who had acquired or opted for citizenship under the 1961 Constitution after less than a year.[28]
- A person born in Sierra Leone of a 'negro African' mother could not qualify for citizenship by birth if that person's father or grandfather were not of 'negro African descent'; however, a person with a 'negro

24 Hale and M'Cormack-Hale, "Statelessness, Nationality, and Citizenship," 325 and Lina Beydoun, "The Complexities of Citizenship among Lebanese Immigrants in Sierra Leone," African Conflict & Peacebuilding Review 3, no. 1 (2013): 115, https://doi.org/10.2979/africonfpeacrevi.3.1.112.

25 Significant changes introduced by the Constitution (Amendment) Act, 1962 and entrenched in the Citizenship Act, 1973. Citizenship Act, 1973, S. 14(1).

26 Citizenship Act, 1973, S. 2, 3, 5 and 8.

27 Citizenship Act, 1973, S. 8(1).

28 Citizenship Act, 1973, S. 14(1) and (2).

African' mother could apply to register as a citizen on a discretionary basis.[29]

- A registered citizen did not qualify to hold elected office, including being a Member of Parliament, unless he or she had been a resident or served in the army for 25 years.[30]

The amendments restricted ius soli acquisition both at and after independence with the requirement that the person's father and grandfather had to be of 'negro African descent.' They also introduced restrictions for the registration and naturalisation of those not of 'negro African descent' so that persons of mixed race like Akar could only apply to acquire citizenship by naturalisation, a discretionary process and a preclusion for naturalised citizens from holding political office.[31] As Manby argues, the amendment to the citizenship law was directly aimed at reducing the political influence of persons of Syrian Lebanese descent who aspired for political office.[32]

From 1973 to date, Sierra Leone's current citizen regime is governed by the Sierra Leone Citizenship Act of 1973 as amended by the 2006 and 2017 Citizenship (Amendment) Acts. This section explores the political dynamics that shape these laws and Sierra Leone's current citizenship regime. It draws attention to citizenship legislation from 1973 to the post-war period. The continuities and changes to the citizenship regimes of these legislations are also considered. Three key factors shaped Sierra Leone's citizenship laws: reducing the political influence of Syrian-Lebanese and other groups born in Sierra Leone, particularly those with Sierra Leonean mothers, as championed by John Akar; promoting reconciliation and national development in post-war Sierra Leone; and advancing women's and children's rights. The 1971 Republican Constitution omitted citizenship provisions, which were instead enacted in the Citizenship Act of 1973.

Another new constitution was adopted in 1991, but it was quickly followed by the outbreak of civil war and a succession of military coups until a civilian government was restored briefly in 1996 and finally in 2002. After the end of the civil war, there was a need to advance truth and reconciliation and to facilitate the repatriation of Sierra Leoneans who had sought safety

---

29 Citizenship Act, 1973, S. 2, 3, 6, 8.

30 Citizenship Act, 1973, S. 22.

31 Although Citizenship Act, 1973, S. 8(2) provides that the Minister shall grant a naturalization certificate unless he sees reason to the contrary, in practice the granting of citizenship by naturalization has been entirely discretionary.

32 See Manby, Citizenship in Africa, and Khan, "Country Report," 8.

abroad to support national reconstruction and development. The right to Sierra Leonean citizenship based on *ius soli*,[33] *ius sanguinis*,[34] and *ius matrimonii*[35] were misaligned with the residency, family, and marital statuses of many Sierra Leoneans in the diaspora.[36]

Between 1991 and 2002, many Sierra Leoneans sought asylum abroad, particularly in North America, Europe and some parts of West Africa, such as the neighbouring countries of Guinea, Gambia and Liberia.[37] There was a need to encourage Sierra Leone's middle-class professionals who fled the war to live abroad to return home and contribute to national development without fear of losing the citizenship of Western countries they had acquired. There was recognition that Sierra Leonean refugees abroad would have voluntarily renounced allegiance to Sierra Leone due to the atrocities and human rights abuses they suffered from both state authorities and the rebels during the civil war.

Additionally, some countries hosting immigrants, including Sierra Leoneans, would require those seeking naturalisation to renounce the citizenship of their homeland to qualify for the host country's citizenship.[38] Therefore, the need to allow for the 'resumption' of Sierra Leonean citizenship was urgent. After sustained campaign and advocacy by Sierra Leoneans, the 2006 Act was put in place to respond to these socio-political realities of Sierra Leoneans in the diaspora and for the reconstruction and development of the post-war Republic.[39]

The 2006 Citizenship (Amendment) Act amended the law to permit dual citizenship for the first time and to remove gender discrimination in

---

33 A Latin term meaning "right of soil," is a legal principle of nationality law. In simple terms, it is the right of anyone born within the territory of a state to be a citizen of that state, regardless of the nationality or citizenship of their parents.

34 A Latin term meaning "right of blood," is a legal principle of nationality law. It is a system in which an individual's citizenship is determined by the nationality or ethnicity of their parents, rather than by their place of birth.

35 Latin for "right of marriage," is a principle of nationality law where a person can acquire citizenship through marriage to a citizen of a specific country. This is also commonly referred to as "citizenship by marriage" or "jure matrimonii."

36 See Manby, Citizenship in Africa, and Khan, "Country Report," 8.

37 U.S. Committee for Refugees, World Refugee Survey 2002: Sierra Leone, Refworld, June 10, 2002, accessed 20th August, 2025, https://www.refworld.org/reference/annualreport/uscri/2002/en/31872.

38 Countries like Austria, Germany (pre-2024 reforms), Japan, and others, have single-nationality policies. See Henley & Partners, "Countries That Don't Allow Dual Citizenship — And Why It Matters," Henley & Partners, June 27, 2025, https://www.henleyglobal.com/publications/dual-citizenship/countries-dont-allow-dual-citizenship.

39 Khan, "Country Report," 8.

transmitting citizenship for those born in the country. For the first time, the Act recognises dual citizenship and the 'resumption' of Sierra Leone citizenship. In this regard, a citizen of Sierra Leone may hold citizenship of another country in addition to his citizenship of Sierra Leone.[40]

The Act removed gender discrimination in both the definition of 'negro African descent' to include 'a person whose mother or father and any of the grandparents of the mother or father is or was a Negro of African descent' and in the requirement for a parent or grandparent to have been born in the country. This continues to be discriminatory as it excluded those born in Sierra Leone to non-Sierra Leonean parents. This amendment enables a Sierra Leonean mother to extend citizenship to her child born in Sierra Leone if the mother or one of the grandparents was also born in Sierra Leone. However, children born abroad acquired Sierra Leonean citizenship by descent if their father was a Sierra Leonean citizen. Therefore, discriminating against women who are Sierra Leonean citizens with children born abroad.

The Sierra Leone Citizenship (Amendment) Act of 2017 revised the Citizenship Act of 1973 to eliminate gender-based discrimination in the transmission of citizenship by descent, ensuring equal rights for Sierra Leonean women and men to pass citizenship to their children born abroad. Specifically, it repealed and replaced Section 5 of the 1973 Act, which states that:

> 'Every person born outside Sierra Leone on or after the nineteenth day of April 1971 of a father or mother who was or would but for the death of the person have been a citizen of Sierra Leone by virtue of sections 2, 3 and 4, is a citizen of Sierra Leone by birth.'

This amendment removed the prior restriction that limited citizenship by descent to children born abroad to a Sierra Leonean father, explicitly including mothers, thus aligning with the 2006 amendment[41] that granted citizenship by birth through a Sierra Leonean mother under Section 6. The 2017 amendment ensures that children of Sierra Leonean women, including those with foreign husbands, are recognized as citizens by descent, promoting gender equality in nationality laws. This change reflects Sierra

---

40 Amending Section 9, replacing Section 10, repealing Section 11, adding Section 19A, and amending section 16.

41 The Sierra Leone Citizenship (Amendment) Act, 2006, Act No. 11 of 2006, S. 3, https://www.sierra-leone.org/Laws/2006-11.pdf.

Leone's commitment to international standards, such as the Convention on the Elimination of All Forms of Discrimination Against Women (CEDAW), and addresses historical inequalities, particularly impacting women in the diaspora and their children.

5. Pathways To Sierra Leonean Citizenship

In Sierra Leone, citizenship rights are acquired and can be lost pursuant to the Citizenship Acts 1973, amended in 2006 and 2017. Citizenship can be obtained in several ways.

First, citizenship was granted to everyone born in Sierra Leone before 19 April 1971 or resident in Sierra Leone on 18 April 1971 provided that their mother or father, or grandparent was born in Sierra Leone and was a 'person of negro African descent.' Individuals born in Sierra Leone after 19 April 1971 were deemed to be citizens by birth, subject to the same condition.[42] Citizenship is automatically granted at birth to individuals born or residing outside Sierra Leone who are of Negro African descent and have an ancestor born in Sierra Leone.[43] In addition, women now have an automatic right to extend citizenship to children who may have been born or reside outside Sierra Leone.[44] This is quite different in other countries where you only have to be born in the said country irrespective of the citizenship of your parents. It is immaterial whether any parent is a citizen of that country. The only condition is birth. A clear case is that of the United States of America.[45]

Second, citizenship by descent means every person born outside Sierra Leone on or after the nineteenth day of April 1971 of a father who was or would but for his death have been a citizen of Sierra Leone by virtue of sections 2, 3 and 4, is a citizen of Sierra Leone by birth.[46]

Third, with regard to citizenship by marriage, foreign women who were or are married to Sierra Leonean citizens qualify for naturalisation. Thus, 'every woman who is not a Sierra Leonean and who is or has been married to a Sierra Leone citizen, may, on an application being made by her in the manner prescribed, be granted a certificate of naturalisation.'[47] However, the ability of

---

42 Citizenship (Amendment) Act, 2006 S. 8,5, 9 and 10.

43 Citizenship (Amendment) Act, 2006 S. 2 and 4.

44 The Sierra Leone Citizenship (Amendment) Act, 2017, Act No. 17 of 2017, S. 1, https://www.parliament.gov.sl/uploads/bill_files/The%20Citizenship%20(Amendt)%20Act,%202017.pdf.

45 U.S. Const. amend. XIV, § 1, cl. 1.

46 Citizenship Act, 1973, S. Section 4 of the 1973 Citizenship Act.

47 Citizenship (Amendment) Act, 1976 S. 7,8 and 9.

Sierra Leone women to pass along citizenship to a foreign spouse continues to be missing.[48] This is also a significant issue of discrimination.

Fourth, individuals who do not meet the automatic right to acquire Sierra Leone citizenship may do so by naturalisation. This includes children of Sierra Leone mothers 'of negro African descent' who were born outside Sierra Leone but whose fathers were not of 'negro African descent' and whose mothers did not take citizenship of another state.[49] Individuals under the age of twenty-one have a discretionary right to acquire citizenship by naturalisation if one of the parents is a naturalised Sierra Leone citizen and born outside Sierra Leone on or after the date the father or mother became a citizen.[50]

Under the current citizenship laws, all other persons of 'negro African descent' who are born and have been continuously resident in the country for not less than eight years to apply to become a Sierra Leonean citizen.[51] All other individuals of 'negro African descent' who are of full age and capacity, resident in Sierra Leone and have been continuously so resident for a period of not less than fifteen years may, on an application being made by him or her in the manner prescribed, be granted a certificate of naturalisation if he satisfies the Minister[52] that he is qualified for naturalization.

Other conditionalities for applicants to meet and subject to Ministerial approval include knowledge of a language in use in Sierra Leone, a good character would be a good citizen, (if negro African, or would make a useful and substantial contribution to the advancement, progress and well-being of Sierra Leone, if not of negro African descent.[53]

There are also provisions granting executive powers to reject an application for Sierra Leone citizenship. For instance,

> 'Every person of negro African descent born in Sierra Leone after the eighteenth day of April 1971, may on application being made by him in the manner prescribed, be granted a certificate of naturalisation. Provided that a person shall not be granted a certificate by virtue of this section if at the time of his birth— (a) neither of his parents was a citizen of

48 Citizenship (Amendment) Act, 2006 S. 4.

49 Citizenship (Amendment) Act, 2006 S. 4.

50 Citizenship (Amendment) Act, 2006 S. 8(4) and 7.

51 Citizenship (Amendment) Act, 1976 S. 8(3) & 9.

52 Under the Citizenship Act, 1973, the 'Minister' is defined in Section 1 as 'the member of Cabinet charged with responsibility for matters relating to citizenship.'

53 Citizenship (Amendment) Act, 1976 S. 9.

> Sierra Leone and his father possessed such immunity from suit and legal process as is accorded to an envoy of a foreign sovereign power accredited to Sierra Leone, or (b) his father was an enemy alien and the birth occurred in a place then under occupation of the enemy.'[54]

Naturalised citizens may not hold certain public offices.[55]

6. Examining the Grounds for Deprivation of Citizenship in Sierra Leone

Citizenship may be lost through voluntary renunciation, but since dual citizenship is now permitted in Sierra Leone, automatic loss of citizenship by operation of law no longer applies. There are, however, provisions to enable renunciation of citizenship. Any Sierra Leonean may renounce their citizenship subject to approval by the Executive. The set process for effecting this is as follows:

> 'Where any citizen of Sierra Leone who is of full age and capacity makes a declaration renouncing his citizenship of Sierra Leone, the Minister shall if he is satisfied that the person is (a) a citizen of a Commonwealth country, or the Republic of Ireland; or (b) a national of a foreign country, cause the declaration to be registered, and thereupon that person shall cease to be a citizen of Sierra Leone.'[56]

Under Sierra Leone's citizenship framework, deprivation of citizenship applies exclusively to naturalised citizens and is governed by the National Drugs Control Act 2008 and the 1973 Citizenship Act, as amended in 2006. Section 14 of the 2008 Act permits a Minister to deprive a naturalised citizen of their citizenship if they are deemed disloyal to the Republic through acts or speech, or if, within seven years of naturalisation, they are sentenced in any country to imprisonment of at least twelve months for offences involving fraud or dishonesty. [57] The 2006 amendment to the 1973 Citizenship Act[58] marked a significant shift by removing dual citizenship

---

54 Citizenship Act, 1973, S. 8(1).
55 Citizenship Act, 1973, S. 22.
56 Citizenship Act, 1973, S. 15.
57 Citizenship Act, 1973, S. 17.
58 Citizenship Act, 1973, S. 9, 10, and 16.

as a ground for deprivation, instead introducing a broader provision allowing the Minister to revoke citizenship if they are satisfied that the individual's continued citizenship is 'not conducive to the public good.'[59] This discretionary power, while legally permissible, raises concerns about potential abuse, particularly in politically motivated cases. The broad ministerial discretion in citizenship deprivation, combined with judicial flexibility in sentencing, underscores systemic vulnerabilities to executive influence.

Another basis for depriving Sierra Leone citizenship is when a person who is ordinarily resident in a foreign country for a continuous period of seven years fails to register annually in the prescribed manner at a Sierra Leone Consulate or notify the Minister in writing of his intention to retain his Sierra Leone citizenship.[60] This provision only applies to citizens who acquire citizenship by naturalization.

7. A Critical Review of the Discriminatory Nature of the 1973 Citizenship Act and its Amendments

The 1973 Citizenship Act, as amended, forms the cornerstone of Sierra Leone's citizenship legal framework. The Act interfaces directly with constitutional provisions that govern political participation and civic responsibilities. The 1991 Constitution of Sierra Leone, Act No. 6, explicitly ties citizenship to core democratic rights, stipulating under sections 40 and 76(1) that only citizens may vote or stand for election in presidential and parliamentary contests.[61]

Section 13 further delineates the responsibilities of citizens, mandating adherence to the Constitution, respect for national institutions, and the cultivation of nationalism over sectional or ethnic loyalties. It also obliges citizens to protect public property, uphold the dignity and rights of others, contribute to community welfare, and participate in democratic processes. While these provisions aim to foster a cohesive national identity, they have been critiqued for their discriminatory undertones, particularly in how citizenship is defined and applied, which has significant implications for access to justice and democratic inclusion.

---

59 Citizenship (Amendment) Act, 1976 S. 16.

60 Citizenship Act, 1973, S.18.

61 The Constitution of Sierra Leone, 1991, S. 13, 40, and 76 (1).

The 1973 Citizenship Act initially entrenched a restrictive and patriarchal framework, limiting citizenship by descent to the paternal line and imposing stringent conditions on naturalisation. This framework, rooted in colonial-era legal traditions, disproportionately excluded women and members of the diaspora, raising concerns about equality and inclusivity. The 2006 amendment to the Act marked a significant step towards reform by removing gender discrimination, allowing citizenship to be conferred through both maternal and paternal lines. This change aligned Sierra Leone's laws with international human rights standards, such as those enshrined in the Convention on the Elimination of All Forms of Discrimination Against Women (CEDAW). However, despite this progress, the Act retains exclusionary elements, notably the prohibition on dual citizenship for natural-born citizens seeking elected office, as outlined in section 76(1)(a) of the 1991 Constitution. This restriction, which disqualifies individuals who voluntarily acquire foreign citizenship or pledge allegiance to another state, has been a flashpoint in high-profile cases.

In citizenship cases, courts have frequently adopted a narrow, positivist approach, prioritising statutory compliance over substantive justice. For instance, the disqualification of candidates on citizenship grounds has often been upheld without rigorous scrutiny of procedural fairness or constitutional principles, eroding public trust in the judiciary as an impartial arbiter.

Moreover, the restrictive citizenship framework exacerbates access to justice barriers, particularly for marginalised groups. The high costs of legal proceedings, combined with the complexity of citizenship litigation, deter many Sierra Leoneans from challenging unlawful denials of citizenship or related rights. This issue is compounded in rural areas, where access to courts is limited, and legal literacy is low. The Truth and Reconciliation Commission (TRC) identified such structural deficiencies as contributing to the pre-war erosion of the rule of law, yet post-conflict reforms have only partially addressed these challenges. A comparative perspective, such as South Africa's post-apartheid citizenship reforms, which prioritise inclusivity and judicial oversight, suggests that Sierra Leone could benefit from a more progressive approach to citizenship adjudication, ensuring that courts actively protect constitutional rights rather than serve as gatekeepers for the executive's policy.

The persistence of exclusionary citizenship laws also raises questions about Sierra Leone's commitment to international human rights norms. The African Charter on Human and Peoples' Rights, ratified by Sierra Leone, emphasises equality and non-discrimination, principles that the current citizenship framework arguably undermines.[62] The judiciary's role in interpreting and applying these laws is critical, yet its capacity to do so impartially is constrained by systemic vulnerabilities, including corruption and resource constraints, as highlighted in the concluding chapter of this book.

To address these issues, reforms must focus on liberalising citizenship laws, enhancing judicial independence, and improving access to justice. Specific measures could include amending section 76(1)(a) to permit dual citizenship for elected office, establishing specialised citizenship tribunals to expedite disputes, and increasing funding for legal aid to support marginalised groups. Such reforms would not only align Sierra Leone's laws with global standards but also reinforce the judiciary's role as a guardian of democratic principles, fostering greater public trust and national cohesion.

The 1973 Citizenship Act, as amended, represents a pivotal yet contentious framework for defining citizenship in Sierra Leone, shaping access to democratic participation and intersecting with constitutional guarantees under the 1991 Constitution, Act No. 6. Sections 40 and 76(1) of the Constitution restrict eligibility for presidential and parliamentary elections to citizens, while section 13 outlines civic duties, including adherence to the Constitution, respect for national institutions, and fostering nationalism over ethnic or sectional loyalties. These provisions aim to unify the nation but have been criticised for perpetuating exclusionary practices rooted in the 1973 Citizenship Act's restrictive definitions of citizenship, particularly concerning race, gender, and dual citizenship. The Act's evolution through amendments in 1976, 2006, and 2017 reflects efforts to address these discriminatory elements, yet persistent judicial and structural challenges continue to undermine equitable access to citizenship and, by extension, justice and democratic rights.

The 1973 Citizenship Act entrenched a highly discriminatory framework, retaining colonial-era restrictions based on race and gender while introducing new barriers to citizenship acquisition. It limited citizenship by birth to individuals of 'negro African descent'[63] whose father or grandfather was also

---

62 African Charter on Human and Peoples' Rights, adopted June 27, 1981, OAU Doc. CAB/LEG/67/3 rev. 5 (1981), arts. 2 and 3, https://www.achpr.org/legalinstruments/detail?id=49. Ratified by Sierra Leone in 1983, Article 2 provides that non-discrimination; Article 3 states that equality before the law) sets binding human rights standards. Sierra Leone's citizenship laws, particularly the 'negro African descent' requirement in the Citizenship Act, 1973 as amended, arguably violate these principles by discriminating against non-African descent groups, such as Lebanese-Sierra Leoneans.

63 Defined as those with a father and paternal grandfather of African origin.

born in Sierra Leone.[64] This dual requirement of racial and territorial lineage excluded many born in the country, particularly those with non-paternal or non-African ancestry. For those born abroad after the 1971 Republican Constitution, citizenship could only be acquired through the father, reinforcing patriarchal biases. The Act extended citizenship to stateless children of Sierra Leonean mothers,[65] but only as a fallback to prevent statelessness, not as a recognition of equal maternal rights. Naturalisation provisions further entrenched gender disparities, allowing foreign women married to Sierra Leonean men to apply for citizenship but offering no equivalent pathway for men married to Sierra Leonean women. [66]

The 1976 amendment exacerbated these inequalities by differentiating naturalisation requirements. Individuals with at least one parent of negro African descent faced a lower residency threshold, eight years compared to others, fifteen years. Additionally, it permitted naturalisation for those under 21 if one parent was a naturalised citizen born abroad post-naturalisation but relegated all other applicants to a stringent process overseen by the Minister.[67]

The judiciary's handling of citizenship disputes reveals systemic vulnerabilities, particularly its susceptibility to executive influence and reluctance to prioritise substantive justice. In citizenship cases, courts have often adopted a positivist approach, strictly interpreting statutory provisions without robustly scrutinising their compatibility with constitutional or human rights principles. For instance, the disqualification of candidates on dual citizenship grounds, as seen in the Yumkella case, has been upheld with minimal consideration of procedural fairness or the broader implications for democratic inclusion.

To address these challenges, comprehensive reforms are needed. First, amending section 76(1)(a) to allow dual citizenship for elected office would enhance democratic inclusivity, particularly for the diaspora. Second, establishing specialised citizenship tribunals could expedite disputes and reduce judicial backlog. Third, increasing funding for legal aid, as recommended in the 2012 Legal Aid Act, would support marginalised groups in accessing justice. Finally, integrating customary and statutory systems, could ensure culturally sensitive yet rights-compliant citizenship adjudication. These reforms would strengthen the judiciary's role as a guardian of constitutional

---

64 Citizenship Act, 1973, S. 2 and 3.

65 Citizenship Act, 1973, S. 6.

66 Citizenship Act, 1973, Section 8.

67 Citizenship Act, 1973, S.14.

principles, fostering public trust and aligning Sierra Leone's citizenship framework with global standards of equality and justice.

8. Unraveling Discriminatory Threads – An Analysis of the Judicial Decisions

The law of Sierra Leone has a history of discriminating against some citizens. The aforementioned prejudice has become more pervasive, negatively affecting people who fall under the purview of the constitutional and statutory laws governing citizenship. These restrictions have prevented many citizens from participating in presidential and parliamentary elections and exercising key fundamental rights. One cannot tell the history of discriminatory citizenship laws in Sierra Leone without examining the case of John Akar. Since 1961, these cases have spurred debates and prompted changes to the Constitution and the Acts of Parliament to grant a certain group of people those rights that all citizens currently enjoy.

Depending on the manner in which it was acquired, certain citizens are deprived from voting or holding some public office. Apart from the limit imposed by the law, there is a general sense of 'xenophobia' against certain naturalised citizens holding positions of public trust.[68]

Section 40 of the Sierra Leone Constitution, Act No. 6 of 1991, provides for citizenship as a requirement, among other, to contest for the presidency. Citizenship, in this case, refers to citizenship by birth. In respect of holders of dual citizenship vying for public office such as the presidency and members of parliament, the case of *David Fornah v Kandeh Yumkella*[69] and the 2006 Constitutional amendment have provided a turning point.

According to section 76(1) of the Constitution, a naturalised citizen shall not be entitled or qualified to contest for presidential and parliamentary elections. Additionally, the general law, according to section 27 (1) of the Sierra Leone Constitution, is that '...no law shall make provision which is discriminatory either of itself or in its effect.'

However, there are exceptional cases where there can be discriminatory provisions against registered or naturalised citizens as prescribed by section 27 (4) (c), which states that 'section 27 (1) shall not apply to any law so far as that law makes provision... with respect to persons who acquire citizenship

[68] Hale and M'Cormack-Hale, "Statelessness, Nationality, and Citizenship," p. 331.

[69] *David Fornah v Alhaji Kandeh Yumkella.*

of Sierra Leone by registration or by naturalisation, or by resolution of Parliament.'[70] Therefore, in terms of section 27 (4) of the Constitution, the protection against discrimination embedded in section 27(1), is subject to limitations by law in respect of registered or naturalised citizens. This provision supports some discriminatory policies and laws against registered and naturalized citizens in Sierra Leone. However, section 27(4)(c) of the 1991 Constitution permits exceptions to the anti-discrimination protections of section 27(1), allowing laws to impose restrictions on registered or naturalised citizens, thereby enabling discriminatory policies that have historically barred such individuals from holding key political offices, such as the presidency, in Sierra Leone.

9. Analyzing the Impact of Akar v Attorney-General on Sierra Leonean Citizenship

The Plaintiff brought an action against the defendant challenging the validity of certain amendments of the Constitution. John Akar was born in Sierra Leone to a Sierra Leonean mother. His father, a Lebanese man, lived in Sierra Leone most of his life and never visited Lebanon. This background led to a legal challenge regarding his citizenship and political rights.[71] When Sierra Leone became independent on April 27, 1961, Akar automatically became a citizen by operation of the Constitution as both he and one of his parents had been born in Sierra Leone. Early in 1962, Parliament amended the citizenship provision of the Constitution with retrospective effect to the date of independence to provide in effect two classes of citizens. The first class was for those whose father's fathers were of African descent. They were citizens as of right and could inter alia contest as candidates in national and local elections. The second class was those who, like Akar, were Negro of African descent on their mother's side only. They might apply for citizenship, but if granted, they might not contest as candidates in the national and local elections until they had resided in Sierra Leone for 25 years.

At the time of the proceedings, John Akar lived in Freetown. He was the substantive director of Broadcasting, Director of the National Dance Troupe and Secretary of the Hotels and Tourist Board. On the 27th day of April 1961, John Akar became a citizen of Sierra Leone with full rights and the right

70 Constitution of Sierra Leone, S. 27 (4).

71 Manby, Citizenship in Africa.

to unlimited political participation. That was a result of section 1(1) of the Constitution of Sierra Leone of 1961, which provides that:

> 'Every person, who having been born in the former colony or Protectorate of Sierra Leone, was on the twenty-sixth day of April 1961, a citizen of the United Kingdom and colonies or British protected person shall become a citizen of Sierra Leone on the 27th day of April 1961.'

Following that, the Appellant, John Akar, claimed a declaration that the amendment to section 1 of the Constitution by Act No. 12 of 1962 and Act No. 52 of 1965 was ultra vires the Constitution and, therefore, null and void. Section 2 of Act No. 12 of 1962 provides for the Amendment of the Constitution. Section 2 amended section 1 of the Constitution by inserting the words negro African descent. Section 3 provides for the meaning of negro African Descent. Therefore, in this case, John Akar's father and father's fathers were not of negro African descent. So that automatically precluded him, just like many others born in Sierra Leone of fathers of Asian descent such as the Indians, Lebanese and Syrians, from contesting in national and local elections. The Chief Justice decided that certain Amendments of the Constitution were ultra vires the Constitution and, therefore, null and void.

The central issue here concerns the validity or otherwise of certain enactment that will affect the Appellant's status as a citizen if valid; and whether section 2 of Act No 12. of 1962 and no. 52 of 1965 were discriminatory and ultra vires the Constitution and, therefore, null and void.

According to the Appellant, the provision was discriminatory because his father and his father's father are or were not of negro African descent. The Appellant relied on section 23 of the Constitution of Sierra Leone of 1961, which prohibits protection from discrimination on the grounds of race. However, at the Court of Appeal, many questions were raised as to whether the content of section 2 of Act No.12 was discriminatory within the meaning of subsection 3 of Section 23 of the 1961 Constitution of Sierra Leone.

i) *Court of Appeals Judgement*

The Lordships agreed with the result rendered by the learned Chief Justice. They are:

a. The Amendment to Section 1 by Act No.12 of 1962 and Act No. 53 of 1965 was ultra vires the Constitution and, therefore, null and void.

b. That the purported amendment Act No. 36 of 1962 of Section 23 was ultra vires the Constitution and therefore null and void.

c. All amendments to other sections of the Constitution were ultra vires and void.

The Judicial Committee, with unanimous agreement,[72] endorsed the reasoning and judgement of Tejan-Sie, CJ, and accordingly allowed Mr Akar's appeal. The Committee noted that the Constitution of Sierra Leone 1961, as amended, expressly provided for citizenship. Upon Sierra Leone's transition to a republic in 1971, the Constitution of Sierra Leone 1971[73] did not include provisions addressing citizenship. This was left to subsequent legislation.[74] This matter was subsequently resolved by the Sierra Leone Citizenship Act 1973. The Supreme Court determined that the Plaintiff's claim must prevail, declaring that the purported amendment to section 1 of the Constitution by the Constitution (Amendment) (No. 2) Act 1962 was ultra vires the Constitution and thus null and void. Similarly, the purported amendment to section 23 of the Constitution by the same Act was deemed ultra vires and consequently null and void. The Court accordingly granted a declaration in the Plaintiff's favour.

The effect of the judgement was to address discriminatory provisions that had precluded Sierra Leoneans of non-Negro descent from participating in politics at the highest levels. However, the Sierra Leone Citizenship Act 1973 reversed this outcome by reintroducing the requirement that citizenship be restricted to 'a person of Negro African descent' and further stipulating that either the father or grandfather must have been born in Sierra Leone. This provision excluded numerous individuals born in Sierra Leone who had no other nationality to claim, including those born to fathers born in Sierra Leone but not of Negro African descent, even where their mothers were Sierra Leonean citizens or of Negro African descent. Consequently, the 1973 Citizenship Act rendered the decision in Akar's case nugatory and without practical effect.

---

72 Save for Lord Guest's dissent on a single issue.

73 Constitution of Sierra Leone, http://www.sierra-leone.org/Laws/1971-constitution.html.

74 Manby, Citizenship in Africa confirms that the 1971 Republican Constitution omitted citizenship provisions, deferring to the Sierra Leone Citizenship Act 1973, which introduced the 'negro African descent' requirement and other restrictions.

10. Democracy on Trial - Insights from the Case of Fornah v Yumkella and Others Case

The case of *Fornah v Yumkella and Other*[75] constitutes a landmark decision in Sierra Leone's constitutional and electoral jurisprudence, addressing the critical issue of whether individuals holding dual citizenship are eligible to contest parliamentary and presidential elections. Initiated by an Originating Notice of Motion filed on 5 February 2018 by the Plaintiff, David Fornah, the case sought to interpret key provisions of the Constitution of Sierra Leone 1991[76] and the Citizenship Act 1973, as amended, concerning dual citizenship and electoral qualifications. This analysis explores the procedural history, legal issues, judicial reasoning, and broader implications of the Supreme Court's ruling, highlighting its significance in shaping constitutional framework and reflecting evolving societal attitudes towards inclusivity.

The action was brought before the Supreme Court of Sierra Leone in the first instance,[77] presided over by a panel of five Justices: N.C. Browne-Marke, E.E. Roberts, G. Thompson, Alusine S. Sesay, and Sengu M. Koroma. The Plaintiff initially named several Defendants, including Alhaji Dr Kandeh Kolleh Yumkella, the 1st Defendant, the Attorney-General and Minister of Justice, Mohamed N'fah Allie Conteh, and the National Electoral Commission (NEC). Subsequently, through a joinder application, Dr Dennis Bright, Francis Hindowa (deceased), and the National Grand Coalition (NGC) party were added as Defendants.

The Plaintiff's Originating Notice of Motion sought declarations on the eligibility of individuals with dual citizenship to contest elections under sections 41, 75, and 76 of the 1991 Constitution, as well as sections 5, 7, 10, and 11 of the Sierra Leone Citizenship Act 1973, as amended by Act No. 11 of 2006. The proceedings faced significant procedural challenges. The Plaintiff filed his statement of case on 15 February 2018, with Defendants required to respond within ten days, creating a timeline that clashed with the presidential and parliamentary elections scheduled for 7 March 2018.

On 27 February 2018, Dr Dennis Ayodele Bright, the 5th Defendant, Francis Hindowa, now deceased, the 6th Defendant, and the National Grand Coalition, the 7th Defendant, applied to be joined as parties, an interlocutory

---

75 *David Fornah v Alhaji Kandeh Yumkella.*

76 Constitution of Sierra Leone.

77 The Supreme Court of Sierra Leone serves as the court of first instance for constitutional matters.

matter heard by a three-Justice panel on 1 March 2018, as mandated by section 47(3) of the Public Elections Act 2012 (PEA 2012). However, section 126 of the 1991 Constitution requires a five-Justice panel for final determinations in civil matters, rendering decisions by a three-Justice panel subject to review. On 2 March 2018, objections to the composition of the full bench led to the recusal of two Justices, necessitating reconstitution of the panel by 5 March 2018. This delay made it impossible for the Court to deliver a decision within the 30-day period prescribed by section 47(3) of the PEA 2012, exposing a conflict between the PEA 2012 and the 1991 Constitution.

Ultimately, the Plaintiff sought to discontinue the action, a request granted by the Court. However, the 7th Defendant, NGC, urged the Court to issue a declaration on the citizenship issue to provide clarity for future electoral contests. The Court agreed, delivering a pronouncement that addressed the core issue of dual citizenship and electoral eligibility.

The case centred on two primary sets of legal questions. First, the Plaintiff sought interpretation of sections 41, 75, and 76 of the 1991 Constitution to determine whether a naturalised citizen of Sierra Leone is disqualified from being elected as a Member of Parliament and, consequently, as President; whether a Sierra Leonean citizen who is also a citizen of another country, either voluntarily or under a declaration of allegiance to that country, is similarly disqualified; and, if so, the legal effect of such a citizen contesting parliamentary or presidential elections.

Second, the Plaintiff requested interpretation of sections 5, 7, 10, and 11 of the Sierra Leone Citizenship Act 1973, as amended by Act No. 11 of 2006, to ascertain whether, prior to the 2006 amendment, a person holding both Sierra Leonean and another citizenship simultaneously ceased to be a Sierra Leonean citizen by operation of law, and whether a person who, upon attaining the age of 22, held dual citizenship ceased to be a Sierra Leonean citizen. Additionally, the Plaintiff sought declarations that Dr Yumkella was disqualified from contesting parliamentary or presidential elections due to his alleged dual citizenship.

The fundamental issue was whether holding dual citizenship disqualifies a person from being elected as a Member of Parliament and, by extension, as President of Sierra Leone. The Supreme Court's analysis was rooted in a detailed examination of the 1991 Constitution, the Sierra Leone Citizenship Act 1973 (as amended), and relevant domestic and comparative case law. The Court's reasoning addressed several key aspects.

The Court first clarified jurisdictional boundaries. Challenges to parliamentary election eligibility fall under the High Court's jurisdiction pursuant to section 78(1) of the 1991 Constitution and the PEA 2012, with appeals limited to the Court of Appeal. However, challenges to presidential election eligibility, particularly concerning citizenship, fall within the Supreme Court's original jurisdiction under section 127(1) of the 1991 Constitution, which permits the Court to interpret enactments alleged to be inconsistent with the Constitution. The Court identified a conflict between section 47(3) of the PEA 2012, which allows a three-Justice panel to hear objections to presidential nominations, and section 126 of the 1991 Constitution, which mandates a five-Justice panel for final determinations in civil matters.

The Court held that the Constitution takes precedence, rendering section 47(3) inconsistent in this respect.[78] On the issue of dual citizenship and electoral eligibility, the Court examined section 76(1)(a) of the 1991 Constitution, which disqualifies a person from parliamentary election if they are a naturalised citizen of Sierra Leone, a citizen of another country (having become so voluntarily), or under a declaration of allegiance to another country. Section 41 links presidential eligibility to parliamentary eligibility, requiring a candidate to be qualified to be elected as a Member of Parliament. The Court reviewed section 2 of the Sierra Leone Citizenship Act 1973, which deems a person born in Sierra Leone before 19 April 1971, or resident on 18 April 1971, and of Negro African descent with a father or grandfather born in Sierra Leone, to be a citizen by birth. Dr Yumkella, born in Sierra Leone in 1966 to Sierra Leonean parents of Negro African descent, satisfied these criteria.[79]

The Court considered the impact of the Sierra Leone Citizenship (Amendment) Act 2006, which recognised dual citizenship, removing the prohibition on Sierra Leoneans holding another nationality. This amendment was deemed consistent with section 173 of the 1991 Constitution, which grants Parliament discretion to legislate on citizenship matters without requiring a two-thirds majority for amendments to citizenship laws.[80] The Court rejected the Plaintiff's argument that Dr Yumkella's acquisition of United States citizenship in or around 1995 disqualified him. Dr Yumkella had renounced his US citizenship on 22 November 2017, as evidenced by a certificate of loss of nationality and an oath of renunciation,[81] prior to his nomination for the

78 *David Fornah v Alhaji Kandeh Yumkella*, paras 10-11, 13.

79 *David Fornah v Alhaji Kandeh Yumkella* para 65.

80 *David Fornah v Alhaji Kandeh Yumkella.*

81 Exhibits 'KKY4' and 'KKY5.'

presidential election, satisfying section 76(1)(a). Moreover, the Court held that, even without renunciation, the 2006 amendment meant that holding dual citizenship does not automatically disqualify a Sierra Leonean citizen by birth from contesting elections. The prohibition in section 76(1)(a) applies only to naturalised citizens or those who voluntarily acquire foreign citizenship and remain under a declaration of allegiance to that country post-2006.

The Court drew on comparative jurisprudence, notably from Kenya. In case of *Bishop Donald Kisaka v Attorney-General & Others*,[82] the Kenyan Court of Appeal held that the 2010 Kenyan Constitution's recognition of dual citizenship did not disqualify a dual citizen from contesting elections unless they held a state office, a distinction overlooked by the trial judge. Similarly, the Supreme Court in Fornah held that the 2006 amendment eliminated the mischief targeted by section 76(1)(a), rendering dual citizenship permissible for electoral purposes. The Court also referenced *Akar v Attorney-General*, where the Judicial Committee of the Privy Council upheld the plaintiff's citizenship rights under the 1961 Constitution, declaring amendments that deprived him of citizenship ultra vires, reinforcing the judiciary's role in protecting constitutional rights.

Adopting a progressive approach, the Court viewed the 1991 Constitution as a 'living document' that must adapt to societal changes. It held that Parliament's intent in enacting the 2006 amendment was to promote inclusivity, reflecting evolving attitudes towards citizenship, race, and other identities. The Court emphasised its duty to interpret laws in a manner consistent with parliamentary intent and societal progress, ensuring no group is excluded from political participation. The Court clarified that section 76(1)(a)'s disqualification now applies only to naturalised citizens, as citizens by birth who hold dual citizenship are no longer barred post-2006, aligning with section 173's grant of legislative discretion on citizenship matters.

Regarding costs, the Defendants sought punitive costs, arguing the Plaintiff's action was frivolous. The Court, however, declined to impose punitive costs, noting that the Plaintiff's counsel acted promptly to discontinue the action upon instruction. Referencing *Palmer v The Governor*[83] and *Palmer v Stooke & Attorney-General*,[84] where no costs were awarded due to the public

---

82 *Bishop Donald Kisaka v Attorney-General & Others*, Civil Appeal No. 280 of 2013, [2014] eKLR.

83 *Palmer v The Governor*, CIVIL CASE 241 of 1952, [1952] SLSC 19 (Nov. 18, 1952), https://sierralii.gov.sl/akn/sl/judgement/slsc/1952/19/eng@1952-11-18.

84 *Palmer v Stooke & Attorney-General*, 1950-56 ALR SL 325, https://sierralii.gov.sl/akn/sl/judgement/slsc/1953/2/eng@1953-01-12.

interest nature of the litigation, the Court ordered the Plaintiff to bear costs only up to the date of discontinuance, excluding the 2nd Defendant, who did not actively participate, and the 5th and 6th Defendants joined at the 1st Defendant's instance.

The Supreme Court granted the 7th Defendant's declaration, stating: 'Any person who upon attaining the age of twenty-two years was or is a citizen of Sierra Leone and also a citizen of any other country did and does not by operation of law or any other means cease to be a Sierra Leonean.'[85] This declaration affirmed that dual citizenship does not automatically disqualify a Sierra Leonean citizen by birth from contesting parliamentary or presidential elections. The Court further held that Dr Yumkella, a citizen by birth who had renounced his US citizenship, was qualified to contest the 2018 presidential election under sections 41, 75, and 76 of the 1991 Constitution.

The decision in *Fornah v Yumkella and Others* has far-reaching implications for Sierra Leone's constitutional and electoral framework. The Court's endorsement of the 2006 amendment aligns Sierra Leone with progressive jurisdictions that recognise dual citizenship, removing barriers for diaspora Sierra Leoneans to participate in political processes without renouncing foreign citizenships. This promotes inclusivity and strengthens democratic participation.

The characterisation of the 1991 Constitution as a 'living document' underscores the judiciary's role in interpreting laws to reflect societal evolution. The Court ensured that constitutional provisions align with legislative reforms by harmonising section 76(1)(a) with the 2006 amendment, fostering an inclusive political system. The case also clarifies the supremacy of the 1991 Constitution over conflicting statutory provisions, such as section 47(3) of the PEA 2012, highlighting the need for legislative alignment with constitutional mandates.

While the decision liberalises electoral eligibility for citizens by birth, it maintains the disqualification of naturalised citizens under section 76(1)(a), raising questions about potential discrimination that may prompt future legislative or constitutional amendments. The Court's approach to costs reflects a balanced consideration of public interest litigation, encouraging bona fide challenges to electoral laws while discouraging frivolous actions.

---

85 *David Fornah v Alhaji Kandeh Yumkella*, para 81(1).

11. Conclusion

Sierra Leone's citizenship regime has a contentious history, marked by discriminatory laws that have historically curtailed the rights of certain groups, particularly those of non-negro African descent. Despite amendments, such as the 2006 and 2017 Citizenship Acts, which addressed gender disparities and permitted dual citizenship, the legal framework remains inherently exclusionary, perpetuating barriers to full civic participation and undermining democratic inclusivity. These persistent inequities, rooted in restrictive provisions like section 76(1)(a) of the 1991 Constitution, which bars dual citizens from elected office, highlight the judiciary's critical role in either challenging or reinforcing systemic discrimination.

The courts of Sierra Leone have made notable progress in interpreting citizenship laws to mitigate discrimination, particularly by aligning with international human rights standards, such as those in the Convention on the Elimination of All Forms of Discrimination Against Women (CEDAW) and the African Charter on Human and Peoples' Rights.

This societal resistance to embracing individuals of non-negro African descent as equal citizens stands in stark contrast to global examples of inclusive leadership. Sierra Leoneans celebrated Barack Obama, a Black man with a Kenyan father elected President of the United States in 2009,[86] and Rishi Sunak, of East African-Indian descent, who became Prime Minister of the United Kingdom in 2022.[87] Yet, individuals like John Akar, whose families have contributed significantly to Sierra Leone's economic, social, cultural, and educational sectors across generations, face criticism and exclusion from political participation due to their ethnicity, surname, or family background. This dissonance reveals a profound miscarriage of justice, where the colour of one's skin or ancestral origin overshadows merit and character, contradicting the vision of equality articulated by Martin Luther King Jr.: 'I have a dream that my four little children will one day live in a nation where they will not be judged by the color of their skin but by the content of their character.'[88]

---

86 Barack Obama, Dreams from My Father: A Story of Race and Inheritance (New York: Three Rivers Press, 1995).

87 Parveen Akhtar, "It Matters that Rishi Sunak Has Become the UK's First Prime Minister of Indian Descent," The Conversation, October 24, 2022, accessed on 25th August 2025 https://theconversation.com/it-matters-that-rishi-sunak-has-become-the-uks-first-prime-minister-of-indian-descent-193154.

88 Martin Luther King Jr., "I Have a Dream," (speech, Lincoln Memorial, Washington, D.C., August 28, 1963), in A Testament of Hope: The Essential Writings and Speeches of Martin Luther King,

Throughout the 20th century, families of Indian, Lebanese, and Syrian descent settled in Sierra Leone, choosing it as their home and contributing substantially to its development. They built businesses, schools, and cultural institutions, fostering a shared national identity. Yet, discriminatory laws and societal attitudes continue to deny their descendants equal opportunities to shape their destiny, particularly in political spheres. This exclusion undermines the principles of fairness and inclusivity that are essential for a cohesive and democratic society. Addressing these injustices requires comprehensive reforms such as amending section 76(1)(a) to allow dual citizenship for elected office, establishing specialised citizenship tribunals to expedite disputes, and increasing legal aid funding to enhance access to justice for marginalised groups. Moreover, public education campaigns and judicial training on human rights norms can challenge societal prejudices and empower courts to uphold equality.

Throughout the 20th century, individuals of Indian, Lebanese, and Syrian descent settled permanently in Sierra Leone, making significant contributions to its economic and social fabric. Committed to the nation, they envisioned a future where their children and grandchildren could thrive. Sierra Leone's citizenship laws should ensure equal opportunities for all born in the country, judged by their character and contributions, not by race, surname, or ancestry.

Jr., ed. James M. Washington (San Francisco: HarperCollins, 1991), 217–20, https://kinginstitute.stanford.edu/encyclopedia/i-have-dream-speech.

PART TWO:

SYSTEMIC CHALLENGES TO ACCESS JUSTICE

LOCUS STANDI AS A SMOKESCREEN - HOW COURTS IN SIERRA LEONE USE THE DOCTRINE OF LEGAL STANDING TO AVOID DEALING WITH CASES ON THEIR MERITS

YADA H. WILLIAMS

1. Introduction

This chapter is a discourse on and analysis of the extent to which the courts of Sierra Leone have used *locus standi*, if at all, to avoid dealing with the merits of cases. It features thought-provoking arguments and postulations and draws references and inferences from international perspectives on 'legal standing' or '*locus standi*' notably from Nigeria, Malaysia and the international human rights framework. These references and inferences serve as a natural harbouring ground for the comparative analyses that traverse the length and breadth of this work. Finally, it hypothesizes the liberalisation of the traditional principles of *locus standi* in the interest of public interest and better access to justice. It does so by drawing references from the migration from a conservative approach to a more flexible approach.

2. *Locus Standi* and How It Inhibits a Case from Proceeding on its Merits

Locus standi is a Latin phrase that can simply be translated as 'a place of standing.' It is commonly referred to as 'the doctrine of standing' as it delineates and determines not only the jurisdiction of the courts to entertain matters brought before them but also the competence of a plaintiff to initiate civil proceedings in a court of law against the defendant. Where a court adjudges that an applicant has no *locus standi* to commence the action that applicant will be seen as an 'incompetent plaintiff.' The doctrine of standing, intended to ensure judicial efficiency and prevent frivolous litigation, requires plaintiffs to demonstrate a direct, personal interest in a case, thereby restricting access to courts for individuals with genuine grievances who lack sufficient legal standing. This right of access to the courts is a key principle that has been embedded in the idea and ethics of constitutional governance since at least the Magna Carta.[1] It is a value that the courts are prepared implicitly to recognise and employ even if to do so effectively entails disobedience to a statute.[2] Thus, it is deeply entrenched that a litigant who fails to satisfy the 'interest' and 'injury' test will be denied legal standing to challenge any perceived act of unconstitutionality.

The concept of *locus standi* is highly relevant to administrative law and has been of importance in the various aspects of European and English law and the broad spectrum of human rights law.[3] *Locus standi* may also be regarded as an essential tool for realizing human rights. The concept of standing is intertwined with the right of access to justice. Furthermore, effective access to justice is considered as the most basic requirement of a legal system, which purports to guarantee legal rights.[4] 'Traditionally, it implies that, to sue successfully in the public interest, seek a court order to declare a law unconstitutional or challenge the actions of the government or its agencies, an applicant must possess sufficient interest in the matter.'[5] This traditional approach to the common law principle of *locus standi* has been restrictive and inflexible when applied to prevent litigants from flooding the court. Where a litigant was not able to prove a direct relationship or a sufficient interest in the action, they were turned away even before the 'merits of their case' were heard.

1 Maurice Sunkin, "The Problematical State of Access to Judicial Review," in Judicial Review: A Thematic Approach, ed.Brigid Hadfield (Gill & McMillan, 1995).

2 *Anisminic v Foreign Compensation Commission*, [1969] 2 AC 147.

3 Institute of Human Rights and Development in Africa, "Judicial Colloquium on Locus Standi in Administrative Justice and Human Rights Enforcement" (paper, Judicial Colloquium, Banjul, The Gambia, May 26, 2001), https://www.ihrda.org/2001/05/judicial-colloquium-on-locus-standi-in-administrative-justice-and-human-rights-enforcement/ and S. M. Thio, Locus Standi and Judicial Review (Singapore: University Press, 1971), 1.

4 Lovemore Chiduza and P. N. Makiwane, "Strengthening Locus Standi in Human Rights Litigation in Zimbabwe: An Analysis of the Provisions in the New Zimbabwean Constitution," Potchefstroom Electronic Law Journal 19, no. 1 (2016): 4.

5 Alex Cyril Ekeke, "Liberalization of the Rule on Locus Standi before Nigerian Courts: Lessons from India," Journal of African Law 66, no. 2 (2022): 341, https://doi.org/10.1017/S0021855322000055.

The consequences where it is held that a litigant does not have *locus* standing in a matter was succinctly put by Justice A. Renner-Thomas CJ in the case of *Samuel Hinga Norman v Dr. Sama S. Banya & 2 Others.*[6] The judgement delivered on 31st August 2005 it was stated as follows:

> 'This test is of crucial importance for the Plaintiff's case because where a court reaches the conclusion that a plaintiff lacks *locus standi* or legal capacity to institute the particular proceedings before it the court is obliged to strike out the action without going into the merits of the case … According to the editors of the 'Constitutional Law of South Africa,' an authority cited by Dr. Jabbie, in Chapter 8, page 8.3 thereof:
>
> 'The concept of standing is concerned with whether a person who approaches the court is a proper party to present the matter in issue to the court for adjudication … An inquiry into standing should thus focus on the party who brings the matter before the court, not on the issues to be adjudicated.''

As already stated, a litigant not meeting the interest and injury test underpins the strictness, narrowness and inflexibility that characterized the court's application of the doctrine. For a very long time, the only exception to this narrow interpretation and application was seemingly the writ of habeas corpus available to a stranger or a next friend:

> 'The only exception is in the case of the writ of habeas corpus. This writ is issued to liberate a person from illegal detention. It may happen that the person held in such illegal detention is not in a position to move the court and therefore a stranger or the next friend is given *locus standi* to move the court for such a writ. Such a stranger or next friend may trigger the judicial process after showing that the impugned action or law resulted in denial of a person's liberty.'[7]

---

6 *Samuel Hinga Norman v Dr. Sama S. Banya*, S.C. No. 2/2005.

7 Satyaranjan Purushottam Sathe, "Judicial Activism: The Indian Experience," Washington University Journal of Law & Policy 6 (2001): 71.

This exception firmly rooted in section 28(1) of the Constitution of Sierra Leone[8] states that:

> 'Subject to the provisions of subsection (4), if any person alleges that any of the provisions of sections 16 to 27 (inclusive) has been, is being or is likely to be contravened in relation to him by any person (or, in the case of a person who is detained, if any other person alleges such a contravention in relation to the detained person), then, without prejudice to any other action with respect to the same matter which is lawfully available, that person, (or that other person), may apply by motion to the Supreme Court for redress.'

Historically, the concept of *locus standi* was mainly restricted to private law such as contract, civil liability, land law and property and family law, however, the common law principle of *locus standi* became technically a preliminary one for the judicial review of administrative action.[9] In England, the Senior Court Act 1981 was promulgated, providing in its Section 31(3) that:

> 'No application for judicial review shall be made unless the leave of the High Court has been obtained in accordance with rules of court; and the court shall not grant leave to make such an application unless it considers that the applicant has a sufficient interest in the matter to which the application relates.'[10]

Thus, *locus standi* became the medium through which the courts determine who may be an applicant for judicial review. The English provision, therefore, aimed to limit the number of challenges to administrative decisions, which would otherwise cause unnecessary interference with the administrative process. However, it simply created very restrictive outcomes for applicants who could not prove their interests to the courts.[11]

---

8 Constitution of Sierra Leone.

9 Peter Cane, Administrative Law, 5th ed. (Oxford: Oxford University Press, 2011).

10 Senior (Supreme) Courts Act 1981, c. 54, S. [section number], https://www.legislation.gov.uk/ukpga/1981/54/pdfs/ukpga_19810054_en.pdf.

11 Ian Loveland, "16. Locus Standi," in Constitutional Law, Administrative Law, and Human Rights: A Critical Introduction, 9th ed., ed. Ian Loveland (Oxford: Oxford University Press, 2021).

The question whether a plaintiff has *locus standi* to bring an action raises an issue of jurisdiction which ultimately threatens adjudication on the merits of a matter before the court. In the Nigerian case of *Attorney-General of Lagos State v Attorney-General of the Federation (2004),* <?> the Supreme Court held that when a Plaintiff has been found not to have the standing to sue, the question whether other issues in the case had been properly decided or not does not arise. This is because the trial court had no jurisdiction to entertain the claim. According to the Court,

> 'The correct position of the law therefore is that where a plaintiff is held to lack the locus standi to maintain his action, the finding goes to the jurisdiction of the court and denies jurisdiction to determine the action.'<?>

The issue of *locus standi* is technically a preliminary issue. However, the courts have held that, in cases where the applicant's interest is so tenuous that standing can easily be denied prior to the hearing of the merits, standing will generally be determined alongside the merits of the case.

In other words, in some cases, standing can be denied without hearing the merits of the case and sometimes standing may be determined alongside the merits of an applicant's case. The case of *R v IRC, ex p National Federation of Self Employed and Small Businesses*<?> had to do with a dispute in relation to the taxation of casual print workers on national newspapers in which they had avoided paying income tax by falsifying information provided to the tax authorities. The Inland Revenue Commission granted them amnesty on the condition that they registered for tax. The National Federation of Self-Employed (NFSE), who were the claimants, argued that the Inland Revenue Commission had exceeded its power or, if it had the power, exercised it improperly by granting an amnesty and sought a declaration or mandamus order. The House of Lords, however, held on the facts that the claimant did not have standing to pursue its claim. Their Lordships noted that the claimant had no particular interest in the case.

They held that it was unfortunate that the courts below had taken *locus standi* as a preliminary issue. They opined that whilst there might be simple cases where it was appropriate at the earliest stage to find that the applicant

---

12 *Attorney-General of Lagos State v Attorney-General of the Federation*, (2017) 8 NWLR (PT 1566) 20 at p. 55 para. D.

13 *Attorney-General of Lagos State v Attorney-General of the Federation*, at p. 31.

14 *R. v IRC*, at 625.

for judicial review had no interest at all or no sufficient interest to support his application thereby refusing leave to apply, in other cases like the present one, that should not have been the case. It was their position that the question of sufficient interest must be construed together with the legal and factual context of the application since Rules of the Supreme Court (R.S.C.), Ord. 53, r. 3 (5) required the applicant to show sufficient interest in the matter to which the application is related. The matter in the present case included the question of the statutory duties of the revenue and the breach or failure of those duties that the federation complained of.

The Divisional Court allowed the appeal. It found the federation, as a group of taxpayers, lacked sufficient interest to justify relief. [15] The federation failed to prove the revenue acted ultra vires or unlawfully. [16] It also did not show the revenue neglected its statutory duty, warranting no further court proceedings. [17]

In this case, the House of Lords had varying thoughts with several important features emerging from the decision. Lord Wilberforce reiterated that it was unfortunate that standing was decided as a preliminary point without consideration of the merits of the case in the Divisional Court and the Court of Appeal. Based on Lord Wilberforce's judgement, standing became a two-stage process to be considered at both the permission and full hearing stages: even if leave was granted, standing could still be denied at the hearing stage upon a full examination of the merits of the case. However, a criticism of this case is that the House of Lords conflated the issue of standing with merits. This case, however, presented a more liberal approach to the application of *locus standi*. This writer is of the opinion that it might have been more useful to keep standing as a distinct concept.

3. *Locus Standi* - A Bar to Justice Before Sierra Leonean Courts?

The principle of *locus standi* has generated many problems in various jurisdictions. Some jurisdictions have abandoned the strict interpretation of this principle and adopted a liberal approach to its application. However, Sierra Leonean courts have mostly continued to apply it narrowly and strictly.

---

15 *R. v IRC*, per Lord Wilberforce, Lord Fraser of Tullybelton and Lord Roskill p. 617.

16 *R. v IRC*, per Lord Diplock p. 635.

17 *R. v IRC*, per Lord Scarman 652.

Sierra Leonean courts inherited and adopted the laws of England, however, jurisprudence in English law has transformed in the last forty years into a more modern and effective system of law. However, Sierra Leone's approach to conferring *locus standi* to plaintiffs in private and public law is still substantially influenced by the English common law system's previous limited and narrow paradigm of *locus standi*. The law on *locus standi*, as openly admitted by an eminent British judge as indeed being 'outdated', is now clearly contrary to the principles of good governance, i.e. 'openness, transparency, integrity, and accountability.'[18]

Due to the impact of the common law adversarial system in Sierra Leone's legal system, *locus standi* concerns do not arise within the lower courts.[19] Discussions of *locus standi* in this chapter will therefore rely on the judgements and rulings of the Supreme Court of Sierra Leone.

4. Sierra Leone Association of Journalists v The Attorney General & Minister of Justice and Another

In the landmark case of *Sierra Leone Association of Journalists v The Attorney General & Minister of Justice & Another*,[20] the Sierra Leone Association of Journalists, the journalists' pressure group, argued that Part V of the 1965 Public Order Act which largely dealt with the crime of seditious libel contravened Section 25(1) of the Constitution of Sierra Leone. They urged the Supreme Court of Sierra Leone to declare that law null and void by virtue of Section 171(15) of the Constitution of Sierra Leone. Their application to the Court was by way of an originating notice of motion and their reliefs prayed for were as follows:

> 'A. The interpretation of Sections 25 of the Constitution vis-a-vis sections 27, 32 - 37 of the Public Order Act 1965, Act No .46 of 1965 for the determination of the following questions.

18 Lord Diplock in *R. v IRC*, p. 654.

19 The concept of locus standi in Sierra Leone's common law adversarial system is straightforward in lower courts, where private law disputes require direct personal interest, but becomes a critical preliminary issue for judicial review in higher courts under the 1991 Constitution's supervisory framework.

20 *Sierra Leone Association of Journalists v The Attorney General & Minister of Justice & Another*, SC 1 of 2020, [2009] SLSC 4, https://sierralii.gov.sl/akn/sl/judgment/slsc/2009/4/eng@2009-11-11.

(i) Whether the provisions of sections 26, 27, 32 - 36 of the Public Order Act criminalizing free speech contravene the right of freedom of expression guaranteed under the entrenched provisions of section 25(1) of the Constitution?

(ii) Whether the provisions of sections 26, 27, 32 - 31 of the Public Order Act can be demonstrably justifiable in the light of Sierra Leone's obligations under the Universal Declaration of Human Rights, the International Convention on Civil and Political Rights and the African Charter on Human and People's Rights?

(iii) If the answer of (i) and (ii) above are in the affirmative whether the provisions of sections 26, 27, 32-36 of the Public Order Act does not fall out of the restriction provision of sections 25(2) of the Constitution.

B. A declaration that sections 26, 27, 32-36 of the Public Order Act criminalizing free speech are unconstitutional and therefore null and void by virtue of section 171 (15) of the Constitution in so far as they violate provisions of section 25(1) of the Constitution.

C. A declaration that the restriction provision to the right of freedom of expression under section 25(2) of the Constitution does not save the provisions of sections 26, 27, 32-36 of the Public Order Act in so far as the said provisions cannot be demonstrably justifiable in a democratic society.

D. Any further and other relief that the Honourable Court may deem fit and just.'

Upon considerations of the reliefs sought by the applicant, Justice Umu H. Tejan-Jalloh, then Chief Justice, had this to say in her judgement with regards to *locus standi* and the standing of the Plaintiff:

> 'The Courts over the years in granting declaratory judgement in respect of constitutional questions had involved principles to guide them. The first is that a declaration will not be

> awarded to a plaintiff or an applicant who is unable to show he is engaged with another party in a Court to which his legal interests are directly affected.
>
> Secondly, the Court will not grant a declaratory judgement unless all the parties interested are before it. Thirdly, the Court will decline to make a declaration affecting the interest of persons who are not before it. Fourthly, an application for a declaration must satisfy a stricter test of *locus standi* than is applied to a Prerogative Order. Fifthly, only a person with *locus standi* is entitled to assail the constitutionality of a legislation meaning that the applicant must prove that he has sustained or is immediately in danger of sustaining some direct injury as a result of its enforcement, and not merely that he has suffered in some infinite way common with people generally.'[21]

Regardless of the arguments canvassed by the Sierra Leone Association of Journalists,[22] the Supreme Court of Sierra Leone dismissed the action.

5. Factual Premises of the Action Which Would Have Warranted A Decision On The Merits – Part A

Three practicing journalists, Richard Olu Gordon, Philip Neville and Dr. Julius Spencer, who were current members of the Sierra Leone Association of Journalists and media practitioners for over twenty years at the time, made averments that formed the basis of the case of the Sierra Leone Association of Journalists. Richard Gordon and Philip Neville were editors-in-chief of Peep

21 Sierra Leone Association of Journalists, SC 1 of 2020 p. 15.

22 In the case, counsel for the Sierra Leone Association of Journalists (SLAJ), Yada Williams Esq, argued that sections 26, 27, and 32–37 of the Public Order Act 1965, which criminalised defamation and seditious libel, were inconsistent with section 25(1) of the 1991 Constitution guaranteeing freedom of expression. SLAJ accepted that freedom of expression is not absolute but maintained that the impugned provisions went far beyond the permissible constitutional limits. They contended that these laws had a chilling effect on journalists and were not necessary in a democratic society. Relying on comparative constitutional jurisprudence and international human rights instruments, SLAJ argued that Sierra Leone should uphold universal rather than narrow local standards when protecting free speech. They further submitted that the burden was on the state to justify any restriction on free expression, and that the restrictions created by the Public Order Act could not be demonstrably justified under section 25(2) of the Constitution, which permits only narrow and necessary limitations such as protecting public order or reputation.

Magazine and Standard Times Magazine, respectively and Dr. Julius Spencer was Managing Director of the Premier Media Consultancy Ltd. and Proprietor of the Premier Newspaper.

Starting with Richard Olu Gordon, he asserted that on the 11th of February 2005, he was summoned to the Criminal Investigations Department on the instructions of the Attorney-General and Minister of Justice in connection with an article captioned 'KABBA SAYS OKERE STAYS' that had appeared in his satirical newspaper Peep Magazine questioning why Marine Minister, Ibrahim Okere Adams had not been sacked after the Anti-Corruption Commission indicted him. He alleged that prior to the article, two other Ministers were promptly dismissed after being indicted by the Anti-Corruption Commission. However, Okere Adams was regarded as President Kabba's 'most reliable Northern ally.' He stated that he was detained at the Criminal Investigation Department for three days and charged with seditious libel but was released on 14th February 2005 without being arraigned before any Court and did not receive any compensation. He apprehended that he could no longer publish contentious articles without first deciding whether he would go to prison or not and that the state of affairs was neither reasonable nor necessary in a democratic society. Finally, he averred that the existence of criminal or seditious libel offences allows for the Government authorities to arrest and detain journalists at their will, disregarding fundamental human rights.

Philip Neville deposed that during the reign of the National Provincial Ruling Council, he was arrested and summarily detained at the Pademba Road Prisons on three occasions for supposedly breaching sections 27 - 36 of the Public Order Act 1965. That on 24th February 1991, he published an article captioned '*Joe* Demby's mercenaries stabbed to kill Mr. Jonah' concerning a plot to assassinate the President of Sierra Leone, Alhaji Ahmed Tejan Kabba, and the then Minister of Finance, Dr. James Jonah, by foreign mercenaries. He was told that his arrest was for a breach of the criminal libel provisions of the Public Order Act 1965. On 8 March 1999, after twelve of detention, he was released without a charge under any of the offences proscribed under sections 26 - 36 of the Public Order Act. On 29th June 2007, he was again arrested after a publication captioned 'Bombshell Gaddaffi Exposes Government' in the Standard Times Newspaper concerning gifts from the Government and the people of Libya to the Government and People of Sierra Leone. He was remanded in custody for two days, charged to Court on 4th July 2007 and was granted bail. He averred that the amount was the toughest bail condition ever set for a criminal libel offence and that he was fretful about publishing contentious articles without deciding whether he was ready to go to prison.

That he has been persecuted by successive Governments merely as a result of disseminating reliable information that came to him in his capacity as a journalist and he was of the view that Sierra Leoneans have the right to be informed about sensitive matters he reports on.

Dr. Julius Spencer averred that on 13th October 1993, he was editor of 'New Breed' Newspaper, which published an editorial based on an article found in the Swedish newspaper 'Expression' captioned 'Redeemer or Villain.' The article focused on the sale of diamonds and the misappropriation of some of the proceeds by the then Government of Sierra Leone. He was charged to Court with seditious libel on a ten-count indictment and was found guilty and fined the Leones equivalent of two thousand United States Dollars. His appeal to the Court of Appeal of Sierra Leone was still pending at the time of filing the action and because of the conviction, he is blemished with a criminal record, and he is chary of being in active media practice, as it had a negative impact on him and his family.

The decision to deny standing and dismiss the action, taking these factual expositions into consideration, reverberated the already growing noise relating to criminal libel laws in Sierra Leone, which criminalised the wrong of defamation and had prompted various media activists to criticize its existence. In 2019, a cabinet meeting was held where the Ministry of Information and Communication and the Ministry of Justice approved a repeal of Part V of the 1965 Public Order Act. This was seen as a success, as various Governments since 1991 had promised and failed to repeal the law, which journalists stated was obnoxious, retrograde and bad for democracy in Sierra Leone. This case depicts very vividly how the Supreme Court relied on *locus standi* to sidestep dealing with the merits of the case. The phrase 'on the merits' implies that decisions must be grounded in law as applied to the particular facts and evidence presented in the case. As various individuals and activists were criticising the law on seditious libel, one could say that the Court should have first dealt with the merits of the case and the facts laid before it rather than base their apathy on the alleged insufficient interests of the litigants and their standing in the matter. *Locus standi* can be abused and misused to simply ignore an applicant who has clear factual evidence presented in the case solely on the basis that they are not competent. What is significant is that *locus standi* undermines two essential elements of the rule of law: the universality of law and equality before the law. The logic of the standing doctrine is that if there is no competent plaintiff, governmental bodies may violate the legal limits of their powers and the courts are powerless to intervene.

6. Samuel Hinga Norman v Dr. Sama S. Banya; Dr. Prince Harding; And Sierra Leone People's Party (SLPP)

In 2005, the plaintiff, a renowned ex-deputy Defence Minister of Sierra Leone, in the matter of *Samuel Hinga Norman v Dr. Sama S. Banya, Dr. Prince Harding and Sierra Leone People's Party (SLPP)* [23] sought a number of declarations and a permanent injunction from the Supreme Court of Sierra Leone against the 1st, 2nd and 3rd defendants in their decision to proceed with the election of the presidential candidate of the Sierra Leone People's Party, the 3rd defendant, for national presidential elections citing violations of the Constitution of Sierra Leone. The plaintiff was a registered and fully paid-up member of the 3rd defendant entity. In a majority decision, the court held that the 'plaintiff lacks *locus standi* to maintain the claim for declarations sought.'[24]

i) *Factual Premises of The Action Which Would Have Warranted A Decision On The Merits – Part B*

The Plaintiff, Samuel Hinga Norman, described himself for the purposes of the action as a member of the Sierra Leone Peoples Party, the 3rd defendant, 'who aspires to be Presidential Candidate at the 2007 Presidential elections, but who is keenly concerned that the democratic credentials and processes of the SLPP are maintained, entered and facilitated in all its internal structure, organization, operations, programmes, activities and functioning.'[25]

The 1st defendant, Dr. Sama Banya, was described as the National Chairman of the SLPP. The 2nd defendant, Dr. Prince Harding, was the National Secretary-General of the SLPP. The SLPP was and is a political party registered pursuant to the provisions of the Constitution of Sierra Leone[26] and the Political Parties Act.[27]

Apparently, sometime in July 2005, the National Executive Council of the SLPP held a meeting in Freetown and decided that a party conference of the SLPP was going to be held in Makeni in the Northern Region of Sierra

---

23 *Samuel Hinga Norman v Dr. Sama S. Banya*, S.C. No. 2/2005.
24 *Samuel Hinga Norman v Dr. Sama S. Banya*, S.C. No. 2/2005.
25 *Samuel Hinga Norman v Dr. Sama S. Banya*, S.C. No. 2/2005.
26 Constitution of Sierra Leone.
27 Political Parties Act, Act No. 3 of 2002, https://www.sierra-leone.org/Laws/2002-3.pdf.

Leone on 19th and 20th August 2005. Among other things, it was proposed to elect the presidential nominee of the SLPP for the 2007 elections who, pursuant to Clause V(2)(c) of the 1995 Constitution of the SLPP, automatically becomes the party leader of the SLPP after such election. According to the Statement of the Plaintiff's Case, the Plaintiff was of the view that it was too premature to choose a presidential nominee for the SLPP any time in 2005 for the Presidential elections due to be held in 2007. Apparently, it was the Plaintiff's dissatisfaction with the decision of the National Executive Council (NEC) of the SLPP to go ahead with the election of the Presidential Nominee of the SLPP at the Party Conference scheduled for 19th - 20th August 2005 that prompted the Plaintiff to institute the proceedings.

The Plaintiff commenced the action by way of an Originating Notice of Motion invoking the original jurisdiction of the Supreme Court pursuant to sections 122, 124(1), 127 and 171 (15) of the Constitution of Sierra Leone and praying amongst other things, for a declaration 'That the positions of Leader and Deputy Leader of the SLPP, in the manner and to the extent that they have been and/or are being held by specified incumbents respectively over the past ten years or so, that is to say, since at least 1996 and uptill now, were and are so held in contravention of the provisions in section 14(1) of the Political Parties Act and sections 35(4) and 76(1)(h) of the National Constitution and so, as held, were and are void and of no effect.'

Apparently, the Court failed to avert its mind to the damning effects of the action about to be taken by the party for which the action was instituted. These effects, as particularized by the plaintiff, included but was not limited to preventing certain members of the SLPP, including the Plaintiff, from becoming potential presidential nominees and eventually President of the nation of Sierra Leone. In effect, they were denied the right to be voted for. The Court shut its eyes to the glaring ramifications beaming before it and adjudged as it did below.

The Chief Justice, Justice A. Renner-Thomas, in his judgement, noted the liberal approach to the concept of *locus standi* in common law jurisdictions:

> 'The courts in some common law jurisdictions have adopted a more modern and liberal approach in conducting the inquiry as to the *locus standi* of the plaintiff in public law litigations. However, in all the common law jurisdictions where this change of approach has taken place the court have done away with the requirement that for a person to

> have *locus standi* in an action to assert a right conferred on the public at large or to enforce a duty owed to the public he must show that he has a special interest which is personal and peculiar to him and which interest has been adversely affected by the act or omission which he seeks to challenge. Invariably, what the courts have done is to take a liberal view of what constitutes the required interest.
>
> For example, in the Canadian case of *Minister of Justice of Canada v. Borowski* the only interest alleged by the plaintiff was that he was a concerned citizen who wanted the issue in contention to be litigated. The Supreme Court of Canada granted him standing, holding that where a plaintiff is seeking a declaration that a statute is invalid, if there is a serious issue as to its invalidity, that person need only show that he is affected by it directly or that he has a genuine interest as a citizen in the validity of the legislation and that there is no other reasonable and effective manner in which the issue may be brought before the court.
>
> … Dr. Jabbie has urged this Court to adopt the liberal approach in applying the common law principle. This would involve in effect giving *locus standi* to a plaintiff who claims relief not in his own personal interest but in the public interest or in the interest of a section of the public as happened in the Canadian case of *Minister of Justice of Canada v Borowski* cited earlier in this judgement.'[28]

Justice Muria, then Justice of the Supreme Court, in a separate concurring judgement, stated in a similar vein:

> 'In the present case, if this court were to accept the liberal approach to the test of standing urged upon it by Dr. Bu-Buakei Jabbie, the plaintiff must show, not only that he has sufficient interest in the matter that he brings to the court, but that this liberal test of 'sufficient interest' is the appropriate test to be adopted in Sierra Leone. No case decided by our courts here had been cited by counsel on

[28] *Samuel Hinga Norman v Dr. Sama S. Banya*, S.C. No. 2/2005 at p. 28.

> this issue. However, when looking at the cases on the test of standing from other jurisdictions, it is clear that the position is not uniform. Thus, the courts in Sierra Leone, in particular the Supreme Court, will have to decide the path to follow on the standing of a party who seeks to invoke the judicial review jurisdiction of the Court. The Court must do so on legal grounds. My searches in the National Constitution, statutes and Rules of Courts have not shown any express legislative formula in this jurisdiction for the liberal approach to standing as urged by counsel. Apart from the clear test to invoke the Court's jurisdiction under section 28 of the National Constitution, the general tenor as to the approach to be taken by the Courts in Sierra Leone is one where the applicant for a judicial review in the nature here claimed, the applicant must show that he has an interest in the subject matter before the court. That interest must be one that is personal to him and one which has been adversely affected by the action complained of a general interest which the applicant possesses in common with all members of the public or in common with other members of a section of the community cannot confer standing on him.'[29]

Justice M. E. Tolla-Thompson, then Justice of the Supreme Court, in his separate concurring judgement, differed with his colleague justices on the issue of *locus standi,* stating that because the plaintiff was a fully paid-up member of the 3rd defendant entity, this was sufficient reason to grant him *locus* in the said matter:

> 'In this regard, I am inclined to adopt a liberal approach to this question. The Plaintiff is a Sierra Leonean and a fully paid-up member of SLPP. He is an aspirant for the Presidential Election in 2007. In my humble view, I think this is enough to vest the plaintiff with standing and I so hold.'[30]

The approach taken by Justice Tolla-Thompson was brilliant and laudable and quite clearly a radical but correct departure from those taken

---

29 *Samuel Hinga Norman v Dr. Sama S. Banya,* S.C. No. 2/2005 at p. 5.

30 *Samuel Hinga Norman v Dr. Sama S. Banya,* S.C. No. 2/2005 at p. 14.

by his brothers. Such an opinion should have formed the basis of a dissenting judgement, not a concurring one.

Later in the same year, the plaintiff, Samuel Hinga Norman, in *Samuel Hinga Norman v SLPP*,[31] brought similar claims against the same political party, the Sierra Leone Peoples' Party (the first defendant). The Supreme Court struck out his case again on similar grounds of standing as in the earlier action. In a unanimous decision, the Court maintained the narrow application of the principle of *locus standi* even though they commended counsel for the plaintiff for his thorough and extensive research into the modern liberal approach to *locus standi*. Chief Justice Ade Renner-Thomas opined as follows:

> 'The second method by which the strict common law principle that a private person has no *locus standi* in an action to assert or vindicate a right conferred in the public at large has been modified is by way of statutory intervention. This time we do not have to go very far for an example. Right here in Sierra Leone, in 1991, our Parliament by enacting the provisions contained in section 127 of the National Constitution made it possible for the first time for a private litigant to institute proceedings to challenge the constitutional validity of any enactment as well as to challenge the constitutional validity of anything done under the authority of the National Constitution or any other law without any requirement that the person should show that he has a legal right or interest personal or peculiar to him which has been adversely affected by the act or omission which he seeks to challenge..' [32]

The Chief Justice, in the said judgement, also considered the 'two gateways' argument raised by counsel for the plaintiff under sections 28 and 127(1) of the Constitution of Sierra Leone –

> 'Section 28(1): Subject to the provisions of subsection (4), if any person alleges that any of the provisions of sections 16 to 27 (inclusive) has been, is being or is likely to be

[31] *Samuel Hinga Norman v SLPP, SC 3 of 2005*, [2006] SLSC 4 (Sept. 7, 2006), https://sierralii.gov.sl/akn/sl/judgment/slsc/2006/4/eng@2006-09-07.

[32] *Samuel Hinga Norman v SLPP*, [2006] SLSC p. 27.

> contravened in relation to him by any person (or, in the case of a person who is detained, if any other person alleges such a contravention in relation to the detained person), then, without prejudice to any other action with respect to the same matter which is lawfully available, that person, (or that other person), may apply by motion to the Supreme Court for redress.
>
> Section 127(1): A person who alleges that an enactment or anything contained in or done under the authority of that or any other enactment is inconsistent with, or is in contravention of a provision of this Constitution, may at any time bring an action in the Supreme Court for a declaration to that effect.'[33]

In respect of the above provisions, he held that:

> 'A person's standing under the section 28(1) 'gateway' presents no qualm at all. He has to show that the alleged breach was in relation to him although section 127(1) gives no express guidance as to the ambit of the words 'a person who alleges' used in that provision, the language of the section does not inhibit the power of this court, as the ultimate court of final appeal to insist on the requirement that a person who wishes to bring a constitutional challenge before the court must be a 'proper party.' Since the standing to bring a matter before the court is the first procedural criteria that a person must accomplish before he can be heard on any issue he may wish to raise, however so pressing such issue may be.'
>
> The position both in SC. 2/05 and the present case (SC03/05) is that the plaintiff is alleging that a political party and its officers have contravened the provisions of the SLPP Constitution as well as those of the National Constitution. The law provides the statutory machinery under section 27 of the Political Parties Act which grants the Political Parties Registration Commission the right (and so, the standing) to

[33] *Samuel Hinga Norman v SLPP*, [2006] SLSC p. 25.

> invoke the original jurisdiction of the Supreme Court. There has been no evidence, whether before or after 31st August 2005, that the Commission had exercised its power under that section, nor is there any evidence to show that it had refused or neglected or failed to exercise its power under the Act. It would, therefore, be difficult to accord the plaintiff standing in those circumstances. He would not be a proper party to invoke the jurisdiction of the Court under 127(1) of the National Constitutional in this case.'[34]

The Supreme Court in 2011 in the matter of *Dr. Bu-Buakei Jabbie v The Sierra Leone Peoples' Party and Others*[35] granted standing to the plaintiff, the same person who acted as the plaintiff's counsel in both actions in 2005 on behalf of Samuel Hinga Norman. The Chief Justice, Justice Umu H. Tejan-Jalloh, delivering the judgement of the Court on the 28th day of February 2011, did not provide any reasoning for the shift in approach by the Supreme Court, especially so when the facts, in this case, were substantially the same as those in the 2005 actions. In her words:

> 'As regards his capacity or standing to institute the action, he submitted that he had the capacity to do so. He also relied on the decision of *Hinga Norman & Others...*
>
> We have considered the submission of both sides, and have come to the conclusion that the objection is untenable and is accordingly overruled. Reasons for overruling the objection will be given later.'[36]

7. Similar Factual Basis, Different Timelines & Suspicions of Political Considerations

Before dismissing the Plaintiff's case in *Samuel Hinga Norman v Dr. Sama S. Banya & 2 ORS*[37] on the basis of his paucity of standing, the Learned Chief Justice Ade Renner-Thomas made an extensive analysis of the concept of

---

34 *Samuel Hinga Norman v SLPP*, [2006] SLSC p. 29.

35 *Jabbie v Sierra Leone People's Party and 3 others*, SC MISC APP 1 of 2011, [2011] SLSC 1 (Feb. 28, 2011), https://sierralii.gov.sl/akn/sl/judgment/slsc/2011/1/eng@2011-02-28.

36 *Jabbie v SLPP*, [2011] SLSC p. 4.

37 *Jabbie v SLPP*, [2011] SLSC p. 1.

standing as applicable in common law jurisdictions and at the time, in Sierra Leone, which he used as the anchorage for holding that the Plaintiff lacked *locus standi*. He stated as follows:

> 'First, I think it is important to recognize that there is a distinction between standing at common law and the various statutory provisions relating to standing in different common law jurisdictions such as England, South Africa, Nigeria, Canada, India and, of course, locally.
>
> Secondly, according to the authorities, a distinction ought to be made between the requirement of standing in private law litigations brought, for example, to enforce private rights in contract, tort or property on the one hand and the requirement for standing in public law litigation, particularly in the field of administrative law. An example of the latter type would be an action seeking a judicial review of administrative action. In England, in particular, the question of *locus standi* in actions seeking a judicial review is now governed entirely by statute, to wit, the English Supreme Court Act 1981. This is exhaustively dealt with in Chapter 2 of De Smith, Woolf & Jowell's 'Principles of Judicial Review' that Dr. Jabbie relied on very heavily but which, in my opinion, is not relevant in the instant case.
>
> I shall now deal with the position at common law. The principle in English law is that in an action to enforce a private right legal capacity to sue accrues only to a person who has a legal right or whose legal right has been adversely affected or who has suffered or is likely to suffer special damage in consequence of an alleged wrong.
>
> In an action to assert or protect a public right or to enforce the performance of a public duty, it is only the Attorney-General, as the guardian of public interest who has the requisite standing to sue. Such proceedings can either be brought at the instance of the Attorney-General or he can consent to a private person bringing a 'relator action' in the name of the Attorney-General.

> In private law litigations, whether a person has locus standi or not seldom presents any problem. However, it is in the area of public law that there has been some major developments in most common law countries. Over the years, there has been a shift from the strict common law principle of *locus standi* in public law litigation which has occurred in two ways.
>
> First, the courts in some common law jurisdictions have adopted a more modern and liberal approach in conducting the inquiry as to the *locus standi* of the plaintiff in public law litigations. However, in all the common law jurisdictions where this change of approach has taken place the courts have not done away with the requirement that for a person to have *locus standi* in an action to assert a right conferred on the public at large or to enforce a duty owed to the public he must show that he has a special interest which is personal and peculiar to him and which interest has been adversely affected by the act or omission which he seeks to challenge. Invariably, what the courts have done is to take a liberal view of what constitutes the required interest.'[38]

With regards to the liberal view taken by the courts, the Learned Chief Justice made reference to the Canadian case of *Minister of Justice of Canada v Borowski*,[39] where the only interest alleged by the plaintiff was that he was a concerned citizen who wanted the issue in contention to be litigated. The Supreme Court of Canada granted him standing, holding that where a plaintiff is seeking a declaration that a statute is invalid, if there is a serious issue as to its invalidity, that person need only show that he is affected by it directly or that he has a genuine interest as a citizen in the validity of the legislation and that there is no other reasonable and effective manner in which the issue may be brought before the court,

He also referred to the Nigerian case of *Senator Abraham Adesanya v The President of Federal Republic of Nigeria and Others*[40] where the action

---

38 *Samuel Hinga Norman v SLPP*, [2006] SLSC p. 26.

39 *Minister of Justice of Canada v Borowski*, [1981] 2 SCR 575, https://www.canlii.org/en/ca/scc/doc/1981/1981canlii34/1981canlii34.html.

40 *Senator Abraham Adesanya v The President of the Federal Republic of Nigeria and Others*, [1981] 2 NWLR 358, https://nigerialii.org/akn/ng/judgment/ngsc/1981/3/eng@1981-05-15.

was brought by the appellant challenging the constitutional validity of an appointment made by the President of Nigeria. The Nigerian Supreme Court dismissed the action on the sole ground that the appellant had no *locus standi* to bring the action as there were no rights peculiar or personal to him which had been infringed or injured. However, the Supreme Court of Nigeria departed from this narrow approach and adopted the modernized liberal view in the case of *Fawehinmi v Akilu*.[41]

In granting *locus standi* to the appellant, who had sought leave to apply for an Order of mandamus to compel the Director of Public Prosecutions to decide whether or not to prosecute, Nnamani JSC had this to say about section 6(6)(b) of the Nigerian Constitution which provision is in actual fact a codification of the common law principle on *locus standi*:

> 'It is my view that in these matters which are interlinked with the criminal law, our interpretation of Section 6(6)(b) of the Constitution must be approached with a true liberal spirit in the interest of society at large. The appellant has *locus* to make the application he has brought to court, and if all other conditions are fulfilled, to initiate criminal proceedings. He also has an obligation which the courts must determine and protect. In the circumstances of this case, can it be seriously argued that the appellant is not on a higher pedestal than any person to whom the law has given *locus* in the wider interest of the society?'[42]

In delivering his judgement in the Fawehinmi case, Eso J.S.C. expressly conceded that the decision was 'a departure from the narrow attitude of the Supreme Court of Nigeria in the *Abraham Adesanya's* case and subsequent decisions.'[43]

The Learned Chief Justice Renner Thomas seemed to have gone to lengths to distinguish the *Fawehinmi* case from the case of *Nwanko v Nwanko*,[44] where the parties were a divorced couple and the dispute concerned the proprietorship of a business registered in the couple's joint names under the Nigerian Registration of Business Act 1961. The husband

---

41 *Col. Halilu Akilu v Chief Gani Fawehinmi*, SC. 215/1988 & SC. 216/1988, [1989] NGSC 2 (Mar. 5, 1989), https://nigerialii.org/akn/ng/judgment/ngsc/1989/2/eng@1989-03-05.

42 *Col. Halilu Akilu v Chief Gani Fawehinmi*, [1989] NGSC 2.

43 *Col. Halilu Akilu v Chief Gani Fawehinmi*, [1989] NGSC 2.

44 *Nwanko v Nwanko*, (1995) 2 SCNJ 44.

was a civil servant and by virtue of paragraph 2(b) of the 5th Schedule of the 1979 Nigerian Constitution, he was not allowed to 'be engaged or participate in the management or running of any private business, profession or trade.'[45] Paragraphs 15 and 17 of the said 5th Schedule set up a Code of Conduct Bureau and a Code of Conduct Tribunal to deal with any breach of the provisions set out in the said Schedule.

Mrs. Nwanko instituted an action against her ex-husband, claiming, inter alia, an injunction restraining the husband from interfering with the running and management of the business. The Supreme Court of Nigeria held that the provisions of the said paragraph 2(b) of the 5th Schedule of the Nigerian Constitution did not create a private right or interest for which the plaintiff could claim a relief, that the purpose of the provisions was to protect the public interest and that she, therefore, had no *locus standi* to claim a relief against the husband as a result of his contravention of the said provision of the Nigerian Constitution. The Court accordingly struck out the matter. Understandably, the Court may have ruled as it did, not because it wanted to constrict the liberal approach hitherto adopted and applied and thereby create a messy jurisprudential affair but simply because Mrs. Nwanko did not identify any personal interest at all as was done in the Fawehinmi case and as Mr. Samuel Hinga-Norman himself did.

The purport of the liberal approach is not for the plaintiff/applicant not to identify any interest in the matter at all. It is merely to do away with the restrictive common law requirement that the plaintiff/applicant must be one with a legal right or whose legal right has been adversely affected or who has suffered or is likely to suffer special damage in consequence of an alleged wrong. The plaintiff merely has to show that he or she has an interest in the matter or the issues to be litigated.

It is obvious from the submission of Dr. Bu-Buakei Jabbie that since other common law jurisdictions, notable Nigeria, had not thought it far-fetched to extend the test of interest to be satisfied by the Plaintiff, there was no legal or moral barricade preventing our Supreme Court from localizing that same liberal blueprint. However, this is what the presiding judge retorted:

> 'Dr. Jabbie has urged this Court to adopt the liberal approach in applying the common law principle. This would involve

45 The Constitution of the Federal Republic of Nigeria, 1979, https://constitutionnet.org/sites/default/files/nig_const_79.pdf.

> in effect giving *locus standi* to a plaintiff who claims relief not in his own personal interest but in the public interest or in the interest of a section of the public as happened in the Canadian case of *Minister of Justice of Canada v Borowski* cited earlier in this judgement.
>
> For reasons which will soon become obvious, I do not believe it is necessary in the circumstances of the instant case for me to dispose of the issue of standing on that basis and I do not desire to do. I, therefore, make no pronouncement on whether or not this Court should adopt the liberal approach in the inquiry for standing as advocated by Dr. Jabbie.'[46]

With respect to the Bench, adopting a liberal approach to the common law principle of *locus standi* would grant standing to a plaintiff seeking relief in the public interest or for a section of the public. However, in this case, Samuel Hinga Norman would not qualify, as his Statement of Case and counsel's arguments show he initiated proceedings to protect his personal interests as a long-standing Sierra Leone People's Party (SLPP) member, fearing disadvantage if the SLPP appointed a presidential nominee two years before the presidential elections. In the *Minister of Justice of Canada v Borowski* case, the Canadian Supreme Court held that it was sufficient if the only interest alleged by the plaintiff was that he was a concerned citizen who wanted the issue in contention to be litigated.

Mr. Samuel Hinga-Norman instituted 'this action as a law-abiding citizen of Sierra Leone and member of the Sierra Leone People's Party (SLPP), who aspires to be Presidential Candidate for the SLPP at the 2007 Presidential elections, but who is keenly concerned that the pristine democratic credentials and processes of the SLPP are maintained, enhanced and facilitated in all its internal structure, organization, operations, programmes, activities and functioning; and that they are always consistently compliant with the valid and lawful provisions not only of its own Party Constitution, Rules, Regulations and Standing Orders but also of the Political Parties Act 2002, the national Constitution, and any other law(s) relevant and pertinent thereto...' [47]

---

[46] *Samuel Hinga Norman v Dr. Sama S. Banya*, S.C. No. 2/2005.

[47] *Samuel Hinga Norman v Dr. Sama S. Banya*, S.C. No. 2/2005 p. 4.

In the third relief sought, Mr. Hinga-Norman prayed for a declaration:

> 'That, without any prejudice whatsoever to the holding of the Party Conference (as such) slated for 19 - 20 August 2005 or at all otherwise in 2005, the nomination, election, selection, choice or identification, as the case may be, whether attempted or purported, of a Presidential Nominee and/or Leader of the SLPP at the said Party Conference, that is to say, almost two years before the Presidential and Parliamentary elections of 2007 are due to be held, has or would have or leads or would lead to the following interpretive consequences, viz:
>
> (ii) it is and will in practice be grossly unfair to certain individual members of the Party and potentially prejudicial to their interests vis-à-vis the Presidency and even to the wider related interests of the Party itself and the nation at large, in that;
>
> a) it does and will tend to operate to prematurely preclude and exclude certain potential aspirants to that or those position(s) who, for reasons of present untimeliness or prematurity or otherwise, may not yet, as at 19 - 20 August 2005 or at any other time in 2005, have indicated their intentions or aspirations in respect thereof, but may be likely as at the due and proper time in 2006 or 2007 to make such intentions or aspirations publicly known at the appropriate time.'[48]

The plaintiff did identify the capacity in which he sued; a law-abiding citizen which, without more, is sufficient as seen in the Borowski case, and, more importantly, a member of the Sierra Leone People's Party. He further particularized his interest as a potential flagbearer and how a premature appointment of a presidential nominee may jeopardize such interest. It is immaterial that he did not refer to himself in the first person but opted for the third person vis-à-vis 'certain individual members of the Party; certain potential aspirants.'[49] He, therefore, had more than sufficient standing first for

48 *Samuel Hinga Norman v Dr. Sama S. Banya*, S.C. No. 2/2005 p. 4.

49 *Samuel Hinga Norman v Dr. Sama S. Banya*, S.C. No. 2/2005 p. 4, 20 and 21.

himself and perhaps other certain members of the party. Borrowing the words of Nnamani JSC in the *Fawehinmi v Akilu* case, 'In the circumstances of this case, can it be seriously argued that the appellant is not on a higher pedestal than any person to whom the law has given *locus* in the wider interest of the society?'[50]

In addition to holding that the liberal approach could not be applied to the Plaintiff's case for reasons which definitely did not become evident, the Learned Chief Justice noted that:

> 'The second method by which the strict common law principle that a private person has no *locus standi* in an action to assert or vindicate a right conferred in the public at large has been modified is by way of statutory intervention. This time we do not have to go very far for an example, Right here in Sierra Leone, in 1991, our Parliament by enacting the provisions contained in section 127 of the National Constitution made it possible for the first time for a private litigant to institute proceedings to challenge the constitutional validity of any enactment as well as to challenge the constitutional validity of anything done under the authority of the National Constitution or any other law without any requirement that the person should show that he has a legal right or interest personal or peculiar to him which has been adversely affected by the act or omission which he seeks to challenge.'[51]

He further stated that the advantage of seeking relief under section 127 of the National Constitution is that contrary to the position at common law, the plaintiff is not required to show that he has a legal right or interest that he is seeking to enforce or protect. As rightly adjudged, the Plaintiff could not claim standing under that section because the 1995 SLPP Constitution could not be regarded as an enactment or subsidiary legislation since there is no suggestion that the SLPP 1995 Constitution was made by Public Notice, Statutory Instrument or Constitutional Instrument or that it was ever laid before Parliament.

---

50 *Samuel Hinga Norman v Dr. Sama S. Banya*, S.C. No. 2/2005 p. 28.

51 *Samuel Hinga Norman v Dr. Sama S. Banya*, S.C. No. 2/2005 p. 29.

Quite apart from section 127, it is rather mind-boggling to understand why the Learned Justice refused to adopt and apply the liberal approach when the Plaintiff had an interest most likely to be affected by the SLPP's action. In *Yambasu and Ors. v Ernest Bai Koroma & Ors*[52] referenced by the Learned Chief Justice, Wright J.S.C. had this to say on the question of *locus standi* and the requirement of an interest likely to be affected:

> 'I disagree with learned counsel for the Defendants that the Plaintiffs do not have a *locus standi* in this matter. In my view, the Plaintiffs in the action do have an interest that is most likely to be affected by this action.'[53]

Referring to the dictum, the Learned Chief Justice stated, 'My understanding of that statement is that, absent such interest, the plaintiffs in that case would have lacked *locus standi*.'[54] It is rather shocking that he found the absence of such interest from Hinga-Norman when Justice M. E. Tolla-Thompson, in what should have been a dissenting judgement, found that the Plaintiff had standing as a fully paid-up member of SLPP and aspirant for the Presidential Election in 2007.

One would have suspected and expected that the Supreme Court may have realized that it made a regrettable mistake and would have resolved to correct and shore it up were it to come up again. As provided in Section 122(2) of the 1991 Constitution, the Supreme Court reserves the right to depart from its previous decisions. It did not do so but decided to dogmatically maintain its stance in the second action instituted by Hinga-Norman despite more revealing and convincing research and arguments for applying the liberal approach unlocked and presented by Dr. Bu-Buakei Jabbie.

Four years later, the opportunity to emancipate the nation's jurisprudence from the restriction and constriction of the principle of standing by the Supreme Court presented itself again, but the Court balked at the chance to do so by voyaging into some imaginary legal construct in the SLAJ case. The matter, as already indicated, concerned the constitutionality, validity and justifiability of sections 26, 27, 32 - 36 of the Public Order Act 1965 in light

52 *John S. Yambasu & 3 Ors v Hon. Mr. Ernest Bai Koroma & 5 Ors*, SC 3 of 2002, [2003] SLSC 2 (Apr. 30, 2003), https://sierralii.gov.sl/akn/sl/judgment/slsc/2003/2/eng@2003-04-30.

53 *John S. Yambasu & 3 Ors v Hon. Mr. Ernest Bai Koroma & 5 Ors*, SC 3 of 2002, [2004] SLSC 2 (Mar. 5, 2004), https://sierralii.gov.sl/akn/sl/judgment/slsc/2003/2/eng@2003-04-30.

54 *John S. Yambasu*, [2004] SLSC 2.

of section 25(2) of the 1991 Constitution, which guarantees and protects the right to freedom of expression.

In denying the Sierra Leone Association of Journalists standing, Justice Umu H. Tejan-Jalloh stated –

> 'The two applications also concern *locus standi* and all the authorities establish that in a constitutional application for declaratory order in a case relating to fundamental rights the Courts will do so only to a person, who is in immediate danger of coming into conflict with a law, or whose normal business or other activities had been directly interfered with by or under the law has sufficient interest to sustain a claim that the law is unconstitutional.

I have searched the several documents, and I am unable to find where plaintiffs have averred its legal rights have been infringed or likely to be infringed nor the exclusive suffering it has sustained or likely to sustain.'[55]

In essence, what she meant is that she was at pains to see how the plaintiff, Sierra Leone Association of Journalists, had suffered any wrong when from the affidavits filed, the only elements of wrongness discerned were those suffered by its members, vis-à-vis, Richard Olu Gordon, Philip Neville and Julius Spencer. In her judgement, the rule in *Foss v Harbottle* took precedence in that the proper plaintiff in an action in respect of a wrong alleged to be done to a Company or Association of persons is prima facie the Company or Association of persons itself. She, therefore, called in aid the Nigerian case of *Otugar Gamiobra and Others v Esezi II, The Onodjie of Okpe and Others*,[56] where Brett, Federal Judge of the Supreme Court said:

> '.... there is a further test to be applied in a case as this one. It is always necessary where the plaintiff claims a declaration that a law is invalid, that the Court should he satisfied that the plaintiff's legal rights have been or are in imminent danger of being invaded in consequence of the law. We dealt with this point of length with *Alawoyin v Attorney-General Northern Region* (1961) ANLR 269, and it will be enough to

55 Sierra Leone Association of Journalists, SC 1 of 2020 p. 15.

56 In *re: Otugor Gamioba and Others v Esezi II, The Onodjie of Okpe, and Others*, FSC 120/1961, [1961] NGSC 36 (Oct. 9, 1961), https://nigerialii.org/akn/ng/judgment/ngsc/1961/36/eng@1961-10-09.

> say here that since the validity of a law is a matter of concern to the public at large the Court has a duty to form its own judgement as to the plaintiff's *locus standi* and should not assume it merely because the defendant admit it or does not dispute it. The plaintiff's *locus standi* in this present case has not been discharged, and if he has not his claim must be dismissed on that ground and it will be unnecessary to decide the question involved in the declaration he claims ...'[57]

Justice U.H Tejan-Jalloh further made particular reference to the House of Lords decision in *London Passengers Transport Board v Moscrop*[58] where their Lordships said

> 'I cannot call to mind any action for declaration in which (as in this case) the plaintiff claimed no right for himself but sought to deprive others of a right which did not interfere with his liberty or his private right. Still less can I think there is any precedent for such an action in the absence of the persons who are interested in opposing the declaration?'[59]

Relying on the above, she concluded –

> 'In this case, the media practitioners appear to be claiming rights for the company, the plaintiffs. This cuts across the principles of law dealing with declaratory judgements. The two declarations fail and I dismiss them accordingly.'[60]

It becomes almost immediately apparent to critical legal minds how the Supreme Court made attempts at ingenuity to deny the Plaintiff's standing. Rather than the media practitioners claiming rights for the company, as the Learned Justice put it, the converse was the truth. It was the Plaintiff claiming rights for its members and, invariably, itself. The Sierra Leone Association of Journalists was founded on 5th June 1971 and as gleaned from its Memorandum of Association, it was so formed, inter alia, 'primarily to promote freedom of expression and the press, to seek the welfare and protection of its members,

57 In *re: Otugor Gamioba*, [1961] NGSC 36. p. 592.
58 *London Passenger Transport Board v Moscrop*, [1942] 1 All ER 972.
59 *London Passenger Transport Board v Moscrop*, at 975.
60 *London Passenger Transport Board v Moscrop*, at 975.

etc.' Richard Olu Gordon, Philip Neville and Julius Spencer were senior media practitioners at the time and members of the Sierra Leone Association of Journalists whose rights to freedom of expression in the performance of their professional duties and as members of the Association had allegedly been violated in a number of instances. Those alleged violations represented a minor percentage of a number of other alleged violations of the Association's members.

Given that the Association was formed to promote freedom of expression and the press and to seek the welfare and protection of its members, any alleged curtailment of the freedom of expression of its members must be perceived as a wrong against the Association for which it can sue. There is no gainsaying the fact that a company has a separate legal personality, but it is its human counterparts that make it functional and, as such, cannot operate without its members. The company will therefore be the proper plaintiff for wrongs done to its members which affect the functionality of the company or which infringe on the company's objects as was the case here. There was, therefore, no reason, legally grounded, to deny the plaintiff standing.

As earlier indicated, in 2011, the Supreme Court radically changed its stance and granted standing in *Dr. Bu-Buakei Jabbie v The Sierra Leone Peoples' Party and Others*[61] to the Counsel who represented Samuel Hinga Norman in the two Hinga Norman matters. It is as though the Supreme Court now thought that there was no reason for the future of *locus standi* to be confined by its previous arbitrary and possibly politically motivated decisions. Whilst practitioners could be tempted to celebrate this decision as a move in a progressive judicial interpretation, its nature being shrouded in unexplained judicial rationale leaves the principle in an uncertain state. The nebulosity of this decision is that the Supreme Court indicated that 'reasons for overruling the objection will be given later.' The wait continues as no such reason has been proffered by the highest court to date some eleven years after.

It beats this writer's imagination that the Supreme Court had it in its locker to liberalize the position of the law on standing but decided to fold its arms and wait this long. What makes it more suspicious is that at least three of the Justices who sat on the bench that granted standing in the *Dr. Bu-Buakei Jabbie v The Sierra Leone Peoples' Party and Others* case sat on the benches that had denied standing to Hinga-Norman and the Sierra Leone Association of Journalists. It should be apparent from this decision and the previous ones in

61 *Jabbie v SLPP,* [2011] SLSC p. 1.

the Hinga-Norman and SLAJ cases that the Supreme Court must have taken other factors into consideration in the manner in which they dealt with the issue of *locus standi*.

The Sierra Leone Peoples Party was the Government in office between the years 1996 to 2007. During that period, Mr. Samuel Hinga Norman instituted the proceedings referred to supra against the sitting Government. It was, therefore, quite convenient for the Supreme Court to shield the Government from judicial scrutiny by using *locus standi* to dismiss his case. However, in 2011 the Sierra Leone Peoples Party had left power and it was then quite convenient for the Supreme Court to make a volte-face to open the same political party when they were now in opposition to the judicial scrutiny they had hitherto deprived Mr. Hinga Norman. As regards the SLAJ case decided in 2009, it is no surprise that standing was denied to persons critical of and vociferous against the Government of the day. As uncomfortable as this may sound, it only stands to reason that the Supreme Court in the Hinga Norman and SLAJ cases personalized the positivist maxim – '*Quod Principi Placuit, Legis Habet Vigorem*' which, when translated, means 'that which pleases the ruler has the force of law.'

This writer cannot fathom any other explanation for the divergence in the decision in *Dr. Bu-Buakei Jabbie v The Sierra Leone Peoples' Party and Others*[62] and the previous two cases. The rulings in three pre-2011 cases suggest the Court prioritised appeasing the Government over applying the law. The Government resisted the scrutiny sought by the plaintiffs. No morally or legally driven Judiciary would have reached such perverse decisions.

8. The Liberalization of the *Locus Standi* Doctrine in the International Hemisphere

In different parts of the world, various jurisdictions have been opting for a more liberal standpoint of the old common law principle of *locus standi*. In Nigerian jurisprudence, the classic authority on the strict rule of *locus standi* in the Supreme Court case of *Senator Abraham Adesanya v President of the Federal Republic of Nigeria & Anor*,[63] showcased an outdated application of *locus standi* in the context of contemporary human rights development. In

[62] *Jabbie v SLPP*, [2011] SLSC p. 1.

[63] *Senator Abraham Adesanya v President of the Federal Republic of Nigeria & Anor, S.C.* 1 of 81, [1981] NGSC 3 (May 15, 1981), https://nigerialii.org/akn/ng/judgment/ngsc/1981/3/eng@1981-05-15.

this case, the plaintiff, who subsequently became the appellant, was a member of the Senate of the National Assembly. The first defendant, who subsequently became the first respondent, was the President of the Federal Republic of Nigeria. Under the 1979 Constitution of Nigeria, the first defendant is empowered to appoint the Chairman of the Federal Electoral Commission, one of the bodies established under section 140 of the Constitution. The Plaintiff/Appellant in this matter sought:

> 1. A declaration that the appointment of the 2nd defendant by the 1st defendant as a member and Chairman of the Federal Electoral Commission is unconstitutional, null and void in that at the time of his appointment by the 1st defendant, Hon. Mr. Justice Ovie-Whiskey (the 2nd defendant) was the Chief Judge of Bendel State and is therefore disqualified from being appointed a member of the Federal Electoral Commission.
>
> 2. An injunction restraining the 1st defendant from swearing in or causing to be sworn in the 2nd defendant as a member and Chairman of the Federal Electoral Commission.
>
> 3. An injunction restraining the 2nd defendant from acting or purporting to act as a member or as a Chairman of the Federal Electoral Commission.

The learned Attorney-General stated that since the plaintiff had no personal interest in the matter, he had no *locus standi* to bring the proceedings where the relief he sought would confer no tangible benefit on him. Fatayi-Williams Chief Justice stated in his judgement that the issue of who had *locus standi* was very crucial to the interpretation of the Constitution and therefore decided to deal with the general issue before dealing with it in relation to the particular facts and circumstances of the instant case. The learned judge opined as follows:

> 'It is of paramount importance and indeed most desirable to encourage citizens to come to Court in order to have the Constitution interpreted. However, this is not to say, with respect that meddlesome interlopers, professional litigants or the like should be encouraged to sue in matters that do not directly concern them. In my view, to do that is to open the

> flood gate to frivolous and vexatious proceedings. I believe that such latitude is capable of creating an undesirable state of affairs.'[64]

However, in the same judgement, Fatayi-Williams C.J.N. further stated that:

> 'With these observations in mind, I take significant cognisance of the fact that Nigeria is a developing country with a multi-ethnic society and a written Federal Constitution, where rumour-mongering is the pastime of the market places and the construction sites. To deny any member of such a society who is aware or believes, or is led to believe, that there has been an infraction of any of the provisions of our Constitution, or that any law passed by any of our legislative Houses, whether Federal or State, is unconstitutional, access to a court of law to air his grievance on the flimsy excuse of lack of sufficient interest is to provide a ready recipe for organised disenchantment with the judicial process.'[65]

This presents the idea that even with the strict application of *locus standi* and the fear of liberalizing it to create and open floodgates, the judge was also aware that solely relying on *locus standi* and to avoid dealing with the merits of a case could be problematic in the long run.

Professor Lawrence Atsegbua articulated that the 'Supreme Court had clearly moved away from the extremely restrictive attitudes formerly adopted by the Nigerian Courts to locus standi. Such a trend towards a more liberal attitude, adopted both in Nigeria and in England, is the most appropriate for the issue of *locus standi*.'[66] He concluded that the liberal approach to *locus standi* would be the best way to go in the future.

In *R v IRC, Exp National Federation of Self Employed and Small Businesses*,[67] it was found that the National Federation lacked *locus standi*. The House of Lords highlighted the distinction between the standing of a person to bring a case and the merits of the case. The Court demonstrated that these

64 *Senator Abraham Adesanya v President*, [1981] NGSC 3, per Uwais, JSC.

65 *Senator Abraham Adesanya v President*, [1981] NGSC p. 20.

66 Lawrence Atsegbua, "The Supreme Court's Approach to Locus Standi," Vanguard, July 11, 2013, https://www.vanguardngr.com/2013/07/the-supreme-courts-approach-to-locus-standi-2/.

67 *R. v IRC*, at 625.

two factors could not always be assessed independently of each other. Lord Wilberforce declared:

> 'There may be simple cases in which it can be seen at the earliest stage that the person applying for judicial review has no interest at all, or no sufficient interest to support the application; then it would be quite correct at the threshold to refuse him leave to apply ... But in other cases, this will not be so. In these it will be necessary to consider the powers or the duties in law of those against whom the relief is asked, the position of the applicant in relation to those powers and duties, and the breach of those said to have been committed.'[<?>]

In this case, the National Federation's inability to prove any illegality in the amnesty granted by the IRC resulted in their failure to establish *locus standi*. However, in the same case, Lord Diplock also emphasized that:

> 'It would, in my view, be a grave lacuna in our system of public law if a pressure group, like the Federation, or even a single public spirited taxpayer, were prevented by outdated technical rules of *locus standi* from bringing the matter to the attention of the court to vindicate the rule of law and get the unlawful conduct stopped ...'[<?>]

In Malaysia, on 12th February 2014, the Federal Court reviewed the law on *locus standi* and ruled that a person needs at least a 'genuine interest' in an issue but no longer needs to prove he has rights affected by it. This decision was made in the ruling in a matter between *Malaysian Trade Union Congress (MTUC) & 13 Ors v Menteri Tenaga, Air Dan Komunikasi & Anor*[<?>] for access to the concessionaire agreement involving Syarikat Bekalan Air Selangor Sdn Bhd (Syabas) and an audit report. In this case, the Court held that for a plaintiff to pass the 'adversely affected' test, he must at least show that he has 'a real and genuine interest' in the subject matter rather than establishing infringement of a private right or the suffering of special damage. The court held as follows:

---

68 *R. v IRC*, at 625 Per Lord Diplock p. 644.

69 *R. v IRC*, at 644

70 *Malaysian Trade Union Congress (MTUC) & 13 Ors v Menteri Tenaga, Air Dan Komunikasi & Anor*, (unreported), https://www.malikimtiaz.com.my/doc/trade-union.pdf.

> 'Looking at the whole legal and factual context of the application, especially the fact that this is a public interest litigation, we are of the view that MTUC had shown that it had a real and genuine interest in the two documents. Hence, MTUC was adversely affected by the Minister's decision.'[71]

This decision was significant as it cast aside the earlier test of *locus standi* set down by the Supreme Court in the 1988 case of *Government of Malaysia v Lim Kit Siang*.[72] In this case, Lim had asked for a declaration that the letter of intent issued by the Government to UEM to construct the North-South Expressway was invalid. The Supreme Court then ruled that Lim had no *locus standi* as he had failed to show that his private right had been infringed or suffered a special damage.

9. *Locus Standi* and its Applicability in International Tribunals

At the international human rights level, human rights committees are established to monitor and implement the International Covenant on Civil & Political Rights (ICCPR) and the International Covenant on Economic, Social & Cultural Rights (ICESCR). Complaints under these instruments are submitted to the differing Human Rights Committees. A communication (complaint) submitted on behalf of an alleged victim may be accepted when it appears that the individual in question is unable to submit the communication personally.[73] Whilst legal persons, including NGOs, cannot act as victims but can represent one or more individuals who claim violations of their rights.

At the African regional level, there is the African Commission on Human and Peoples' Rights charged with the responsibility of, inter alia, promoting and protecting human rights in Africa. Article 55 of the African Charter on Human and Peoples' Rights (the 'African Charter') does not place any restrictions on who can submit cases to the Commission. This provision simply notes that, 'Before each session, the Secretary of the Commission shall make a list of the communications other than those of States Parties to the present Charter.'[74] The Commission has interpreted this provision as giving

---

71 Malaysian Trade Union Congress, (unreported) p. 146.

72 *Government of Malaysia v Lim Kit Siang*, (1988) 2 MLJ 12.

73 Human Rights Committee, Rules of Procedure, Rule 90, adopted under the International Covenant on Civil and Political Rights, https://www.ohchr.org/en/treaty-bodies/ccpr/rules-procedure-and-working-methods.

74 African Charter on Human and Peoples' Rights, adopted June 27, 1981, OAU Doc. CAB/

locus standi to the victims themselves and the victims' families, as well as NGOs and others acting on their behalf.

At the European regional level, Article 34 of the European Convention on Human Rights provides that 'The Court may receive applications from any person, non-governmental organisation or group of individuals claiming to be the victim of a violation by one of the High Contracting Parties of the rights set forth in the Convention or the protocols thereto.'[75]

At the American regional level, Article 44 of the American Convention on Human Rights states that 'Any person or group of persons, or any non-governmental entity legally recognized in one or more member states of the Organization, may lodge petitions with the Commission containing denunciations or complaints of violation of this Convention by a State Party.'[76]

Although these international entities mentioned above are not fully competent courts, they provide useful guidance as to the modern liberal approach to *locus standi*. After all, Sierra Leone has entrenched human rights provisions in its Constitution and is also a state party to the ICCPR and the African Charter. These provisions from the differing human rights instruments have contributed to many legal reforms in several countries worldwide and have inspired the protection of human rights and constitutionalism such as in post-apartheid South Africa.[77] One could rarely find authorities regarding

LEG/67/3 rev. 5, entered into force Oct. 21, 1986, art. 55, https://www.achpr.org/legalinstruments/detail?id=49. Article 55 of the African Charter explicitly states that the African Commission on Human and Peoples' Rights shall consider 'communications other than those of States Parties' before each session, as compiled by the Secretary. This provision imposes no restrictions on who can submit communications (e.g., individuals, NGOs, or groups), unlike stricter standing rules in national systems like Sierra Leone's. see Constitution of Sierra Leone, S. 127.

75 European Convention on Human Rights, art. 34, adopted Nov. 4, 1950, C.E.T.S. No. 5, https://www.echr.coe.int/documents/convention_eng.pdf. Article 34 of the European Convention on Human Rights, titled 'Individual applications,' grants individuals, non-governmental organizations, and groups the right to petition the European Court of Human Rights. This allows them to bring an application to the court if they claim to be a victim of a violation by one of the High Contracting Parties of the rights set forth in the Convention or its Protocols. The article also states that the High Contracting Parties must not hinder the effective exercise of this right in any way.

76 American Convention on Human Rights, adopted Nov. 22, 1969, O.A.S. Treaty Series No. 36, 1144 U.N.T.S. 123, entered into force July 18, 1978, art. 44, https://www.oas.org/dil/treaties_B-32_American_Convention_on_Human_Rights.pdf.

77 The Constitution of the Republic of South Africa, 1996, incorporates international law into its legal framework through Sections 39(1)(b) and 233, significantly enhancing the protection of human rights and access to justice. Section 39(1)(b) mandates that courts, tribunals, or forums interpreting the Bill of Rights must consider international law, ensuring that human rights jurisprudence aligns with global standards, such as those in the ICCPR or African Charter. Similarly, Section 233 requires courts to prefer legislative interpretations consistent with international law over those that conflict, promoting coherence with international human rights norms. These provisions, unique in

the dismissal of complaints or communications on the grounds of *locus standi* in these international human rights tribunals. This is so because these bodies are inclined to grant *locus standi* on a flexible plane to ensure that violations are not prevented from being investigated or brought to light by technical rigidities.[78]

10. Conclusion

If the citizen's right to seek his remedy in court is denied because he is said to lack *locus standi*, the defendant (such as public authorities) may violate or exceed the legal limits of their powers and the courts are powerless to intervene. The courts are allowing the fundamental rights of individuals to be trampled upon by various public institutions and private entities by avoiding to deal with the merits of the case.

The few Sierra Leonean case law authorities cited on the issue of *locus* standing are at odds with the significant development of the law on standing across the English common law jurisdictions. In fact, what is more amazing is the fact that the Hon. Justice A. Renner-Thomas, the Chief Justice then, delivering the judgement in the matter of *Samuel Hinga Norman v Dr. Sama S. Banya & Others,* noted the liberal approach adopted in common law jurisdictions across the world. In that case, the Supreme Court of Sierra Leone painstakingly toiled to find excuses not to liberalise standing by drawing on the dichotomy between 'public law and private law.' The learned Justice Muria (JSC), in his concurring judgement, even though he acknowledged that the

their explicit embrace of international law, contrast with Sierra Leone's 1991 Constitution, which lacks such mandates, and highlight South Africa's post-apartheid commitment to liberal standing rules and constitutionalism, offering a model for reforming Sierra Leone's restrictive locus standi practices to improve access to justice.

78 The flexible approach to locus standi in international human rights tribunals is exemplified in several key cases. In *Verein KlimaSeniorinnen Schweiz v Switzerland* (2024, ECtHR), the European Court of Human Rights granted standing to an association of elderly women challenging Switzerland's climate policies, emphasizing that Article 34 allows groups to claim victim status for widespread rights violations without requiring direct personal harm. Similarly, the African Commission on Human and Peoples' Rights in *Social and Economic Rights Action Center and the Center for Economic and Social Rights v Nigeria* (2001) permitted NGOs to submit communications under Article 55 on behalf of Ogoniland communities affected by environmental degradation, prioritizing the investigation of systemic abuses over strict standing requirements. The Inter-American Commission on Human Rights in *Velásquez Rodríguez v Honduras* (1988) accepted petitions from family members and NGOs under Article 44 for enforced disappearances, underscoring that broad access ensures human rights violations are not shielded by procedural technicalities. These cases demonstrate how tribunals favor inclusive standing to promote accountability and justice, rarely dismissing communications on rigid locus standi grounds.

matter bordered on a public law by its judicial review nature, did not bestow standing on the plaintiff. He opined that:

> '... ...the general tenor as to the approach to be taken by the Courts in Sierra Leone in such a case is one where the applicant must show that he has an interest in the subject matter before the court. That interest must be one that is personal to himself, and one in which he has been adversely affected by the actions complained of. A general interest which the applicant possesses, as in the present case, in common with all members of the public or in common with other members of a section of the community cannot confer standing on him.'[79]

This pronouncement of law is completely out of sync with the current approach to standing in progressive jurisdictions as *locus standi* is granted, especially on the grounds of serious public importance or on the basis of the general public's interest. In that case, the plaintiff alleged constitutional breaches by a political party of which he was a fully paid-up member. Putting aside the issue of exhaustion of remedies available at the Political Parties Registration Commission level, the Supreme Court of Sierra Leone ought to have granted the plaintiff standing on the grounds of public importance since he was alleging serious breaches of the national Constitution by a political party and also because the plaintiff's case substantially falls within the bracket of public law where a more flexible approach to *locus standi* is the norm rather than the exception.

The Court's current view is archaic, has inhibited public interest litigation and has constrained access to justice for a long time. It is clear that the current view of the *locus standi* principle in Sierra Leonean courts is not necessarily attached to the text of the 1991 Constitution. The constitutional prerogative that Government respects the law should prompt the courts to enforce the law whenever the court is properly seised of proceedings instituted for, amongst other things, administrative impropriety and disregard for the law as all citizens have an interest in being governed according to the law. No departure from this principle is justifiable unless there is a well-reasoned and compelling public interest to be preserved, withholding access to the court.

---

79 *Samuel Hinga Norman v Dr. Sama S. Banya*, S.C. No. 2/2005 p13 per Chief Justice Ade Renner-Thomas.

There is no gainsaying that there may be instances in which allowing a case to proceed may be detrimental to the administration of the law, but the court already enjoys an array of procedural rules which can be invoked to either deny leave or withhold a remedy. Therefore, it stands to reason that utilizing the *locus standi* doctrine as a tool of restriction has become redundant, as such restrictions and limitations can adequately be satisfied by resorting to procedural rules. Any other reason advanced for upholding the standing doctrine in public law would ultimately fail the test of conviction. A bona fide party with an arguable case that is not vexatious, frivolous, or an abuse of the process of the court ought to be heard within an adversarial system. It is about time that the Supreme Court of Sierra Leone moves away from the strict application of the 'sufficiency of interest test' by the plaintiff. What must take precedence is the greater constitutionalism growth of the legal system of Sierra Leone and the overriding public interest. The liberalisation of the judicial approach to *locus standi* still has miles to cover to catch up with the rest of the world, but the Court would not be groping in the dark since there are numerous authorities in respect of the flexible interpretation and application of *locus standi*. This would require judicial activism like in Nigeria, India and South Africa.

THE NON-ASSIGNMENT OF CASES: A TRAVESTY OF ACCESS TO JUSTICE IN SIERRA LEONE

AUGUSTINE SORIE-SENGBE MARRAH & MOHAMED JALLOH

1. Introduction

Sierra Leone's judiciary, once a symbol of integrity in West Africa, has been eroded by corruption, compromise, and political interference. The Truth and Reconciliation Commission (TRC) of Sierra Leone identified this decline as a key factor in the nation's civil conflict, criticizing a judiciary weakened by successive governments' manipulations and politically motivated appointments. This chapter examines a critical issue undermining Sierra Leone's justice system, namely, the non-assignment of cases. This practice, which denies citizens access to justice, threatens the rule of law and the nation's fragile democracy. We explore the historical context, current challenges, and urgent need for reform, drawing on the TRC's critiques and contemporary legal scholarship.

This chapter delves into the contemporary predicament of Sierra Leone's justice system, homing in on a critical issue of the non-assignment of cases. A travesty that undermines the very essence of the rule of law and denies citizens their rightful access to justice, the non-assignment of cases poses a profound threat to the fabric of Sierra Leone's nascent democracy. As we dissect this predicament, our exploration will traverse historical critiques, contemporary challenges, and the imperative for reform.

The chapter is structured to unfold the multifaceted layers of the non-assignment of cases in Sierra Leone. We begin by contextualizing the historical trajectory of the justice system, examining pivotal critiques from the Truth and Reconciliation Commission and contemporary reflections by legal scholars.

Our journey then navigates through the role of the courts in a constitutional democracy, especially pertinent in the West African context where consolidating democratic values remains a persistent challenge. We scrutinize the constitutional mechanisms designed to facilitate access to justice juxtaposed against the restrictive policies that impede such access. This section serves as a backdrop for the subsequent analysis of the non-assignment of crucial constitutional cases including election petitions, challenges regarding human rights violations, and more.

The core of this chapter unravels the ramifications of non-assignment, drawing on specific cases that remain in limbo, haunting the corridors of justice. From the Renaissance Movement's struggle for the right of assembly to the Sierra Leone Bar Association's battle against constitutional overreach, each case embodies a struggle for justice deferred. The chapter scrutinizes the impact of unassigned cases on the rule of law, democratic consolidation, and individual rights, presenting a comprehensive narrative of a justice system in peril.

Concluding our exploration, we confront the urgent need for remedies and reforms. Drawing inspiration from global best practices, we propose avenues to address the non-assignment travesty, restoring faith in the Judiciary. As we unravel the layers of the non-assignment of cases, this chapter aims to critique and ignite conversations on the imperatives of a reinvigorated, transparent, and accountable judiciary, one that stands as a true guardian of justice.

The justice system in Sierra Leone has come a long way from being the beacon of light in West Africa in the colonial and early days of independence to being dismantled by corruption, compromises, and political manipulations. The Truth and Reconciliation Commission,[1] which documented the historical episodes of the civil war of Sierra Leone, blamed the judiciary as one of the *casus belli* of the conflict. It stated in an un-euphemized diction as follows:

> 'The judiciary was made weak and corrupt. It had been abused by successive governments; several politically motivated appointments being made by all post-independent governments. This largely compromised the independence of the judiciary…Thus, the independence of the judiciary

[1] Truth and Reconciliation Commission for Sierra Leone, Witness to Truth: Report of the Truth and Reconciliation Commission for Sierra Leone, vol. 1 and 2 (Freetown, Sierra Leone: Truth and Reconciliation Commission, 2004), https://www.sierraleonetrc.org.

> has been systematically destroyed. The judges and lawyers failed to stand up to state tyranny.'[2]

Marrah in an online article titled 'Can A Born-Again Chief Justice Revive the Judiciary?'[3] opined about the judiciary as follows:

> 'It seemed from the TRC's commentary that the judiciary was the wooden tree on which the body politic of our nation was hung. And the men and women of the law were the gladiators who manned the body while it oozed out, drenched in injustice and social failings. Many had hoped that the judiciary should be far from the characterization it was given in the TRC report, considering the many post-civil-war rehabilitation programs. However, the many judicial and social issues which brewed discontent have sadly re-emerged and have been amplified by the devices of technology. Indeed, many steps have been taken in attempting to reform the judiciary post the civil conflict. But many of these strides have fallen short of social resurrection of the ideals of justice and equity. Rather they have targeted the refurbishment of the physical infrastructures of justice. These reforms were and are not altogether inconsequential—as they have, for instance, proliferated the presence of magistrates and judges in places, especially far-flung regions of the country where they were only seen once in a blue moon, analogically as Father Christmas to kids.'[4]

Establishing courts and endowing them with jurisdiction is integral to any constitutional democracy. Section 120(1) of the 1991 Constitution of Sierra Leone vests judicial power in the judiciary. Such jurisdiction should guarantee that litigants can access the courts to check alleged violations, enforce governments' legal obligations, and secure the protection of rights in the Constitution.[5] Various factors continue to inhibit the

---

2 Truth and Reconciliation Commission, Witness to Truth, vol 1 p. 27.

3 Sorie Sengbe Marrah, "The Sorie Sengbe Poser: Can a Born-Again Chief Justice Revive the Judiciary?," sorie-sengbemarrah.com (blog), November 8, 2019, https://sorie-sengbemarrah.com/the-sorie-sengbe-poser-can-a-born-again-chief-justice-revive-the-judiciary%E2%80%A8/.

4 Marrah, "The Sorie Sengbe Poser".

5 Babacar Kante and H. Kwasi Prempeh, Judicial Review Systems in West Africa: A Comparative Analysis, 117 International IDEA Resources on Constitution-Building Processes (Stockholm:

progressive realization of the core values and constitutional principles of the Constitution of Sierra Leone, such as the non-assignment of key constitutional cases, election petitions, cases involving human rights violations, the prolonged determination of these high-profile cases and political interference in the administration of justice to mention a few. For litigants to fully realize the promises that the Constitution offers, the arbitrary limitation to access the corridors of justice, as highlighted above, must be curtailed.

2. The Role of the Courts in a Constitutional Democracy

In West Africa, where strengthening and consolidating the democratic ethos has been a long-time challenge, the desire to establish and institutionalize constitutionalism and the rule of law during the democratization processes of the 1990s sparked renewed interest in institutions with constitutional review oversight such as the Supreme Court and Constitutional Courts.[6] The courts in Sierra Leone were designed with at least two key objectives or considerations in mind. First, they were to serve as adjudicators of 'political' disputes, including those between political institutions. Second, they were to play a central role in protecting human rights as guaranteed in constitutional and legislative instruments.[7]

To accomplish this objective, the constitutions and legal frameworks establishing and regulating the operations of constitutional review institutions in West Africa encompass a diverse array of rules, procedural mechanisms, and institutional arrangements.[8] These provisions collectively delineate the methods and pathways through which individuals may engage with what can be aptly characterized as constitutional justice.[9] In the landscape of constitutional democracies, divergent approaches emerge in shaping the contours of access

International Institute for Democracy and Electoral Assistance, 2016).

6 Kante and Prempeh, Judicial Review Systems, p. 117 and also Charles M. Fombad, "Constitutional Adjudication in Africa: Challenges and Opportunities," African Journal of International and Comparative Law 22, no. 2 (2014): 150, https://doi.org/10.3366/ajicl.2014.0090.

7 Frédéric Joël Aïvo, Le Juge Constitutionnel et l'Etat de Droit en Afrique: L'Exemple du Modéle Béninois (Paris: L'Harmattan, 2006), 222.

8 Marc Böckenförde, Yacouba Ngenge, et al., eds., Judicial Review Systems in West Africa: A Comparative Analysis(Stockholm: International IDEA, 2016), p. 17-25, https://www.idea.int/sites/default/files/publications/judicial-review-systems-in-west-africa.pdf.

9 Henri Akerekoro, "Le procès constitutionnel au Bénin," in ABJC, Revue de Contentieux Constitutionnel, ed. Beninese Association of Constitutional Law and University of Abomey-Calavi Centre for Constitutional Law, I-2013 (Cotonou: University Press of Benin, 2013), 59.

to constitutional justice. On the one hand, certain jurisdictions embrace expansive and permissive standing rules, fostering an inclusive environment that amplifies access to the constitutional realm. Conversely, others adhere to a more restrictive policy, constraining the avenues through which litigants can engage with the constitutional adjudicative processes; when analysing claims before the courts in Sierra Leone, two issues require attention. First, non-assignment of cases bordering on legitimate constitutional questions of public interest and, second, what procedure, if any, must be followed to gain access if the guardian, the Court, has erected a barricade to the corridors of justice.

In any state governed by the rule of law, the control of state power becomes an essential warranty in the administration of justice. This is done by translating the constitutional norms and principles in decided cases to promote democratic tenets, their practical application, the recognition and protection of citizens' rights and freedoms. At the same time, this control guarantees the separation and balance of the state powers. None of the guarantees enshrined in the Constitution would mean anything if matters were not assigned for adjudication.

Control of government excesses is the purview of the judiciary and through unique and specialized bodies in Sierra Leone and other countries. The purpose of judicial bodies is to ensure the supremacy of the law and to cultivate social decorum. Among the guarantees of constitutional supremacy as a harmonious and necessary way for putting the Constitution into practice, is the fundamental task of everyone to comply with constitutional provisions, including the same courts that serve as guardians of the Constitution. As mentioned, the core business of the courts, whether centralized or decentralized, is to uphold the rule of law and ensure compliance with constitutional principles. A vital aspect of this function is the scrutiny of constitutionality, judicial or constitutional review, which aims to uphold constitutional principles and provisions against any legislation, regulation or governmental action that might contravene them.[10] This oversight function can take many forms in different jurisdictions and legal systems.

---

10 Kante and Prempeh, Judicial Review Systems, p. 117.

3. The Crucial Nexus - Access to Justice, The Rule of Law, and The Imperative of Efficient Case Allocation in Sierra Leone

The UN's position on the rule of law and access to justice is clearly articulated as follows:

> 'Access to justice is a basic principle of the rule of law. In the absence of access to justice, people are unable to have their voice heard, exercise their rights, challenge discrimination or hold decision-makers accountable. The UN Declaration of the High-level Meeting on the Rule of Law emphasizes the right of equal access to justice for all, including members of vulnerable groups, and reaffirmed the commitment of Member States to taking all necessary steps to provide fair, transparent, effective, non-discriminatory and accountable services that promote access to justice for all.' [11]

Access to justice is an indispensable pillar of the rule of law, as underscored by the United Nations. The UN Declaration of the High-level Meeting on the Rule of Law emphatically states, 'Access to justice is a basic principle of the rule of law.' The consequences of limited access to justice are profound, hindering the ability of individuals to have their voices heard, exercise their rights, challenge discrimination, and hold decision-makers accountable. A fundamental tenet of the rule of law is the right to equal access to justice for all, including the protection of vulnerable groups. This essay delves into the symbiotic relationship between access to justice, the rule of law, and the imperative of a more efficient, fair, and transparent case allocation system in Sierra Leone's courts.

i) *The Rule of Law and Its Constitutive Demands*

Certain constitutive demands must be met for a society to adhere to the rule of law. First and foremost, there must be a law to replace anarchy, creating a structured framework for societal order.[12] Second, the law should guarantee

---

11 United Nations, "Access to Justice," Rule of Law, https://www.un.org/ruleoflaw/thematic-areas/access-to-justice-and-rule-of-law-institutions/access-to-justice/.

12 Thomas Hobbes, Leviathan, ed. C. B. Macpherson (London: Penguin Classics, 1985), chap. 13. He states as follows 'In such condition, there is no place for Industry; because the fruit thereof is uncertain: and consequently no Culture of the Earth; no Navigation, nor use of the commodities that may be imported by Sea; no commodious Building; no Instruments of moving, and removing such things as require much force; no Knowledge of the face of the Earth; no account of Time; no

physical safety, enforce property control, and facilitate productive enterprise. Additionally, the law should permit proper planning, ensuring predictability and stability. Third, consistent and transparent procedures for applying the law are essential, creating an environment where justice is both delivered and perceived as fair. Fourth, officials, including the judiciary, must be subject to the law, restricting the exercise of arbitrary power. The potential for occasional abuse of judicial power, as evidenced by the non-assignment of cases and prolonged determination, poses a significant threat. In societies lacking access to the Court, governments may act illegally, resulting in a breakdown of the rule of law. Checks and balances are vital to prevent such abuses and uphold the rule of law.

The best conception of the rule of law would require official accountability to law and insist that the courts, as much as other official decision-makers, must inhabit a network of accountability relationships in which their judgements are examinable.[13] Even in societies that are reasonably well-ordered in the sense defined above, the potential for occasional aberrant abuse of judicial power, such as non-assignment and prolonged determination of cases, would remain.

Moreover, abuses of judicial power could cause grave harm, especially in a regime where parties do not have access to the Court. Governments would act illegally and, as a result, there would be a breakdown of the rule of law. Some checks ought to exist. The unfortunate incidents of unassigned cases have provoked a profound intellectual question of who will guard the guardian. Accounts of the rule of law, including that offered by Postema, imagined the reign of an accountable sovereign. Postema's conception begins with the premise that the rule of law requires that those who exercise authority in the name of the law should themselves be not only subject to but also ruled by the law. Postem argues that '(T)he rule of law obtains in a polity just when law rules those who purport to rule with law. Reflexivity, law ruling those who rule with the law and in its name, is the rule of law's *sine qua non*.'[14]

Arts; no Letters; no Society; and which is worst of all, continual fear, and danger of violent death; And the life of man, solitary, poor, nasty, brutish, and short.'

13 John Rawls, Political Liberalism (New York: Columbia University Press, 1993), 48–49 n. 1.

14 Postema, Gerald J., Law's Rule: The Nature, Value, and Viability of the Rule of Law (Oxford University Press, 2022); Gerald J. Postema, "Law's Rule: Reflexivity, Mutual Accountability, and the Rule of Law," SSRN Electronic Journal, 2013, https://doi.org/10.2139/ssrn.2294632 and Richard H. Fallon, Jr., "Judicial Supremacy, Departmentalism, and the Rule of Law in a Populist Age," Texas Law Review 96 (2018): 487.

The question of who guards the guardian becomes particularly pronounced in the context of the rule of law. Postema's conception underscores that the rule of law requires those exercising authority to be subject to and ruled by the law. Reflexivity, where law governs those who claim authority in its name, is the *sine qua non* of the rule of law. In Sierra Leone, the absence of an efficient case allocation system has raised concerns about unchecked judicial power. The non-assignment of cases threatens the principles the judiciary is meant to uphold, necessitating a robust framework for accountability.

4. Access to Justice and its Correlation With Case Allocation

Efficient, fair, and transparent case allocation is pivotal for ensuring access to justice. In Sierra Leone, the absence of a structured allocation system impedes litigants' ability to bring their grievances before the courts promptly. Without access to the Court, the rule of law becomes a theoretical construct rather than a practical reality. The denial of justice through the non-assignment of cases is tantamount to the judiciary abdicating its role as the guardian of the rule of law.

The nexus between access to justice, the rule of law, and the imperative of a more efficient, fair, and transparent case allocation system in Sierra Leone is undeniable. Upholding the rule of law requires not only the existence of laws and procedures but also their equitable application through an accessible judicial system. A comprehensive and accountable judiciary is the guardian that ensures the principles of the rule of law are not mere aspirations but concrete realities. By addressing the challenges posed by the non-assignment of cases, Sierra Leone can forge a path towards a legal system that embodies the principles of justice, fairness, and accountability.

5. The Rampancy of Non-Assignment of Cases

The non-assignment of judicial cases, especially with regard to constitutional matters, undermines both the letter and spirit of the Constitution.

In Sierra Leone, there is no legal provision on who should exercise the power and authority to assign cases for hearing by judges or magistrates. Section 120(1) states that the Chief Justice shall be the head of the judiciary. By this provision, the Chief Justice, as head of the administration of justice, is empowered to allocate cases or delegate someone to perform the task.

Where there are no express provisions, abuse is bound to occur and be institutionalised.

Unfortunately, the judiciary in Sierra Leone, due to long years of indifference to significant legal questions, has consistently over the years formed a tradition that denies citizens the opportunity to enjoy the promises of the Constitution. Let us examine a few significant constitutional matters.

In 2017, the Renaissance Movement, then the most prominent social movement in Sierra Leone, filed an action against the Inspector General of Police in the Supreme Court of Sierra Leone regarding the right of citizens to exercise their right of assembly and protest. As crucial as this action is to constitutional democracy and social rights, it is yet to be assigned for a hearing eight years later.

In 2019, the Sierra Leone Bar Association also challenged the government on its power to establish a Commission of Inquiry, which includes and extends to making its own rules without recourse to the Rules of Court Committee established by Section 145 of the Constitution. The action, which should have guided the Commission from the outset since it touches and affects its legitimacy to carry on with its constitutional function, was never assigned. Consequently, the three commissions established by constitutional instruments proceeded on such a weak foundation and later published their report, which scholars and practitioners have impugned. The Sierra Leone Bar Association also filed a mandamus action against the Chief Justice to compel him to assign the matter. Unsurprisingly, the constitutional action in the Supreme Court and the mandamus action have yet to be assigned for hearing, more than three years later.[15]

In June 2020, an action was filed by a private citizen, Brima Sesay, in the Supreme Court against the Government of Sierra Leone regarding the state of emergency regarding the COVID-19 outbreak declared by the President under the emergency provisions of the Constitution. The Plaintiff challenged the President's unilateral exercise of emergency powers, noting that such exercise touches and affects the fundamental human rights of the citizens. The questions posed for determination in that action were whether the regulations or measures made and taken respectively by the President could come into force or effect or operations without those regulations being laid before and

15 Abdul Rashid Thomas, "Lawyers in Sierra Leone Challenge Legality of Commission of Inquiry at Supreme Court," Sierra Leone Telegraph, January 7, 2019, https://www.thesierraleonetelegraph.com/lawyers-in-sierra-leone-challenge-legality-of-commission-of-inquiry-at-supreme-court/.

not otherwise annulled by a resolution of Parliament and whether or not other persons or authorities can take measures or make regulations for the purposes of a public emergency, without an antecedent legislation. As significant as this action is, it has never been assigned for hearing despite those measures being illegal and enforced against citizens.

In 2019, the main opposition party, All Peoples' Congress (APC), filed three constitutional actions in the Supreme Court in relation to 10 of their members being removed from Parliament and the adverse findings by the Commissions of Inquiry against the former President. Despite being seized of these matters, the country's highest Court is yet to hear and determine them.

In July 2024, the Judiciary of Sierra Leone assigned a Supreme Court case filed by lawyers for Lara Taylor-Pearce, the suspended Auditor-General, following persistent public calls for action. Initially filed on March 16, 2022, the case seeks interpretation of sections 137(4), 137(5), and 137(6) of the 1991 Constitution, challenging the legality of her 2021 suspension and the tribunal investigating her. Taylor-Pearce's lawyers argue the Judicial and Legal Service Commission (JLSC) lacked third-party complaints to initiate the investigation, the tribunal was improperly constituted with unqualified members, and due process was violated by withholding specific allegations.[16]

The rule of law is essential for democratic consolidation and economic development.[17] In its report, the Truth and Reconciliation Commission emphasized that inequitable laws, the existence of separate court systems and lack of access to courts conspired to prevent the application of the rule of law in Sierra Leone.[18] The issues raised by the litigants in all the aforementioned matters are significant because the abuse of executive powers is a permanent threat to democratic consolidation. To date, the matters have not been assigned before the Supreme Court to adjudicate on the interpretation of the questions raised by the litigants.

The existence of an efficient judicial system means that matters challenging the abusive powers of the government should be assigned for hearing and determination. In most instances, they have proferred no explanation for the

---

16 SierraeyeSalone, X post, July 2, 2024, 12:06 p.m., https://mobile.x.com/sierraeyesalone/status/1808170515070169546.

17 Tom Ginsburg, "Review: Does Law Matter for Economic Development? Evidence from East Asia," Law & Society Review 34, no. 3 (2000): 835 and Atlantic Council. "Why the Rule of Law Is the Key to Prosperity: Lessons from Thirty Years of Data." Issue Brief. Washington, D.C.: Atlantic Council, 2025. https://www.atlanticcouncil.org/in-depth-research-reports/issue-brief/why-the-rule-of-law-is-the-key-to-prosperity-lessons-from-thirty-years-of-data/.

18 Truth and Reconciliation Commission, Witness to Truth, Vol 3, 130.

non-assignment. This is a vital element of the rule of law. It reveals the factors that are absent, which could enable courts to fulfill this key function properly in fledgling democracies. In a country like Sierra Leone, where emergency powers have been improperly utilized for several decades, even to the extent of putting the maintenance of the rule of law at risk, the Court must be vigilant in guarding the gates of democracy.

According to the TRC reports, successive governments in Sierra Leone have used emergency powers to silence opposition, suppress activism and clamp down on political dissent.[19] In 1987, president Momoh declared a state of economic emergency, which allowed his officials to violate the property rights of the people.[20]

It is a shared sentiment by academics and activists that internal crises, such as the outbreak of a pandemic or the breakdown of public order, that threaten the very existence of the state or the continuity of socially organized life has posed a difficult dilemma to the rule of law, especially in emergent or precarious democracies.[21] The dilemma can be explained. if you do not authorize governmental emergency powers to deal with the crisis, you face two possibilities, namely, either the State could collapse due to unrest or health emergencies or, more probably, the government would act illegally, with the consequent breakdown of the rule of law. Therefore, constitutional regimes must recognize the existence of emergency powers as a critical tool for addressing crises that threaten national security or public order. These powers are essential because they enable governments to take swift and decisive action when regular legal processes may be insufficient or too slow to respond effectively. These powers temporarily increase governmental powers and authorize the restriction of some constitutional guarantees and fundamental

19 Truth and Reconciliation Commission, Witness to Truth, Vol. 2, p. 426.

20 Truth and Reconciliation Commission, Witness to Truth, Vol. 2, p. 428. During Joseph Saidu Momoh's presidency, the declaration of a state of economic emergency in November 1987 granted government officials broad powers to combat corruption, gold and diamond smuggling, and economic sabotage. This led to violations of property rights, including arbitrary seizures of private assets, confiscation without due process, and interference with ownership rights, as officials were 'licensed' to abuse these rights under the emergency measures. The emergency facilitated a 'culture of grabbing' where property was targeted for economic appropriation, contributing to widespread mistrust and economic decline, with impacts on individuals accused of economic crimes who faced property loss without legal recourse.

21 David Dyzenhaus, The Constitution of Law: Legality in a Time of Emergency (Cambridge: Cambridge University Press, 2011) and John Grogan, "COVID-19, The Rule of Law and Democracy: Analysis of Legal Responses to a Global Health Crisis," Hague Journal on the Rule of Law 14, no. 2–3 (2022): 355, https://doi.org/10.1007/s40803-022-00168-8.

personal rights to defend the constitutional order and reestablish normality.[22] This is necessary for the continuity of the rule of law. But the dilemma emerges because these extraordinary powers, conceived to preserve democracy, have been an instrument that authoritarian governments have used to distort democracy and undermine the rule of law.[23]

In Sierra Leone, section 29 of the 1991 Constitution empowers the President to declare a state of emergency in response to threats like war, imminent invasion, or natural disasters that endanger public safety or societal order. These powers allow the government to enact temporary measures, such as restricting movement, detaining individuals, or suspending certain laws, to protect the constitutional order and restore stability. However, to safeguard the rule of law, such measures must be proportionate, time-limited, and subject to parliamentary oversight. For instance, emergency declarations lapse after 7 or 21 days unless approved by a two-thirds majority in Parliament, and detained persons can seek review by an independent tribunal. Moreover, core rights, such as the right to life, remain protected under international obligations like the International Covenant on Civil and Political Rights (ICCPR), to which Sierra Leone is a signatory. These limitations are critical in emerging democracies like Sierra Leone, where historical abuses, such as the 1998 emergency detentions, highlight the need for robust judicial and legislative checks to prevent executive overreach and uphold constitutional principles.[24]

Emergency powers must be recognized but strictly regulated and controlled to prevent governmental abuses or extra limitations.[25] It is necessary to allow the court, as endowed by law, to determine what kinds of crises allow the use of emergency powers. Governmental powers should be enumerated, and the legitimacy of its use should depend on its conformity to some principles, such as necessity and proportionality. Consequently, effective judicial controls should be established and strengthened.

The first step to achieving this is that cases must be assigned, heard, and resolved by the courts. The non-assignment of cases deprives individuals whose rights have been affected from seeking redress in court. It is the constitutional right of every citizen to approach the court for judicial interpretation where

22 Rodrigo Uprimny, "The Constitutional Court and Control of Presidential Extraordinary Powers in Colombia," in Democratization and the Judiciary: The Accountability Function of Courts in New Democracies, ed. Siri Gloppen, Roberto Gargarella, and Elin Skaar (London: Frank Cass, 2004), 130.

23 Uprimny, "The Constitutional Court," 135.

24 Truth and Reconciliation Commission, Witness to Truth, Vol 2, p. 429.

25 Truth and Reconciliation Commission, Witness to Truth, Vol 2, p. 429.

there are alleged contraventions of the Constitution. In Sierra Leone's current judicial context, the persistent non-assignment of critical constitutional cases, such as challenges to emergency powers and electoral disputes, fuels significant concerns about the erosion of the rule of law, undermining public trust and democratic accountability.[26]

6. Comparative Experiences from Other Jurisdictions

Drawing inspiration from established legal systems, Sierra Leone can benefit from examining practices in other jurisdictions. In this regard, one will discuss the application of automated systems in selected jurisdictions.

Automated Case Allocation in African Courts

In recent years, several African countries have embraced technological solutions to enhance the efficiency and transparency of their judicial systems. Automated case allocation, facilitated by innovative electronic systems, has emerged as a pivotal tool in addressing challenges related to backlog, delays, and overall accessibility to justice. This paper will now explore the automated case allocation systems implemented in Kenya, Rwanda, South Africa, Ghana, and Uganda, highlighting the benefits and challenges of this transformative approach.

Kenya's Integrated Case Management System (iCMS) was launched in January 2020 under the Judiciary's ICT and Integrated Case Management Systems Committee as part of efforts to modernise judicial operations. The web-based system covers the full case lifecycle, from electronic filing to final disposition and appeals, across all levels of court. It assigns cases to judges using predefined criteria such as complexity and urgency, reducing manual allocation and minimising delays. According to the Judiciary of Kenya's 2023 report, the platform has helped reduce case backlogs by 30 percent and increased electronic filings by 50 percent within its first year of operation.[27]

Features like real-time case tracking, virtual hearings, and electronic payments via mobile platforms have eliminated the need for physical court

---

[26] Richard H. Fallon, Jr., "Judicial Supremacy, Departmentalism, and the Rule of Law in a Populist Age," Texas Law Review 96, no. 3 (2018): 589, https://texaslawreview.org/judicial-supremacy-departmentalism-rule-law-populist-age/.

[27] Judiciary of Kenya, State of the Judiciary & the Administration of Justice: Annual Report, 2023–24 (Nairobi, Kenya: Judiciary of Kenya, 2024), 25, https://judiciary.go.ke/wp-content/uploads/2024/11/SOJAR-2023-2024.pdf.

visits, saving litigants time and costs. The system's transparency, with accessible case statuses and digital receipts, has bolstered public trust in the judiciary. However, challenges such as uneven internet access and the need for ongoing training highlight the importance of infrastructure investment, a lesson Sierra Leone must heed to adopt similar technologies.

Rwanda's Irembo e-Justice System, operating within the IremboGov platform since 2015, has modernised judicial administration by linking the Judiciary, National Public Prosecution Authority, and Rwanda Correctional Services. It allows litigants to file cases and pay court fees online, often through mobile money, while cases are automatically assigned to judges based on workload and expertise. With digitised records and standardised processes, case pendency has dropped by 54 percent according to the 2022 Rwanda Governance Scorecard, easing longstanding backlogs. The system also supports virtual hearings via video conferencing, improving access for litigants in remote areas, and features a public dashboard that shows real-time case progress and performance metrics to strengthen accountability. Rwanda's success has relied on investment in ICT infrastructure and nationwide awareness campaigns through radio and television that drove user adoption. For Sierra Leone, the Rwandan model highlights how integrated digital systems could link judicial institutions and reduce delays caused by non-assignment, provided digital literacy training is built into the rollout.[28]

South Africa's CaseLines Electronic Court Management System, fully implemented in the Gauteng Division of the High Court by January 2020, adopts a cloud-based, digital-first approach to case management. CaseLines enables electronic filing, secure document sharing, and virtual hearings, streamlining case allocation and reducing delays caused by lost files or manual processes. Judges' secretaries upload judgements and court orders directly to the platform, ensuring immediate access for litigants, while digital bundling facilitates collaboration among legal professionals. The system has cut operational costs and improved efficiency, with the Judiciary of South Africa reporting enhanced case tracking and reduced fraud incidents, such as disappearing files, as noted by Judge President Dunstan Mlambo in 2020. CaseLines' secure cloud storage ensures long-term record integrity,

---

[28] United Nations Development Programme, "Rwanda Launches Electronic Court System to Deliver Justice for All," blog post, February 15, 2023, https://www.undp.org/rwanda/blog/rwanda-launches-electronic-court-system-deliver-justice-all.

a critical feature for Sierra Leone, where judicial delays undermine trust. However, initial resistance from legal practitioners underscores the need for comprehensive training, a consideration for Sierra Leone's reform efforts.[29]

Ghana's E-Justice System (e-JS), part of the e-Transform Programme, is in its pilot phase at the Accra Law Court Complex as of 2025, focusing on digitizing case filing, tracking, and payment processes. The system allows litigants to file cases online, access court records, and receive instant notifications via SMS or email, reducing the need for physical court appearances. Electronic case allocation, based on judicial availability, aims to minimize delays, with early results showing reduced pendency in pilot courts. The Judicial Service of Ghana reports that e-JS has streamlined fee payments through mobile money, enhancing accessibility for low-income litigants. While still scaling up, the system's holistic approach, integrating various judicial functions, aligns with Sierra Leone's need for a unified platform to address non-assignment. Ghana's challenges, including the digital divide and incomplete rollout, suggest Sierra Leone must prioritize infrastructure and phased implementation.[30]

Uganda's Electronic Court Case Management Information System (ECCMIS), introduced in March 2022 at 18 pilot court stations, was designed to automate case registration, scheduling, and allocation, thereby reducing manual errors and curbing bias. Developed on Synergy International Systems' eCase platform, it offers electronic filing, online fee payments, and real-time notifications. By 2025, the Judiciary of Uganda reported that ECCMIS had generated over UGX 2 billion in non-tax revenue through digital filings. Its phased implementation, with nationwide coverage as the goal, shows how a scalable rollout can work in practice. The system includes automated case number generation and performance reporting, which improve transparency and monitoring of judicial efficiency. Still, by 2025 the system was fully active in only eight courts, underlining the limits imposed by infrastructure. For Sierra Leone, ECCMIS provides lessons on how automation can address non-assignment of cases but also signals the need to pair reforms with investment in digital infrastructure to avoid uneven implementation.[31]

---

29 [1]Khumo Ramotsho, "Gauteng High Courts on a Journey to Go Paperless," De Rebus, November 2020, https://www.derebus.org.za/gauteng-high-courts-on-a-journey-to-go-paperless/.

30 Judicial Service of Ghana, "E-Justice Project: Frequently Asked Questions (FAQ)," 2024, https://judicial.gov.gh/index.php/e-services/ejustice/f-a-q.

31 Zahara Nampewo and Isaac K. Mugabi, "Experience and Impact of Digital Transformation in the Administration of Justice in Uganda: A Critical Analysis," International Journal for Court Administration 15, no. 2 (2024), https://iacajournal.org/articles/10.36745/ijca.580.

Automated systems streamline case allocation, expediting the judicial process and optimizing resource utilization, allowing courts to handle cases more effectively. Digital systems minimize opportunities for corruption and bias, promoting a more accountable judiciary. They make courts more accessible, fostering a quicker and more efficient resolution of cases and providing valuable insights, enabling judiciaries to address bottlenecks and challenges proactively.[32]

However, they face some problems, including reliable internet and technology, which are prerequisites for successful implementation. Staff requires comprehensive training to adapt to new systems effectively. Safeguarding sensitive information is paramount to maintaining public trust, and addressing resistance to new ways of working is crucial for a smooth transition.[33]

Adopting automated case allocation systems represents a paradigm shift in African judiciaries, promising enhanced efficiency, transparency, and access to justice. While acknowledging the challenges associated with this transition, the overall benefits are substantial. To fully realize the transformative potential of automation, African countries must invest in robust infrastructure, comprehensive training programs, and robust data security measures. As these challenges are addressed, the continent's judiciaries can look forward to a future where technology expedites legal processes and contributes to the broader goals of a fair and accessible justice system.

ii) *Automated Case Allocation Further Afield*

In the United Kingdom, the allocation of cases within the civil justice system is meticulously governed by a set of Practice Directions, with the overarching objective of ensuring the efficient and equitable distribution of cases based on their intricacy and resource requirements. Among these,

---

32 Olufunbi Olugasa, "Utilising Technology in Making the Nigerian Administration of Criminal Justice Act Effective for Criminal Trials," International Journal for Court Administration 11, no. 2 (2020), https://doi.org/10.36745/ijca.332.

33 Maxwell Eustace Addadzi-Koom and Jacob Kwasi Bediako, "Implementing an e-justice system in Ghana: Prospects, Risks, Challenges, and Lessons from Best Practices," ResearchGate, 2022, https://www.researchgate.net/publication/347437666_Implementing_an_E-justice_System_in_Ghana_Prospects_Risks_Challenges_and_Lessons_from_Best_Practices; Edgar Kuhimbisa, "Experience and Impact of Digital Transformation in the Administration of Justice in Uganda: A Critical Analysis," International Journal for Court Administration 15, no. 2 (2024), https://iacajournal.org/articles/10.36745/ijca.580 and William A. C. Martin, "Court Administrators and the Judiciary – Partners in the Delivery of Justice," International Journal for Court Administration 6, no. 2 (2014), https://doi.org/10.18352/ijca.158.

Practice Direction 26, titled 'Case Management - Preliminary Stage namely Allocation, Reallocation, Assignment, and Reassignment,' stands as the primary guide in delineating the procedures and considerations underlying case allocation.

Practice Direction 26 comprehensively outlines the factors that judges must consider when determining the allocation of a case to a specific track, such as small claims, fast track, or multi-track. These tracks are designed to accommodate cases of varying complexities, with each track prescribing distinct procedural requirements and timeframes. The value and complexity of a case are pivotal considerations influencing its allocation, and the Practice Direction clarifies the processes of reallocation, assignment to designated judges, and the reassignment of cases.

Further contributing to the nuanced framework of case allocation is Practice Direction 2B, which specifically addresses the 'Allocation of Cases to Levels of Judiciary.' This Practice Direction plays a pivotal role in determining which tier of the judiciary, be it a Circuit Judge or District Judge, will preside over a case, depending on its inherent complexity and nature.

For cases designated to the fast track and intermediate track, additional guidance is available through Practice Direction 28, aptly titled 'The Fast Track and the Intermediate Track.' This directive furnishes detailed insights into the case management procedures pertinent to these tracks, encompassing standard directions and timetables that facilitate the expeditious resolution of such cases.

Several vital points elucidate the essence of these Practice Directions. First and foremost, their overarching purpose is to strike a balance between the efficient administration of justice and the equitable treatment of litigants. The factors contemplated during the allocation process include the financial value of the claim, the complexity of legal issues, the presence of witness evidence, and any exigencies necessitating prompt attention.

Crucially, cases are categorically assigned to specific tracks, each delineated by complexity bands. This nuanced categorization ensures that cases with comparable intricacies are grouped together, allowing for the application of tailored procedural frameworks. In the interest of transparency, judges are encouraged to provide concise reasons for their allocation decisions unless unanimity prevails among all parties involved.

The UK's case allocation system is designed with flexibility, allowing reallocation or reassignment of cases when circumstances, such as new evidence, increased complexity, or urgent timelines, change during litigation.

This adaptability ensures cases are handled by the appropriate judicial track or judge, promoting efficiency and fairness, a model Sierra Leone could adopt to address its non-assignment challenges.

The Practice Directions on case allocation in the UK form a robust framework that upholds the principles of fairness and justice and embodies a proactive approach to managing the complexities inherent in the diverse spectrum of civil litigation.

In Colombia, for instance, there have been many attempts by the Colombian Constitutional Court to control the abuse of extraordinary presidential or emergency powers in the last decade.[34] In March 1987, the Supreme Court of Columbia declared unconstitutional the possibility that civilians were to be tried and convicted by martial courts in the state of emergency periods. This was a significant ruling in that the use of military justice to investigate civilians had been one of the critical elements of the previous state of siege practice.

7. Learning from Global Best Practices

Sierra Leone, like many burgeoning democracies, grapples with the absence of a formal case allocation system, resulting in inefficiencies, delays, and potential miscarriages of justice. Drawing insights from established legal systems, notably the United Kingdom, the United States, Canada, and Singapore, a comprehensive strategy is needed to rectify the deficiency and establish a robust case allocation system tailored to Sierra Leone's unique needs.

To address the absence of a structured case allocation system, Sierra Leone should adopt a clear and objective criteria to guide the allocation process. We must put in place a system that assigns cases based on the expertise of judges in specific divisions of the court. Complex cases should be allocated to experienced judges or specialized courts equipped to handle intricate legal issues. Urgent cases must be prioritized considering imminent harm or time-sensitive matters and factoring in accessibility for parties and witnesses when allocating cases to different court locations.

Establishing a well-defined and transparent allocation process is imperative for ensuring fairness and consistency. Instead of single person allocating cases, we must consider instituting a designated office or committee responsible for overseeing and implementing the case allocation process.

---

[34] Uprimny, "The Constitutional Court," 135.

The judiciary should define and publish clear allocation rules to foster transparency and accountability within the legal system and incorporate a mechanism allowing for the review of allocation decisions to promptly rectify potential errors or biases.

Like other African countries, Sierra Leone should adopt technology to modernize her judicial processes. Electronic case management and random assignment systems can enhance efficiency and transparency, streamline case tracking and workload management, and reduce biases by randomly assigning cases to judges.

8. Conclusion and Recommendations

The non-assignment of cases in Sierra Leone presents a grim outlook for the nation's burgeoning democracy. The denial of litigants' access to challenge state policies or hold entities accountable for their actions is tantamount to judicial tyranny. Such autocratic practices echo the troubling historical account provided by the Truth and Reconciliation Commission (TRC), emphasizing the complicity of the judiciary in the breakdown of law and order in Sierra Leone.

This prevailing situation poses a clear and present danger to the democratic fabric of the nation. The echoes of past missteps, as documented by the TRC, threaten to reverberate if the judiciary continues to deny parties their rightful day in Court. Beyond stifling the evolutionary growth of the legal system, the non-assignment of cases erodes confidence in the judicial branch, a critical pillar of democratic governance.

The ramifications of an ineffectual judiciary are starkly evident when the courts are incapacitated in settling disputes between individuals and the state. Sierra Leone bears the scars of historical barbarism resulting from such incapacities, and the nation cannot afford a recurrence. The non-assignment of cases is a travesty of justice, demanding urgent redress.

However, the narrative need not remain bleak. Sierra Leone has the potential to reshape its judicial landscape and restore faith in the legal system by implementing a comprehensive, efficient, fair, and transparent case allocation system. Such an initiative not only safeguards against miscarriages of justice but also bolsters the foundational principles of access to justice. This, in turn, contributes significantly to the broader legal development of the country, fostering an environment where the rule of law thrives and citizens can trust in the impartiality and efficacy of the judicial process.

Sierra Leone can embrace global best practices but must conscientiously tailor its approach to address its distinct circumstances. The effective implementation of a revamped case allocation system hinges on the availability of an adequate number of judges and court staff. Sierra Leone must proactively address capacity constraints to prevent case backlogs, ensuring the judicial machinery operates smoothly and expeditiously.

A crucial facet of reform is investing in the human capital of the judiciary. Comprehensive training programs for judges and staff are imperative. These initiatives should cover the technical aspects of allocation criteria and foster a nuanced understanding of the socio-legal landscape, enhancing the consistency and quality of decision-making throughout the judiciary. We must also institute a robust framework for continuous evaluation, which is indispensable. Regular assessments of the allocation system's efficacy will enable the swift identification of shortcomings and the implementation of necessary adjustments. This process ensures that the system remains adaptive and responsive to evolving judicial needs.

In amalgamating these considerations, Sierra Leone can pave the way for a more resilient and responsive judiciary. By addressing capacity issues, investing in training, instituting regular reviews, and considering the nation's distinct characteristics, Sierra Leone can forge a case allocation system that aligns with international standards and reflects the intricacies and aspirations of its legal landscape. This comprehensive approach is vital for cultivating a judiciary that is not only efficient but also deeply rooted in the socio-legal context of Sierra Leone, thereby ensuring a more accessible and equitable system of justice for all its citizens.

The call for addressing the non-assignment of cases is not merely a plea for justice. It is an urgent call to fortify the very foundations of Sierra Leone's democratic journey. The time to act is now to ensure that justice prevails and that the promise of a fair and accessible legal system becomes a reality for all Sierra Leoneans.

JUDICIAL REVIEW SAFEGUARDING ACCOUNTABILITY AND RESTRAINING EXECUTIVE OVERREACH

KADIJA KABBAH

1. Introduction

This chapter examines judicial review in executive or administrative[1] action as an essential tool for curbing the excesses and abuse of delegated legislative powers in Sierra Leone. This tool is based on the valid assumption that there is a system of administrative law due to a developed system of judicial review in Sierra Leone. The role of the courts in reviewing the acts and decisions of government departments and other public authorities is found in all common law and other legal systems. Sierra Leone is no exception. The authority of courts to declare actions of legislative or administrative bodies unconstitutional or ultra vires, therefore rendering those actions unenforceable and unlawful remains a live debate especially in the legal and political field. As a result of this, various explanations and classifications have been made as to the meaning of the concept of judicial review.

Burris[2] states that the conceptual framework of judicial review is premised upon the assumption that there is a distinction between the power of the court to review laws to determine whether they are constitutional, as well as the power to review laws to determine if they are good policy decisions. Burris argues that the latter belongs to the political decision process. On the

1 The terms administrative action and executive action are used interchangeably in this chapter as both terms in the Sierra Leonean context have often been synonymous.

2 J. C. Burris, "Some Preliminary Thoughts on a Contextual Historical Theory for the Legitimacy of Judicial Review," Oklahoma City University Law Review 12 (1987): 586.

other hand, the former are decisions within the province and the duty of the judiciary in so far as interpreting what the law is.

Bradley[3] states that judicial review denotes the power of the courts to review acts of the executive and legislature on constitutional grounds. He traced this foundation from the landmark case of *Marbury v Madison,*[4] where the United States Supreme Court declared the Constitution to be the fundamental law, and therefore, laws that are inconsistent with it may be declared null and void. Others are of the view that judicial review was first established by the US Judiciary Act of 1789. This Act put in place all the crucial elements of judicial review, including an explicit authorization to declare federal and state laws constitutional.[5]

Nevertheless, what is clear from the views mentioned above is that the term 'judicial review' is commonly used in relation to both administrative and constitutional review. The process is viewed as the courts' rights to test any legislation or other governmental action against the constitution on procedural or substantive grounds. Most Commonwealth countries with constitutions, with the exception of the United Kingdom,[6] accept that the constitution is the fundamental law which confers certain powers on the legislature, executive and judicial arm of governance. The constitution normally imposes limits on the authority of the legislature and the executive. Further, the Constitution confers power to the courts, for Sierra Leone the Supreme Court, to determine matters pertaining to constitutional law.

However, the origins of judicial review in the United Kingdom, from whom Sierra Leone inherited and adopted a great part of its laws,[7] are linked to certain judicial remedies such as the prerogative orders or writs known as *certiorari, mandamus, prohibition* and *habeas corpus* and also the

---

3 A. Bradley, "Judicial Review" (lecture notes, Themes in Legislative Studies, University of London, 2010), 1, accessed January 22, 2024, http://studyonline.sas.ac.uk/course/view.php?id=18.

4 Marbury v. Madison, 5 U.S. 137 (1803).

5 Mark A. Graber, "Establishing Judicial Review: Marbury and the Judicial Act of 1789," Tulsa Law Review 38 (2002–2003): p. 609-650, at pp. 612-613 and Bradley, "Judicial Review," 1.

6 In the United Kingdom there is no 'written constitution', however acts of parliament are supreme.

7 'These rules were received in Africa under the general reception statutes, by which the British imperial overlords imposed the common law on their new African territories'; see [1]Robert B. Seidman, "Administrative Law and Legitimacy in Anglophonic Africa: A Problem in the Reception of Foreign Law," Law & Society Review 5 (1970–1971): 162–64, 167; Joe A.D. Alie, A New History of Sierra Leone (New York: St. Martin's Press, 1990), 62–63; Christopher Fyfe, A History of Sierra Leone (Oxford: Oxford University Press, 1962), 97; Alexander Peter Kup, Sierra Leone: A Concise History (Vancouver: Douglas David and Charles Limited, 1975), 167 and Constitution of Sierra Leone, S. 170(1) (a-e).

use of *declaration* and *injunctions* against public authorities.[8] These judicial remedies trace their origins to key English common law cases. In *Cooper v Wandsworth Board of Works*,[9] the court ruled that notice must be given before exercising statutory power to demolish a house. In *Associated Provincial Picture Houses Ltd v Wednesbury Corporation*,[10] the court established the test for unreasonableness in administrative decisions. In *Ridge v Baldwin*, [11] the court held that dismissing a chief constable without a hearing violated natural justice. Collectively, these cases shaped the English common law procedure for judicial review applications.

Over the past forty years, judicial review in English law has developed into a robust system of administrative law, serving as a specialized mechanism for seeking public law remedies through the Administrative Court, the busiest division of England's High Court. The cases highlight the judiciary's role in ensuring executive accountability under the rule of law

Prominent cases illustrate this evolution, including *Council of Civil Service Unions v Minister for the Civil Service*,[12] where the House of Lords held that royal prerogative powers, such as the government's ban on trade union membership at Government Communications Headquarters (GCHQ) on the grounds of national security, are subject to judicial review for illegality, irrationality, or procedural impropriety. The exception is extended to matters of national security that are deemed non-justiciable. Similarly, in *M v Home Office*,[13] the Home Secretary defied a court order to halt an asylum seeker's deportation. The court ruled that the Home Secretary must comply with judicial orders, reinforcing judicial authority when the Home Secretary defied a court order to halt an asylum seeker's deportation. These cases highlight the judiciary's role in ensuring executive accountability under the rule of law.

In this light, and given that Sierra Leone inherited and adopted its judicial review system largely from English law, can one assume that Sierra Leone has developed a similarly effective system that curbs abuses and excesses of

---

8 Robert B. Seidman, "Administrative Law and Legitimacy in Anglophonic Africa: A Problem in the Reception of Foreign Law," Law and Society Review 5 (1970–1971): 165 and Henry William Rawson Wade, Administrative Law, 2nd ed. (Oxford: Clarendon Press, 1967), 42, 46

9 *Cooper v Wandsworth Board of Works* [1863] 14 CBNS 180, 143 ER 414.

10 *Associated Provincial Picture Houses Ltd v Wednesbury Corporation* [1948] 1 KB 223.

11 *Ridge v Baldwin* [1964] AC 40 (HL).

12 *Council of Civil Service Unions v Minister for the Civil Service* [1985] AC 374 (HL).

13 *M v Home Office* [1994] 1 AC 377, [1992] 4 All ER 97; [1993] 3 All ER 537. It was noted that '(T) he proper constitutional relationship of the executive with the courts is that the courts will respect all acts of the executive within its lawful province, and that the executive will respect all decision of the court as to what its lawful province is' per Lord Justice Nolan.

delegated legislation in administrative actions? In answering this question, this chapter examines the evolution and application of judicial review in Sierra Leone, analyzing its constitutional and statutory foundations, select case law, and systemic challenges aimed at assessing its effectiveness in promoting executive accountability and upholding the rule of law.

2. Judicial Review in Sierra Leone

Judicial review of administrative action is exercised by the High Court and the Supreme Court, the highest court in the land.[14] Section 134 of the Constitution which empowers the High Court to hear and determine applications of judicial review. It states that:

> 'The High Court of Justice shall have supervisory jurisdiction over all inferior and traditional Courts in Sierra Leone and adjudication authority, and in the exercise of its supervisory jurisdiction shall have power to issue such directions, writs and orders, including writs of habeas corpus, and orders of certiorari, mandamus and prohibition as it may consider appropriate for the purpose of enforcing or securing the enforcement of its supervisory powers.'

On the other hand, section 125 of the Constitution empowering the Supreme Court to for the hearing and determination of judicial review applications. It provides that

> 'The Supreme Court shall have supervisory jurisdiction over all other Courts in Sierra Leone and over any adjudicating authority; and in exercise of its supervisory jurisdiction shall have power to issue such directions, orders or writs including writs of habeas corpus, orders of certiorari, mandamus and prohibition as it may consider appropriate for the purposes of enforcing or securing the enforcement of its supervisory powers.'

The source of power of the courts to hear and determine judicial review applications is enshrined in common law and in the constitution of Sierra Leone as indicated above, and by Sections 171 (11) (a) of the same constitution which provides as follows:

[14] Constitution of Sierra Leone, S. 134 and 125.

'Where any power –

(a) is conferred by this constitution to make any order, regulation, rule or pass any resolution or give any direction or make any declaration or designation, it shall be deemed to include the power, exercisable in like manner and subject to the like conditions, if any, to amend or revoke any such order, regulation, rule, constitutional or statutory instrument, resolution, direction, declaration or designation as the case may be.'

The application and procedure of judicial review is further enshrined under Order 52 of the High Court Rules 2007 which lays down cases appropriate for the application for judicial review,[15] the time for application, the remedies available and the general rules of procedure for the hearing of such application.[16] An application can be made by any person aggrieved by the decision or actions of the ministers, local and statutory authorities, or public officers as the case may be. The High Court and the Supreme Court of Sierra Leone do review the legality of the acts of public authorities and apply the law to those authorities.

It is important to state at this point that when they do sit in such matters, they do not sit in appeal from administrative decision-makers, they review any abuse or excesses perpetuated by these decision-makers. Like most jurisdictions, in Sierra Leone there are matters that are not amenable by judicial review application such as prerogative powers, issues of national security, policies that are highly politicized[17] and decisions without legal effect.[18] The remedies offered by the courts in Sierra Leone on the application for judicial review are the prohibiting or quashing orders of certiorari or mandamus, injunction, declaration and damages as the case may be.[19]

---

15 Sierra Leone High Court Rules, 2007, Order 52, Rule 1.

16 Sierra Leone High Court Rules, 2007, Order 52, Rules 2-10.

17 Constitution of Sierra Leone, S. 4- 12 & 14; Hilaire Barnett, Constitutional and Administrative Law, 12th ed. (London: Routledge, 2017), 689 gave examples of non-justiciable matters which are more or less the same in Sierra Leone. Matters of public policy not for judicial review were also illustrated in the case of Nottinghamshire County Council v Secretary of State for the Environment [1986] A.C.240 (HL).

18 Harry Woolf, Jeffrey Jowell, and Andrew Le Sueur, De Smith's Judicial Review, 6th ed. (London: Sweet & Maxwell, 2007) p. 123.

19 These remedies are clearly stipulated in Sierra Leone High Court Rules, 2007, Order 52, rules 8–10.

It is clear at least from the sources of power and the procedures being laid down by statutes[20] that judicial review has developed gradually to the point that it is being codified in statutes and that it deals with disputes between government and the individual. It is in this light that judicial review is traditionally viewed in Sierra Leone as the court's power to police and oversight the legality of government decisions.[21] It is also referred to as the courts exercising its supervisory jurisdiction.[22] It is evident that the courts are concerned about whether the actions of the executive meet certain legal standards and prevent abuse in the exercise of executive decisions in the law of employment, education, licensing, and immigration.[23]

The reviewing court will often consider whether the agency acted arbitrarily or capriciously or contrary to law.[24] The courts also promote the rule of law and procedural fairness and act in support of parliament.[25] The purpose of the application in Sierra Leone is to test the lawfulness of decisions of ministers, public officers, local councils or public bodies. Having stated these facts, the arguments in favour and against the use of judicial review as a means of curbing the excesses and abuse of executive action are examined and analyzed hereunder.

---

20 Constitution of Sierra Leone, S. 125 and 134 empowers the Supreme Court and High Court, respectively, to exercise supervisory jurisdiction through judicial review, including issuing writs like habeas corpus, certiorari, mandamus, and prohibition.

21 *Kamara v Attorney-General* (unreported), cited in Kadija Kabba, "Judicial Review: An Essential Tool for Curing the Excesses and Abuse of Executive Action in Sierra Leone," European Journal of Law Reform 13, no. 2 (2011): 330 and Associated Provincial Picture Houses v Wednesbury Corporation [1948] 1 KB 223.

22 *Cooper v Wandsworth Board of Works* (1863) 14 CBNS 180.

23 The State v The Honourable Mr. Justice F.C Gbow, Judge (SC MISC APP 6 of 93) [1994] SLSC 5 (22 June 1994) https://sierralii.gov.sl/akn/sl/judgment/slsc/1994/5/eng@1994-06-22; *Alie Basma v The Registrar of Companies and Celtel Limited* [2012] SLHC 182 (12 July 2012), https://sierralii.gov.sl/akn/sl/judgement/slhc/2012/182/eng@2012-07-12; *Ridge v Baldwin* [1964] AC 40 and *Zhou Wenje v Pioneer Power Engineering Company SL Ltd & Others* (MISC APP 001/2025) [2025] SLHCFTCAD 3.

24 Philip P. Frickey, "Judicial Review and the Legislative Process: Some Empirical and Normative Aspects of Due Process of Lawmaking" (paper presented at the Annual Meeting of the American Political Science Association, San Francisco, CA, August 30–September 2, 2001), 2.

25 Michael Fordham, Judicial Review Handbook, 5th ed. (Oxford: Hart Publishing, 2008).

3. Arguments against and in Support of the use of Judicial Review and Analysis of Sierra Leonean Judicial Review Cases Spanning Three Decades

i) *Criticisms of the Use of Judicial Review*

Judicial review has been criticized in many ways. First, that it leaves out many administrative matters that are not amenable to resolution by a court of law, meaning non-justiciable matters.[26] Second, that there is no assurance that administrators learn from the case-law or that they generally refine their behaviour in response to what the reviewing judges say about it.[27] For some administrators, rather than improve, they may adopt undesirable and defensive behaviours designed to minimize the risk of challenge.[28] Hutchinson[29] further stated that judicial review is marginal or peripheral and in some instances, irrelevant. He also observed that viewing judicial review as the solution to restraining abuse of executive actions, reinforces 'the mistaken belief that the courts lie at the heart of the legal and political process and insulates and shields the real sources of bureaucratic maladministration from sustained exposure and eradication.'[30]

Judicial review has been criticized as being backward-looking or negative because instead of building up a positive, prospective picture of what good administration should be, it focuses on past maladministration or past defects in decision-making.[31] De Smith *et al*[32] observed that judicial review is 'sporadic and peripheral' because it is unsystematic. They argue that judicial review ' ….does not occur on a regular or consistent basis, but rather contingent on the appearance of applicants with time, money and standing to pursue particular disputes that happen to interest them.'[33] Besides, Harlow and Rawlings[34] state that '… the number of judicial review cases is

26 Lon L. Fuller, "The Forms and Limits of Adjudication," Harvard Law Review 92, no. 1 (1978–1979): 353.

27 Allan C. Hutchinson, "The Rise and Ruse of Administrative Law and Scholarship," Modern Law Review 48 (1985): 317.

28 Peter Cane, An Introduction to Administrative Law, 5th ed. (Oxford: Clarendon Press, 1996), 378.

29 Hutchinson, "Rise and Ruse," 323.

30 Hutchinson, "Rise and Ruse," 334.

31 Cane, Introduction to Administrative Law, 378.

32 S.A. De Smith, Hon. Lord Woolf, and Jeffrey Jowell, Judicial Review of Administrative Action, 5th ed. (London: Sweet & Maxwell, 1995).

33 Cane, Introduction to Administrative Law, 378.

34 Carol Harlow and Richard Rawlings, Law and Administration (London: Weidenfeld and Nicolson, 1984), 258.

infinitesimal compared with the millions of decisions taken daily by public authorities.' Judicial review is inappropriate because adjudication is unsuited to many kinds of administrative action particularly the complex decision-making that is so common in administrative processes.[35] It is inaccessible in the same manner as many other court-based processes, being slow, expensive and deeply mysterious to the layperson.[36]

Judicial review is further criticized as undemocratic in that it permits the judiciary to usurp the powers of the executive.[37] It is generally understood that parliament delegates power to the executive to implement policies based partly on the expertise of administrators. Judges however generally lack this expertise but are permitted to interfere with executive decisions by applying the various grounds of judicial review to them. It is in this light that judicial review of executives' actions is viewed as undemocratic and threatens the separation of powers.[38] Griffith[39] argues for a much more limited conception of judicial review, stating that 'review of substantive policy decisions made by public authorities acting within the four corners of their statutory or prerogative powers should be out of bounds to the courts.'

4. Arguments in Support of the Use of Judicial Review

Woolf *et al*[40] state that judicial review seeks to achieve broader political accountability. According to them, judicial review proceedings may prompt parliamentary action into rectifying the delegated legislative powers that may have been abused. It is further highlighted by Woolf, *et al.*,[41] that judicial review 'also goes some way to answering the age-old question of 'who guards the guards?' by ensuring that public authorities responsible for ensuring accountability of government do so within the boundaries of their own lawful powers.' Put in another way the judiciary by the use of judicial review acts as guardian of parliament's will, seeking to ensure that the exercise of power is in accordance with the scope and purpose of parliament's enactments.[42]

35 Fuller, "Forms and Limits," 353.
36 Cora Hoexter, "The Future of Judicial Review in South African Administrative Law," South African Law Journal 117 (2000): 490.
37 J. A. G. Griffith, "The Political Constitution," The Modern Law Review 42, no. 1 (1979): 42-67.
38 Griffith, "The Political Constitution, 63-64.
39 Griffith, "The Political Constitution, 63-64.
40 De Smith, Woolf, and Jowell, Judicial Review, p. 6.
41 De Smith, Woolf, and Jowell, Judicial Review, p. 7.
42 De Smith, Woolf, and Jowell, Judicial Review, p. 226.

Barnett[43] argues that it is through judicial review that the requirements of legality of the exercise of powers by public bodies is tested; because how else would an individual or body of persons aggrieved by an administrative or executive decision and whose rights have been adversely affected, seek redress? Woolf *et al*[44] also observes that judicial review is essential in that it improves the quality of decisions and decision-making processes by promoting compliance with law, law in this sense encompasses procedures set in legislation and the broad principles that are articulated through the common law.[45] Bickel[46] argues that judicial review contributes to a government that derives its legitimacy from democratic participation because it advances the interests that citizens share in a government. He further observed that, the court by judicial review enforces the principles people share but which are sometimes ignored by the legislature due to their inability to achieve 'the creative establishment and renewal of a coherent body of principled rules.'[47]

In supporting the practice of judicial review, Fordham[48] observed that 'it is an important control ventilating a host of varied types of problems ranging from matters of grave public concern to those of acute personal interest; from general policy to individual discretion; from social controversy to commercial self-interest; and anything in between.' He also argued that judicial review ensures that public bodies are not 'above the law.' It outweighs any inconvenience or chaos caused in governance[49] and it acts as a protection to the individual from injustice and oppression.[50]

---

43 Barnett, Constitutional and Administrative Law, 690.

44 De Smith, Woolf, and Jowell, Judicial Review, p. 226-227.

45 De Smith, Woolf, and Jowell, Judicial Review, p. 226-227.

46 Alexander M. Bickel, The Least Dangerous Branch: The Supreme Court at the Bar of Politics (Indianapolis: Bobbs-Merrill, 1982), 23–28.

47 Bickel, Least Dangerous Branch, 30.

48 Fordham, Judicial Review Handbook, 10.

49 In *R (Refugee Legal Centre) v Secretary of State for the Home Department* [2005] 1 WLR 2219 (CA), 8, it was stated that: 'Government is not entitled to sacrifice fairness on the altar of speed and convenience, much less of expediency; and whether it has done so is a question of law for the courts.'

50 In *Nagle v Feilden* [1966] 2 QB 633 (CA), at 654F–G, Lord Justice Salmon stated that: 'one of the principal functions of our courts is, whenever possible, to protect the individual from injustice and oppression. It is important... that we should not abdicate that function.'

5. Analysis of Arguments and Cases of Judicial Review Application in Sierra Leone

Courts do not interfere by judicial review when powers are intra vires, as the central idea here is that in reviewing government action, the courts are merely doing parliament's bidding by enforcing the limits upon power which are found, expressly or impliedly, in statute.[51] Judicial review today cannot be described as sporadic and peripheral as the principles developed through judicial review over the years have become central to all of public administration insofar as they seek to enhance both the way decisions are reached and the quality of the decisions made.[52]

The argument that judicial review's costs outweigh its benefits in curbing maladministration is misguided in Sierra Leone's context. The ten-year civil war, driven by gross executive mismanagement, incurred far greater costs, human, economic, and social, than establishing an effective judicial review system. While implementing principles of good governance and ensuring fairness through judicial oversight may be expensive, the price of inaction, as seen in our history, is exponentially higher, making judicial review a vital and worthwhile investment.

The criticism that judges must confine themselves to questions of process and procedure and not the merits of the administrative decision may be unrealistic because 'in the end all but the narrowest zone of choice could be deemed to be a matter affecting the legality of the decision and not its merits.'[53] This is as a result of the popularity of administrative power and administrative relationships in modern times, and the simultaneous breadth of the grounds of judicial review.[54] The area of government with which administrative law is chiefly concerned, to wit, the executive, is responsible for the practical running of the country on a daily basis with unfettered discretionary powers vested in them by the legislation. These decisions have an impact on the rights of

[51] Mark Elliot, Jack Beatson, and Martin Matthews, Administrative Law: Text and Materials, 3rd ed. (Oxford: University Press, 2005), 12.

[52] De Smith, Woolf, and Jowell, Judicial Review, p. 226-227.

[53] Lawrence Baxter, Administrative Law (Cape Town: Juta, 1984), 306.

[54] *R v Nat Bell Liquors Ltd.* [1922] 2 AC 128 (PC). See also J. Skelly Wright, "Courts and the Rulemaking Process: The Limits of Judicial Review," Cornell Law Review 59, no. 3 (1974): 375; Agape Henry & Crux, "What Is the Difference between Merits Review and Judicial Review?," Agape Henry & Crux Lawyers, January 24, 2025, https://www.ahclawyers.com/news-articles/25/01/24/what-is-the-difference-between-merits-review-and-judicial-review and Kenneth Culp Davis, Administrative Law Treatise (St. Paul, MN: West Publishing Company, 1958) 640.

members of the public. Therefore, to balance this grand scale empowerment of administrators and the propensity of their decisions affecting citizens, the grounds and scope of judicial review of judges in administrative abuse and excesses is very essential to maintain balance and restraint in the executive in Sierra Leone.

From the early 1970s to the mid-1980s, judges in Sierra Leone largely neglected the hearing and determination of judicial review applications. This neglect was influenced by an authoritarian style of governance. The absence of effective judicial oversight contributed, in part, to the conditions that later fuelled the rebel war.

Today, it is more difficult for the courts to resist intervening on behalf of an aggrieved party who has no other remedy.[55] The judiciary has shown greater willingness to subject the actions of public authorities to judicial review. In certain cases, the courts have also reviewed the conduct of bodies performing both public and private functions.

An example is the case of *Alie Basma v The Registrar of Companies and Celtel Limited*[56] In that matter, the Registrar-General, acting as Administrator, refused to register the Applicant's company, which was the first to apply under a particular name. Instead, she registered the second Respondent, who had applied later, under the same name, without offering any legal or other justification for her decision. The presiding judge in his ruling stated that:

> '...It is argued that in refusing the applicant's application for registration, she was merely carrying out an administrative function, my answer to that argument would be that in the absence of any new machinery to address administrative complaints... the applicant has no alternative but to utilise that which is presently available, judicial review...'[57]

Considering the critiques discussed above, any negative effects of judicial review in Sierra Leone are minimal and far outweighed by its benefits. Far from being destructive, judicial review establishes binding legal precedents that promote consistent, predictable rulings, enhancing accountability and fairness. The Supreme Court, acting under Section 125, applies principles

55 D. J. Galligan, "Judicial Review and the Textbooks Writers," Oxford Journal of Legal Studies 2 (1982): 269.

56 *Alie Basma v The Registrar of Companies and Celtel Limited* [2012] SLHC 182 (12 July 2012), https://sierralii.gov.sl/akn/sl/judgment/slhc/2012/182/eng@2012-07-12.

57 *Alie Basma v The Registrar of Companies*, 8.

from earlier cases to similar disputes, reinforcing governance and safeguarding justice while demonstrating that its role outweighs the risks and costs of unchecked maladministration.[58]

6. Analyses of Sierra Leone Judicial Review Cases

From the mid-1970s to the early 1990s, Sierra Leone's one-party dictatorship stifled judicial review, as judges, fearing for their lives, operated under executive influence, resulting in few and biased decisions. After the 1992 military government took power, [59] judicial review applications increased, with courts granting remedies more impartially. In *Kamara v The Attorney General,*[60] the Supreme Court issued an order of certiorari, quashing a tribunal's decision for violating natural justice. Similarly, in *The State and Hon. Justice Gbow v Julius Spencer & Others,* [61] the Supreme Court fearlessly granted mandamus, prohibition, and certiorari orders, overturning an inferior court's ruling against the applicants for alleged seditious publication and defamation under the National Provisional Ruling Council. These cases demonstrate judicial review's critical role, empowered by Section 125, in upholding justice and accountability, far outweighing its costs compared to the devastation of unchecked maladministration, such as the civil war fueled by governance failures. [62]

It is important to state that while the High Court and the Supreme Court of Sierra Leone hears, determines and grants remedies of judicial review without fear or favour to all who were aggrieved by abuse of power, they also did not allow citizens to abuse the process, Cases in point include *The State v Alghassim Jah,*[63] *The State v LT. COL. C. N. Deen,*[64] and *Dr. Harry Will v Attorney-General.*[65] This stance by the Court also included lawyers who wasted

58 Cane (1996), p. 5.

59 The National Provisional Ruling Council (NPRC) took power from the one-party dictatorship of the All Peoples' Congress (APC) Government in a coup-d'etat in 1992.

60 *Isatu Kamara v The Attorney-General* (SC MISC APP 4 of 1992) [1992] SLSC 5 (11 August 1992), https://sierralii.gov.sl/akn/sl/judgment/slsc/1992/5/eng@1992-08-11.

61 *The State v The Honourable Mr. Justice F.C Gbow, Judge* (SC MISC APP 6 of 93) [1994] SLSC 5 (22 June 1994), https://sierralii.gov.sl/akn/sl/judgment/slsc/1994/5/eng@1994-06-22.

62 *The State v Gbow.*

63 *The State v Alghassim Jah* (SC MISC APP 1 of 1994) [1995] SLSC 7 (1 January 1995), https://sierralii.gov.sl/akn/sl/judgment/slsc/1995/7/eng@1995-01-01.

64 *The State v LT. COL. C. N. Deen* [1995] MISC. APP. 1/95.

65 *Dr Harry Will v Attorney General & Minister of Justice* (SC MISC APP 7 of 1999) [2000] SLSC 22 (23 March 2000), https://sierralii.gov.sl/akn/sl/judgment/slsc/2000/22/eng@2000-03-23.

the court's time[66] and judges who thought they were above the law as was demonstrated in the case of *Honourable Justice Muctaru Ola Taju-Deen v The Commissioner of the Anti-Corruption Commission and The Anti-Corruption Commission and The State.*[67] In this case, the above-named judge was charged on a 12-count indictment from the Anti-Corruption Commission and charged to court by the Attorney-General and Minister of Justice. While his trial was ongoing, he applied to another judge of the High Court for leave to proceed on certiorari for the report of the Commission on him to be quashed. Leave to make the application was granted but the application itself was later dismissed. He made another *ex parte* application for certiorari to the Supreme Court in which he failed to make full and frank disclosure of the material fact that he had already made such application to the High Court and was denied the prayers sought. The Supreme Court which was not aware of the preceding circumstance granted the order based on the available facts. The Attorney-General upon being served the order granted to the applicant by the Supreme Court, immediately made an application for the order to be discharged by the Supreme Court to which they upon hearing the full facts 'discharge the Order Nisi pronounced by this court on 19th December 2000.'[68]

Nevertheless, the review of the executives' actions is ineffective if the courts themselves are not vigilant.[69] The judiciary needs to be committed and efficient in dealing with matters under review and must be courageous to provide remedies in respect of maladministration, arbitrariness and injustice, otherwise the role of judicial review will be defeated. This is the reason why the increasing growth of judicial review of administrative action has been seen by many as a valuable development and that an independent, impartial and informed judiciary holds a central place in the realization of a just and accountable government which the ordinary citizen is entitled to in Sierra Leone.

---

66 *Hon. Kakpindi Jamiru and Hon. Joseph Sallu Conteh v Dr. John Karefa-Smart*, [2000], SC3/ 97.

67 *Ex Parte Muctaru Ola Taju-Deen v Commissioner, Anti-Corruption Commission & Ors* (SC MISC APP 6 of 2000) [2001] SLSC 7 (3 April 2001), https://sierralii.gov.sl/akn/sl/judgment/slsc/2001/7/eng@2001-04-03. A further application for Prohibition was also dismissed by the Supreme Court.

68 *Ex Parte Muctaru Ola Taju-Deen.*

69 *Jalloh v National Insurance Co. Ltd* (SC MISC APP 2 of 1986) [1986] SLSC 1 (18 March 1986), https://sierralii.gov.sl/akn/sl/judgment/slsc/1986/1/eng@1986-03-18. In this case, the applicant's application was refused. It was the period of a one-party dictatorship in Sierra Leone, and the case was between a government company and a poor widow whose matrimonial home was ordered to be given to the company.

The foregoing analysis of cases, such as *Kamara v Attorney-General*[70] and Alie Basma v Registrar of Companies,[71] demonstrates that judicial review has emerged as a dynamic and vital mechanism in Sierra Leone for addressing executive maladministration and abuse of power. The civil war (1991–2001), marked by governance failures that contributed to its outbreak, has significantly spurred judicial intervention through review, as courts have increasingly asserted their supervisory jurisdiction under Sections 125 and 134 of the 1991 Constitution to ensure accountability.[72] Prior to the war, judicial review applications were rare, but their marked increase in recent years reflects a robust response to post-conflict governance challenges.[73] Given its growing effectiveness, as evidenced by the courts' impartial issuance of remedies like certiorari and mandamus, judicial review is likely to remain Sierra Leone's primary tool for combating maladministration and upholding the rule of law in the foreseeable future.[74]

The core principle of delegated legislation is that parliament assigns specific decision-making functions to designated individuals or bodies, intending for those entities alone to exercise such authority. In practice, however, the demands of governance often require civil servants or public officers to carry out these functions on behalf of the designated authority. Judicial review serves as an essential tool to ensure that these delegated powers are exercised lawfully and fairly, preventing abuse or overreach by public officials, as mandated by Sections 125 and 134 of the 1991 Constitution of Sierra Leone.[75] These delegated powers can be so powerful that decisions can be discretionary. For instance, some acts provide that the empowered executive may exercise his discretion as 'he thinks fit and proper.'[76] Such wide discretion such as the power to interpret a statute contains inadequate

---

70 *Kamara v The Attorney-General*, at 8.

71 *Alie Basma v The Registrar of Companies*, 10.

72 Constitution of Sierra Leone 1991, sections 125 and 134.

73 *Alhaji Abdulai Bangura v Sierra Leone National Petroleum Company Limited & Others* [2006] SC. MISC. APP. 4/2006. In this case the Supreme Court asserted their authority to hear and determine judicial review application and Kadija Kabba, "Judicial Review: An Essential Tool for Curing the Excesses and Abuse of Executive Action in Sierra Leone," European Journal of Law Reform 13, no. 2 (2011): 337.

74 Bu-Buakei Jabbi, "'Autonomic Judicial Review': Powers in Search of Identity and Assertion," Journal of African Law 43, no. 1 (1999): 99-111, https://doi.org/10.1017/S0021855300008743.

75 Ian McLeod, Identifying the Scope of Statutory Provisions in the Context of Judicial Review (lecture notes on Themes in Legislative Studies, 2009), 14.

76 For instance, section 24 of the Mines and Minerals Act 2009 (Act No. 3) provides, 'authorises the minister as 'he may determine' authorise any person to undertake non-commercial investigations into the geological or mineral resource of Sierra Leone.'

guidelines wherein the executive may fall back on political and bureaucratic perspective which may clearly encourage impartiality, nepotism and abuse of power. It must be noted, however, that 'every act of delegated authority, contrary to the tenor of the commission under which it is exercised, is void.'[77]

Furthermore, judicial review provides the citizens with an indication of the nature of the rights to which they are entitled to and what actions the government, or any other institution or individual is prohibited from engaging in at the expense of the individual's rights. It is for such reasons mentioned above that the remedy and protection that judicial review offers are widely used and seen as an essential mechanism. It is mind-boggling to speculate what would be the fate of citizens when they become affected by such unchecked discretions and without a remedy. Thus, the courts through judicial review applications play a supervisory role by ensuring that there is limited or no excess or abuse of executive power. This exercise by the judiciary does not mean that it is usurping the powers of the executive. It merely delineates the executives' permissible scope of discretions.

It is in this vein that Lord Diplock in the case of *Council of Civil Service Unions v Minister for the Civil Service*[78] stated that 'judicial review provided the means by which judicial control of administrative action is exercised.' It is also in this light that Lord Hailsham of St. Marylebone said that the court is:

> '... not intended to take away from those authorities the powers and discretions properly vested in them by law and to substitute the courts as the bodies making the decisions. It is intended to see that the relevant authorities use their powers in a proper manner.[79]'

The courts in Sierra Leone have consistently exercised their supervisory jurisdiction over legislative actions, ensuring compliance with constitutional and legal standards. Similarly, the judiciary is equally empowered to oversee executive actions, particularly those involving the implementation of policies derived from legislative delegation. Given that executive powers to enact delegated legislation stem from parliamentary authority, these actions must also be subject to judicial review to prevent abuse and ensure adherence to the

77 E. M. Cogan, "Executive Non-acquiescence: Problems of Statutory Interpretation and Separation of Powers," Southern California Law Review 60 (1986–1987): 1154.

78 Cogan, "Executive Non-acquiescence," 1156.

79 Cogan, "Executive Non-acquiescence," 1156.

rule of law, as demonstrated in cases like *Kamara v Attorney-General*[80] and *Alie Basma v Registrar of Companies.*[81]

7. The Importance of Judicial Review in Curtailing Excesses and Abuse of Executive Actions

From the arguments and analyses above, one can deduce that judicial review is inherently essential to protect politically powerless individuals against majoritarian excesses.[82] Arbitrariness in official action offends the rule of law.[83] The rule of law is the backbone of judicial review making it a means of checking abuse of those with the reins of power, lest they forget that no one is above the law.[84] It is the foundation in attaining equity, fairness, justice and democracy.

The executive's dual role in creating and adjudicating day-to-day regulations creates an inherent conflict, as its decisions may prioritize regulatory compliance over broader legal principles, such as fairness and justice. This conflict often leaves individuals with limited protection in administrative adjudications, where executive overreach was challenged. Consequently, judicial review, empowered by Sections 125 and 134 of the 1991 Constitution, enables the judiciary to exercise its supervisory jurisdiction to ensure executive actions align with statutory intent and legal standards, free from bias. The legislature, focused primarily on enacting laws, lacks the resources to monitor every executive action and thus delegates authority to the executive. Without robust judicial review to check abuses of this delegated power, executive actions risk becoming unchecked, undermining the rule of law. The judiciary's impartiality, unswayed by political pressures, makes it uniquely suited to resolve such disputes, ensuring fidelity to legal requirements over populist demands.[85]

Judicial review is entirely consistent with democratic practices for the actions of government to be scrutinized by the courts at the instance of citizens, to ensure that decisions taken and administrative practices comply

---

80 *Kamara v The Attorney-Gen*eral, at 8.

81 *Alie Basma v The Registrar of Companies*, at 10.

82 John Hart Ely, Democracy and Distrust: A Theory of Judicial Review (Cambridge, MA: Harvard University Press, 1980), 73–179.

83 William H. MacLauchlan, "Some Problems with Judicial Review of Administrative Inconsistency," Dalhousie Law Journal 8 (1984): 435.

84 Fordham, Judicial Review Handbook, 122.

85 Cogan, "Executive Non-acquiescence," 1156.

in all respects with the constitution, relevant statute and other laws. Also, with respect to administrative practices administrative decisions must be taken fairly, reasonably and according to law. It brings the laws' practical application into step with how these laws should be practised. It does not merely require that the courts make sure that constitutional principles are followed, but also that statutory laws and delegations to the executive are carefully restricted to prevent any abuse of discretion notwithstanding the fact that the standards of review differ from country to country.

Another important rationale is that by providing for judicial review of administrative or executive actions, the law provides not only a means for citizens to seek redress where they believe they have a grievance against official action, but also for good administrative practice to be actively promoted. The level of relevance of judicial review was summarized by Lindley MR in the case of *Roberts v Gwyrfai District Council*[86] when he said: 'I know of no duty of the court which it is more important to observe, and no power of the Court which is more important to enforce, than its power of keeping public bodies within their rights.'

8. Judicial Review and Systemic Challenges

Judicial review, as a mechanism for scrutinising the actions of the executive and other public authorities, holds profound implications for addressing systemic challenges in Sierra Leone. It operates not only as a tool for enforcing accountability but also as a safeguard for fundamental rights and democratic principles. Among its most significant contributions are its roles in enhancing access to justice, fortifying judicial independence, and rebuilding trust in public institutions. These dimensions are interrelated and central to the development of a just and equitable society.

Access to justice is a cornerstone of the rule of law and a fundamental requirement for the protection of individual rights. Judicial review enhances this principle by providing individuals with a means to challenge administrative decisions that infringe upon their rights or fail to comply with the law. In Sierra Leone, judicial review serves as a critical mechanism for rectifying grievances, particularly in cases where other remedies are unavailable or insufficient.

The courts' supervisory jurisdiction under Sections 125 and 134 of the 1991 Constitution empowers them to review decisions of public authorities

[86] *Roberts v Gwyrfai Rural District Council* [1899] 2 Ch 608 (CA), at 614.

and ensure adherence to legal standards. This oversight is especially vital in areas such as land disputes, immigration, and public service delivery, where executive decisions often have far-reaching consequences for citizens. For instance, in *Kamara v The Attorney General*,[87] the court quashed a decision that violated the principles of natural justice, underscoring the importance of judicial review in ensuring procedural fairness.

However, the practical accessibility of judicial review remains a challenge. The high costs of litigation, procedural complexity, and a lack of public awareness limit its reach, particularly for marginalised groups. These barriers must be addressed to realise the full potential of judicial review as a tool for achieving justice. Simplified procedures, legal aid schemes, and public education campaigns could help bridge the gap between the availability of judicial review and its effective utilisation.

Judicial independence is an essential component of the rule of law, ensuring that courts can act impartially and without external influence. Judicial review strengthens this independence by reinforcing the judiciary's constitutional mandate to oversee and limit the actions of the executive and legislature. In Sierra Leone, where judicial independence has historically been undermined during periods of authoritarian rule, judicial review serves as a vital assertion of the judiciary's autonomy.

Through landmark cases such as *Julius Spencer v Justice Gbow*,[88] the courts have demonstrated their ability to resist executive interference and uphold the principles of justice. Such decisions bolster public confidence in the judiciary, affirming its role as an impartial arbiter and a guardian of constitutional rights. Moreover, judicial review ensures that the executive operates within the bounds of the law, thereby reinforcing the separation of powers.

Nonetheless, judicial independence in Sierra Leone faces ongoing threats, including limited resources, political pressures, and perceptions of bias. Strengthening the judiciary's capacity to exercise its review powers without fear or favour is critical. This requires reforms to improve the security of tenure of judges, enhance financial independence, and provide comprehensive training on emerging legal challenges.

Trust in public institution is integral to the stability and legitimacy of democratic governance. In Sierra Leone, years of political turmoil, corruption,

---

87 *Kamara v The Attorney-General*, at 8.

88 *The State v Gbow.*

and conflict have eroded public confidence in state institutions. Judicial review plays a crucial role in rebuilding this trust by promoting transparency, accountability, and adherence to the rule of law.

Judicial review deters abuses of power and ensures that government decisions comply with legal and constitutional standards by holding public authorities accountable for their actions. For instance, in *Basma v Registrar of Companies*,[89] the court's intervention in an administrative dispute demonstrated its commitment to ensuring fairness and legality in public administration. Such decisions reinforce the perception that public institutions are subject to legal scrutiny and can be held accountable for their actions.

Furthermore, judicial review enhances transparency by compelling public authorities to justify their decisions. This transparency fosters a culture of accountability, encouraging government officials to act lawfully and responsibly. The judiciary's active role in addressing grievances and rectifying injustices also provides citizens with a sense of justice, further strengthening public trust in state institutions.

However, the judiciary's ability to rebuild trust is contingent upon its own integrity and effectiveness. Allegations of corruption, delays in adjudication, and inadequate enforcement of judicial decisions undermine confidence in the courts. Addressing these issues requires concerted efforts to improve judicial efficiency, enhance ethical standards, and ensure the timely implementation of court rulings.[90]

9. Conclusion and Recommendations

Judicial review is undeniably an essential mechanism in Sierra Leone's legal framework, providing a critical safeguard against the abuse and excesses of executive power. Despite the challenges and limitations identified, its role in maintaining the rule of law, ensuring accountability, and protecting individual rights remains indispensable. This chapter has demonstrated that judicial review functions as an effective tool for overseeing the actions of the executive and public authorities, ensuring their compliance with constitutional and legal standards while upholding principles of fairness, natural justice, and equity.

---

89 *Alie Basma v The Registrar of Companies*, 8.

90 Emmanuel Saffa Abdulai and Ina Kubbe, eds., The Diverse Facets of Corruption in Sierra Leone (Cham, Switzerland: Springer Nature Switzerland, 2024).

The analysis highlighted the dual nature of judicial review, a check on executive power and a means of securing justice for aggrieved citizens. It ensures that decisions taken by public authorities are consistent with the law and that citizens are not arbitrarily deprived of their rights. However, it also highlights that systemic challenges, such as resource constraints, procedural complexities, and accessibility barriers, limit its effectiveness. Addressing these issues is vital to unlocking the full potential of judicial review in Sierra Leone.

One of the critical insights from this discussion is that judicial review alone cannot guarantee good governance. While it is an essential safeguard, it must be complemented by broader reforms to enhance the quality of administrative decision-making. Investments in civil service capacity, specialised training for administrators, and increased public awareness of legal remedies are necessary to create an environment where judicial review can thrive as a corrective and preventive mechanism.

Moreover, the independence of the judiciary emerges as a foundational requirement for the effective functioning of judicial review. Sierra Leone's history of political instability and governance challenges underscores the need for a judiciary that is both impartial and courageous in its oversight of executive actions. Strengthening judicial independence through secure tenure, adequate resources, and protection from political interference is imperative for ensuring that judicial review remains a robust instrument of accountability.

Judicial review has also demonstrated its capacity to rebuild trust in public institutions by holding decision-makers accountable and fostering transparency. This trust is essential for the stability and legitimacy of democratic governance in Sierra Leone. By affirming the principles of fairness and legality, judicial review enhances public confidence in the judiciary and other state institutions, contributing to the overall strengthening of the rule of law.

In conclusion, judicial review is more than a legal mechanism. It is a pillar of democratic governance and an instrument for social justice. Its role in Sierra Leone's post-conflict recovery and democratic consolidation is particularly significant, as it provides a means for addressing grievances, curbing executive overreach, and ensuring that public authorities act within the confines of the law. To maximise its impact, sustained efforts must be made to address systemic challenges and enhance the capacity of both the judiciary and the administrative apparatus.

PART THREE:

FROM CHALLENGES TO CHANGE – FORGING A FAIRER JUSTICE SYSTEM

RECONCILING THE PAST, REFORMING THE FUTURE – SIERRA LEONE'S TRC AND POST-CONFLICT REFORM

SARAMBA KANDEH

1. Introduction

This chapter provides a comprehensive evaluation of the impact of Truth and Reconciliation Commission (TRC) recommendations on Sierra Leone's justice sector. It examines the post-conflict initiatives aimed at fortifying the judiciary and scrutinizes whether these measures have fostered greater accountability and responsiveness to citizens' needs. The analysis encompasses an overview of the TRC process, its findings and recommendations regarding human rights, the rule of law, and the judiciary.

A critical aspect of this exploration is the examination of unaddressed structural issues within the 1991 Constitution that pose challenges to judicial independence. The chapter delves into key areas, including the appointment and tenure of judges, the independence of the Judicial and Legal Service Commission, budgetary allocations for the judiciary, and the long-standing proposal to separate the office of the Attorney-General from that of the Minister of Justice.

The chapter dissects donor support for justice sector reforms and probes whether successive post-conflict governments have effectively addressed the core justice issues and grievances that fueled the protracted civil war. It scrutinizes the political will to confront and rectify constitutional structural challenges, emphasizing the imperative of governmental commitment to fostering judicial independence.

The chapter concludes with a compelling argument for the removal of executive influence over the judiciary and the reinforcement of the rule of law to instill trust among citizens and preserve the hard-earned peace. It underscores the potential repercussions of neglecting these reforms, warning against perpetuating the injustices and grievances that fueled the civil war and threatening the nation's stability and development.

The Government's unwavering political will to uphold judicial independence and respect court decisions, even in politically challenging circumstances, is posited as a prerequisite for lasting peace. The chapter advocates for sustained efforts to nurture and fortify an independent judiciary, positioning it as the cornerstone for upholding the rule of law, ensuring justice, and fostering a stable, democratic society in Sierra Leone.

The decade-long civil war in Sierra Leone[1] formally ended in January 2002 following peace negotiations and international interventions.[2] The brutality of the war is well documented[3] and it is widely recognized for its ghastly atrocities committed against civilians by all factions involved.[4] A report by Mary Karldor, with James Vincent, evaluating UNDP's assistance to Sierra Leone estimated that around 70,000 lives were lost during the conflict,

1 The conflict began on March 23, 1991, when fighters of the Revolutionary United Front (RUF), with the support of Liberian and Burkinabe mercenaries, attacked the town of Bomaru in Kailahun District. The RUF, led by Foday Sankoh, a former army corporal, and backed by the Liberian leader Charles Taylor, aimed to overthrow the one-party Government of President Joseph Saidu Momoh and the All Peoples' Congress (APC) political party, which had ruled Sierra Leone since 1968. The Government of Sierra Leone and the RUF signed a Peace Agreement in Lome, Togo in July 1999. The deal proposed power-sharing in exchange for peace and deploying a UN peacekeeping force (UNAMSIL) to monitor the truce and disarm the RUF and other fighters. However, the rebels failed to comply with the agreement and resumed fighting around Freetown in May 2000. With support from ECOMOG, British troops and the United Nations, the Sierra Leone army eventually defeated the RUF, and UNAMSIL successfully disarmed fighters. The war ended on January 18, 2002, when President Ahmad Tejan Kabbah declared peace at a ceremony in Lungi. For a detailed overview of the civil war.

2 For a detailed overview of the civil war, see Ismael Rashid, "The Sierra Leone Civil War and the Remaking of ECOWAS," Research in Sierra Leone Studies (RISLS)1, no. 1 (2013): 2.

3 See, Aline Leboeuf, "Sierra Leone: List of Extremely Violent Events Perpetrated during the War, 1991–2002," Online Encyclopedia of Mass Violence, 2008.

4 The executive summary of the TRC report describes the violence during the civil war as follows: 'Reports emerged of indiscriminate amputations, abductions of women and children, recruitment of children as combatants, rape, sexual slavery, cannibalism, gratuitous killings and wanton destruction of villages and towns. This was a war measured not so much in battles and confrontations between combatants as in attacks upon civilian populations. Its awesome climax was the destruction of much of Freetown in January 1999.'

and 2.6 million people were displaced from their homes, comprising half of the country's population at the time. [5]

Following the official end of the civil war, the Government of Sierra Leone and its development partners embarked on a post-conflict reconstruction process that encompassed national reconciliation, reconstruction of state institutions, and other peacebuilding activities.[6] A Peace Agreement between the Government of Sierra Leone and the defunct Revolutionary United Front (RUF) signed in Lomé, Togo on 7 July 1999 called for establishing a Truth and Reconciliation Commission ('TRC' or 'Commission') as part of the national reconciliation process.[7] The Commission's primary objective was to create an impartial historical record of the armed conflict in Sierra Leone.[8] One of its core functions was to investigate and report on the causes, nature, and extent of the violations and abuses that occurred during the conflict, including the context in which they occurred.[9]

Among several other findings, the TRC found that the failure of the Judiciary as an institution helped to fuel the 11-year civil war that afflicted the country. The report stated that 'institutions meant to uphold human rights, such as the courts and civil society, were thoroughly co-opted by the executive.'[10] The report went on to make scathing indictments of the Judiciary and legal practitioners, pointing out that institutions such as the Judiciary had become mere pawns in the hands of the executive. Corruption in the Judiciary was rife. Lawyers and judges failed to stand up to the systematic violation of the rights of the people; they failed to stand up to state tyranny and to give any meaningful content to the rule of law.[11]

The Commission, therefore, concluded that the Judiciary shared responsibility for the outbreak of civil war in Sierra Leone. A strong indictment for an institution supposed to be the bedrock of democracy and sustainable

---

5 See Mary Kaldor and James Vincent, "Evaluation of UNDP Assistance to Conflict-Affected Countries: Case Study Sierra Leone" (report, UNDP, Geneva, 2006). These statistics, although not entirely accurate, are a heartbreaking reminder of the human cost of conflict.

6 See, Proscovia Svärd, "The International Community and Post-War Reconciliation in Africa: A Case Study of the Sierra Leone Truth and Reconciliation Commission," African Journal on Conflict Resolution 10, no. 1 (2010): 2.

7 See Peace Agreement between the Government of Sierra Leone and the Revolutionary United Front of Sierra Leone, signed at Lomé, Togo, July 7, 1999, art. XXVI.

8 Sierra Leone Truth and Reconciliation Commission, Final Report.

9 Sierra Leone Truth and Reconciliation Commission, Final Report.

10 Sierra Leone Truth and Reconciliation Commission, Final Report, Vol 2, Chap. 2, p.27.

11 Sierra Leone Truth and Reconciliation Commission, Final Report, Vol 2, Chap. 2, p.27.

development. Accordingly, the TRC recommended addressing the critical justice issues that were the main drivers of the conflict immediately.

Rebuilding justice institutions, therefore, became a central element of the post-conflict reform process in Sierra Leone. The TRC's findings partly spurred significant support for justice strengthening, especially from the UK Department for International Development (DFID). Other institutions, such as the United Nations (UN), the European Union, the World Bank, and GIZ,[12] also significantly contributed to strengthening the justice sector by initiating a range of programs to enhance the Ministry of Justice; rebuild, train, and equip the police; rebuild courts and train the Judiciary; undertake legislative reform; provide paralegal assistance and alternative dispute resolution mechanisms; improve the quality of justice within local courts, and establish oversight mechanisms. [13]

However, they could not transform the judicial system meaningfully. Two decades after the official end of the war, Sierra Leone is still grappling with a weak and compromised judicial system resulting in a lack of citizens' trust in justice delivery. There are visible pre-war patterns in the administration of justice, such as interference by the executive, corruption, and compromised oversight institutions.

2. Overview Of The TRC

The TRC originates from the Lomé Peace Agreement. The negotiators of the peace agreement explained the rationale for setting up the TRC as follows:

> 'Sierra Leoneans needed to express and acknowledge suffering, a need to relate their stories and experiences, a need to know who was behind the atrocities, a need to explain and contextualise decisions and conduct, a need to reconcile with former enemies, a need to begin personal and national healing and a need to build accountability in order to address impunity.'[14]

[12] The Deutsche Gesellschaft für Internationale Zusammenarbeit GmbH, often simply shortened to GIZ, is the main German development agency.

[13] Castillejo, Building Accountable Justice.

[14] Sierra Leone Truth and Reconciliation Commission, Final Report, Vol 1, Chap. 2, p.27.

Accordingly, article 26 of the peace agreement called for the Commission's establishment within ninety days after its signing.[15]

However, the TRC's establishment, mandated by the 1999 Lomé Peace Agreement, was delayed due to renewed conflict shortly after the agreement was signed.[16] The Commission became operational in 2002 following improved stability in the country. Section 6 of the TRC Act mandated the Commission to 'create an impartial historical record of violations and abuses that occurred during the conflict, to address impunity, to respond to the needs of the victims, to promote healing and reconciliation and to prevent a repetition of the violations and abuses suffered.'[17] The Act further required investigation into the roles of internal and external factions in the conflict since the war in Sierra Leone was greatly influenced by external factors such as the war in Liberia.[18]

The Commission had seven commissioners, four Sierra Leoneans and three internationals. A significant task of the commissioner was to interview victims, perpetrators and witnesses and report on what they found. The TRC began its hearings on 14 April 2003 after collecting over 7,100 statements from victims, perpetrators and witnesses to the atrocities. The Commission held one week of public hearings for individual statement givers in each of the country's twelve districts headquarter towns, including one day of closed hearings for children and victims of sexual violence to testify privately.[19] In addition to individual hearings, the TRC process included a series of thematic, institutional, and event-specific hearings in Freetown.

The Commission concluded its work in October 2004 and issued a report of over 500 pages in four volumes. The report highlighted internal and external factors that led to the conflict and concluded that 'years of bad governance, endemic corruption and the denial of basic human rights created the deplorable conditions that made the conflict inevitable.'[20] The TRC report

15 Special Court for Sierra Leone, "Overview of the Sierra Leone Truth & Reconciliation Report," ReliefWeb, October 2004, https://reliefweb.int/report/sierra-leone/overview-sierra-leone-truth-reconciliation-report-oct-2004.

16 Sierra Leone Truth and Reconciliation Commission, Final Report.

17 The Truth and Reconciliation Commission Act 2000, No. 4 (Sierra Leone), https://www.sierra-leone.org/Laws/2000-4.pdf.

18 Truth and Reconciliation Commission Act 2000, sec. 6.

19 Sierra Leone Truth and Reconciliation Commission, Final Report Vol 1, Ch 5, para 194-198.

20 Sierra Leone Truth and Reconciliation Commission, Final Report. 'Background to the recommendations matrix.' (2013). Available at: https://www.sierraleonetrc.org/index.php/background-to-the-recommendations-matrix [Accessed 9 September 2024].

contains this profound summary of the state of Sierra Leone prior to the outbreak of war,

> '...Successive regimes became increasingly impervious to the wishes and needs of the majority. Instead of implementing positive and progressive policies, each regime perpetuated the ills and self-serving machinations left behind by its predecessor. By the start of the conflict, the nation had been stripped of its dignity. Institutional collapse reduced the vast majority of people into a state of deprivation. Government accountability was non-existent. Political expression and dissent had been crushed. Democracy and the rule of law were dead. By 1991, Sierra Leone was a deeply divided society and full of the potential for violence. It required only the slightest spark for this violence to be ignited.'[21]

The Commission accordingly called for the protection of human rights, the establishment of the rule of law, the fight against corruption, the building of the national justice system, reparations, reconciliation that included guiding principles and reconciliation activities, and a national vision of going forward, among other things.[22] These recommendations were designed to help build a new Sierra Leone based on the values of human dignity, tolerance, and respect for the rights of all persons. 'In particular, the recommendations were to help create an open and vibrant democracy in which everybody is equal before the law.'[23]

In June 2005, the Government of the late President Kabbah issued a White Paper on the TRC report. However, civil society found the Government's response to the recommendations disappointing.[24] While the White Paper welcomed most of the recommendations, it failed to establish a timeline to implement them. As a result, civil society wrote an open letter to the late President Kabbah, noting that the 'white paper' does not reflect any

---

21 Sierra Leone Truth and Reconciliation Commission, Final Report.

22 Sierra Leone Truth and Reconciliation Commission, Final Report.

23 UN Integrated Office in Sierra Leone (UNIOSIL), "Summary of the Findings and Core Recommendations of the Sierra Leone Truth and Reconciliation Commission," ReliefWeb, May 24, 2007, https://reliefweb.int/report/sierra-leone/summary-findings-and-core-recommendations-sierra-leone-truth-and-reconciliation.

24 See, Amnesty International, Sierra Leone Government Urged to Implement the Recommendations of the Truth and Reconciliation Commission (TRC), Public Statement, 2005, https://www.amnesty.org/en/wp-content/uploads/2021/08/afr510122005en.pdf.

serious engagement with the TRC process.'[25] The Government also rejected a crucial recommendation on the separation of the office of the Minister of Justice and Attorney General, which remains a critical issue in the judicial system that allows for audacious interference by the executive even in the present day.[26]

3. TRC Findings and Recommendations with Respect to Human Rights, the Rule of Law, and the Judiciary

With respect to human rights and the rule of law, the TRC's findings 'ranged from the failure of lawyers and judges to stand up to systematic violations of the rights of the people, the misuse of the death penalty, abuse of emergency powers to suppress political dissent, widespread use of illegal detention, rampant corruption in the judiciary, to political interference from the executive branch.' [27]

Regarding the Judiciary, the Commission found that the Judiciary was understaffed and underpaid. Influential members of society could sometimes select judges to hear cases, a practice which brought the judicial process into disrepute. Successive governments abused the judicial appointment process, which severely compromised the independence of the Judiciary. Lack of security of tenure of judges permitted the Government to interfere at will with the Judiciary. The practice of employing retired judges on a contract basis compromised judicial independence. Lack of financial autonomy impoverished the administration of justice, the majority of Sierra Leoneans lacked access to the courts and corruption permeated all levels of the Judiciary. Moreover, the Commission found that the office of the Attorney-General had not been and was not free from political interference from the executive arm of Government.[28]

The Commission accordingly made wide-ranging recommendations to strengthen the rule of law and institutions of accountability. With respect to human rights and the rule of law, it called for, among other recommendations, the abolishment of the death penalty; no ouster of the court's jurisdiction

---

[25] Sierra Leone: Civil Society Criticises 'Vague' Government Plan for Post-war Reform," The New Humanitarian, July 13, 2005, September 9, 2024, https://reliefweb.int/report/sierra-leone/sierra-leone-civil-society-criticises-vague-government-plan-post-war-reform.

[26] Sierra Leone Truth and Reconciliation Commission, Final Report, 'Background to the recommendations matrix.'

[27] Sierra Leone Truth and Reconciliation Commission, Final Report.

[28] Sierra Leone Truth and Reconciliation Commission, Final Report.

in public emergencies; enshrining human dignity as a fundamental right; avoiding criminal sanction in the sphere of expression; repealing of Section 27(4)(d) of the Constitution;[29] establishment of a national human rights commission; ratification of human rights treaties; codification of customary law; creation of a new constitution for Sierra Leone.[30]

Regarding the Judiciary, it recommended creating a binding code of conduct for judges; separation of the offices of the Attorney General and Minister of Justice; creation of an autonomous Judiciary with budgetary independence; the incorporation of local courts into the judicial system; introduction of alternative forms of dispute resolution, and the simplification of legal rules and procedures, among others.[31] These recommendations were partly responsible for the substantial contribution toward strengthening the justice sector.

4. Donor Support for Reform of the Justice Sector

The Government and development partners built on these findings to reform the justice sector with 'quick-fix interventions and long-term strategic planning.'[32] DFID, through its Justice Sector Development Programme (JSDP), predominantly funded broader justice sector reforms in Sierra Leone. The United Kingdom (UK) led the security sector reform in Sierra Leone since the second half of the 1990s. The UK contributed significantly to police reform through the Commonwealth Community Safety and Security Project (CCSSP).[33] In the justice sector, DFID first started with a Law Development Project, which operated in parallel to the CCSSP. The first half of the project focused on logistics and infrastructure, encompassing building refurbishment and equipment supply to the main

29 Section 27 (1) of the 1991 Constitution prohibits discrimination. However, Section 27 (4) (d) explicitly states that protection from discrimination does not apply in relation to laws regarding 'adoption, marriage, divorce, burial, devolution of property on death or other interests of personal law', all of which are particularly relevant to women. The TRC recommended the repeal of this section because it negates not only the provisions for fundamental human rights in section 15 of the Constitution, but also all other legislation that has been enacted to advance women's rights.

30 Sierra Leone Truth and Reconciliation Commission, Final Report.

31 Sierra Leone Truth and Reconciliation Commission, Final Report.

32 Mohamed Suma, "Sierra Leone: Justice Sector and the Rule of Law" (review by AfriMAP and the Open Society Initiative for West Africa, [2014), https://www.academia.edu/44912807/A_review_by_AfriMAP_and_the_Open_Society_Initiative_for_West_Africa_Sierra_Leone_Justice_Sector_and_the_Rule_of_Law.

33 Peter Albrecht and Paul Jackson, Security System Transformation in Sierra Leone, 1997-2007 (GFN-SSR, 2009).

Law Courts Building in Freetown and the combined magistrate courts in Bo and Kenema. Albrecht and Jackson recount that in 2002, 'it was noted that the process had a significant psychological effect, representing a process towards restoring normality and the rule of law.'[34] The second half of the project focused on capacity building, training 20 court registrars, undersheriffs, and bailiffs.

In 2005, DFID established a comprehensive Justice Sector Development Programme (JSDP) and allocated more than 25 million pounds over five years for a major reform of the justice sector. With the support of the JSDP, in 2007, the Government of Sierra Leone published a Justice Sector Reform Strategy and Investment Plan (JSRIP), which sets out a platform for a 'coherent, prioritised and sequenced set of activities' to reform the operations of the justice system in Sierra Leone. This strategy recognised that the formal justice system is inaccessible to much of the population and prioritised the strengthening of primary justice.[35] DFID further provided 19 million pounds over four years (2011–2014) for a new Improved Access to Security and Justice Programme (ASJP),[36] and another (JSRSIP III: 2015 -2018), was endorsed by Cabinet in July 2015.[37]

Several other development partners contributed substantially to reconstructing and strengthening the justice sector. For instance, the UN, the United Nations Development Programme (UNDP) and the United Nations Integrated Peace Building Office in Sierra Leone (UNIPSIL) supported the justice sector by building the infrastructure and operational capacity of justice institutions and addressing justice delays. UNDP implemented various projects to support the Judiciary, including constructing new court buildings, logistics and top-up salaries for magistrates.[38] Also, UNIPSIL supported institutions in

34 Albrecht and Jackson, Security System Transformation, p7.

35 See, Claire Castillejo, Building accountable justice in Sierra Leone (Madrid: Fride, 2009). The strategy, launched in 2008 by then President Ernest Bai Koroma, identified the following priorities for reform: Updated laws and procedures; developing a multi-sector approach; addressing overcrowding in prisons and improving prison conditions; addressing delays in court; reforming juvenile justice; improving community relations with the police; supporting mechanisms that facilitate access to justice for the poor, and research and information.

36 Suma, "Sierra Leone: Justice Sector."

37 See, Sierra Leone, Judiciary Strategic Plan 2016–2021, June 22, 2016, Accessed, 22 September 2024, https://www.judiciary.gov.sl/wp-content/uploads/2021/07/Judiciary-Strategic-Plan-2016-2021-22062016-1.pdf.

38 These projects include, 'Access to Justice, 2004–2007; Administration of the Peace Building Fund (UNPBF), 2007–2009; and 'Improving Access to Justice' in partnership with the Bureau of Conflict Prevention and Recovery, 2009–2011. Top-up for magistrates means supplementary payments provided to magistrates.

the justice sector, such as the Constitutional Review Commission, the prisons, the Law Reform Commission, Human Rights Commission, and the local courts.[39]

Furthermore, the German International Cooperation (GIZ) supported the justice sector through its 'Promoting the Rule of Law and Justice Project' by providing equipment for the Legal and Judicial Training Institute (LJTI), the Law Reform Commission and Customary law officers. It also funded training for judicial personnel, paralegals, and police officers and transportation support for magistrates during mobile court hearings and salary top-ups. The Commonwealth Secretariat supported the drafting of legislation and the hiring of judges and prosecutors. Also, the World Bank funded the human capacity in the Ministry of Justice, and the European Commission supported civil society human rights organisations through the European Union Initiative for Democracy and Human Rights (EIDHR).[40]

5. Post-Conflict Reforms and their Impact on the Justice Sector

The collaboration between development partners and the Government of Sierra Leone in building and reforming justice institutions after the civil war somewhat improved the justice sector compared to its tattered state when the war was officially declared over. In the immediate aftermath of the conflict, there were improvements in infrastructure, transportation, logistics and training of judicial personnel. In subsequent years, successive post-conflict governments have made efforts to implement some of the recommendations of the TRC, especially with respect to legislations expected to protect rights and institutions meant to strengthen the justice sector.

Parliament has enacted and amended several laws recommended by the TRC. For instance, the Citizenship Act of 1973 was amended in 2006. It repealed relevant sections and removed gender discrimination, meaning citizenship can now be passed through both the paternal and maternal lines. The Government has also made major reforms in terms of legislation to increase the protection afforded to vulnerable groups. In 2007, three gender

---

39 Claire Castillejo, Building accountable justice in Sierra Leone Supra p. 3.

40 Suma, "Sierra Leone: Justice Sector."

acts[41] and the Child Rights Act were passed to protect the rights of women and children. A Sexual Offences Act was passed in 2012 to combat impunity for sexual offences. In addition, the Convention on the Rights of Persons with Disabilities[42] was ratified with the enactment of the Disability Act in 2011 to protect the rights of persons with disabilities.

Furthermore, the Local Courts Act was enacted in 2011, which transferred oversight functions of local courts from the Ministry of Local Government and Rural Development to the office of the Chief Justice. A Legal Aid Act was passed in 2012 to improve access to justice for indigent Sierra Leoneans. Also, Parliament voted to abolish the death penalty in July 2021, and President Bio signed the law banning the practice in October 2021.[43]

In addition, the Judiciary established several specialized courts to expedite certain claims and complaints. These include the Fast track Commercial Court, established in 2010 to reduce the time taken to resolve commercial disputes; the Sexual Offences Model Court commissioned in 2020 with witness protection facilities to ensure that victims' identities are protected; the National Social Security and Insurance Trust (NASSIT) Court established in 2020, to deal with cases relating to the non-compliance of certain institutions to pay social security contributions for their workers; and Small Claims Commercial Court, which deals with claims below Le 50,000 (Fifty Thousand Leones).

Regarding institutions and oversight mechanisms, a code of conduct for judges and magistrates was adopted in September 2005, which prescribed formal processes for public complaints against the Judiciary. The Human Rights Commission of Sierra Leone (HRCSL) was established in 2004 as called for by the Lomé Peace Agreement and further recommended by the TRC. In addition, the Anti-Corruption Commission (ACC) Act of 2008 and the 1991 Constitution were amended to confer prosecutorial powers on the ACC Commissioner as recommended by the TRC.[44] A Family Support

41 The three Gender Acts of 2007 are: 1) The Domestic Violence Act; 2) The Devolution of Estates Act; 3) The Registration of Customary Marriage and Divorce Act.

42 Convention on the Rights of Persons with Disabilities, opened for signature March 30, 2007, G.A. Res. 61/106, U.N. Doc. A/RES/61/106 (Dec. 13, 2006), https://www.ohchr.org/en/instruments-mechanisms/instruments/convention-rights-persons-disabilities.

43 See Sierra Leone, Abolition of the Death Penalty Act, 2022, Act 6 of 2022, April 21, 2022, https://sierralii.gov.sl/akn/sl/act/2022/6/eng@2022-04-21.

44 Note that the establishment of the Anti-Corruption Commission was not initially linked to the TRC. Corruption was a major concern early in the Kabbah government, and it was the initiative of Former President Kabbah (late)to approach DFID for help in setting up the Anti-Corruption Commission (ACC). Legislation was passed in early 2000, the ACC began work a bit later.

Unit (FSU) was established as an arm of the police to combat sexual violence and cruelty against women and children, and a Complaint, Discipline and Internal Investigations Department (CDIID) was established and charged with handling and investigating complaints from the public regarding police abuse, and disciplining members of the police in some instances.[45]

While these reforms are laudable and well-intentioned, many of them only succeeded in creating an illusion of development but failed to alleviate the challenges that beset the Judiciary and the broader justice sector. While many new laws have been enacted, their effectiveness is questionable, as the political will and resources necessary for implementation and enforcement are lacking. Similarly, setting up institutions has been easy, but many have failed to achieve their goals due to poor funding, reliance on donor assistance, or political interference. As a result, the reforms have not trickled down to the daily life of Sierra Leoneans, and they have not made the justice sector more accountable and responsive to the needs of ordinary citizens. The reforms within the Judiciary do not challenge the existing power dynamics and fail to target the core justice issues that led to the conflict, stemming mainly from structural provisions in the 1991 Constitution discussed below.

6. Unaddressed Structural Issues in the 1991 Constitution that Undermines Judicial Independence

A major underlying issue responsible for the war in Sierra Leone is the persistence of executive influence over the Judiciary. It is impossible to guarantee the rule of law without minimum judicial guarantees, which include independence from factors external to the Judiciary. It may be recalled that the TRC found that 'the judiciary had become mere pawns in the hands of the executive' before the outbreak of war.[46] Successive governments abused the judicial appointment process, which severely compromised the independence of the Judiciary. Lack of security of tenure of judges permitted the Government to interfere at will with the Judiciary and the practice of employing retired judges on a contract basis compromised judicial independence. Lack of financial autonomy impoverished the administration of justice. Sadly, these

However, it was the TRC that suggested the Anti-Corruption Commission be authorised to pursue its own prosecutions independently from other organs of the state.

45 Note that the TRC did not make specific recommendations with regard to the police.

46 Sierra Leone Truth and Reconciliation Commission, Final Report Vol. 3A, Chap 2: Governance. https://www.sierralii.gov.sl/documents/trc-report.

issues still affect the Judiciary twenty years after the end of the conflict. Surprisingly, the Constitution itself, the 'grundnorm' of Sierra Leone, enables executive influence over the Judiciary.

The Constitution is fraught with contradictions, as it gives with one hand and then takes with the other. Section 120(4) of the Constitution guarantees an independent judiciary as follows:

> 'In the exercise of its judicial functions, the Judiciary shall be subject to only this Constitution or any other law and shall not be subject to the control or direction of any other person or authority.' [47]

Despite this strongly worded provision that guarantees the independence of the Judiciary, the same Constitution grants extensive powers to the executive that undermines judicial independence in practice. The executive has control over the appointment and tenure of judges, as well as their salaries, budget, and promotion, as discussed below.

7. Appointment and Tenure of Judges

The TRC made the following analysis regarding the appointment and tenure of judges:

> 'The way in which judges are appointed and subsequently promoted is essential to their independence. Judges must not be appointed for political reasons, but only for reasons of competence and political neutrality. The public must have confidence that judges are chosen on merit and for their integrity, not as a reward for party service or as a tactic by the executive to ensure a friendly face on the bench.'[48]

Section 135 of the 1991 Constitution gives power to the President, acting on the advice of the Judicial and Legal Service Commission (JLSC) and subject to the approval of Parliament, to appoint the Chief Justice and all other judges. By the same token, section 53 (3) of the Constitution provides that courts cannot inquire into whether the President received or acted in accordance with the advice of any person or authority. In effect, the provision that the

[47] Constitution of Sierra Leone.

[48] Sierra Leone Truth and Reconciliation Commission, Final Report Vol 2, Ch 3, para. 138.

President appoints judicial officers with the advice of the JLSC is useless, as the President can choose to ignore such advice, and there would be no consequences.[49]

As Kaifala postulates:

> 'This provision leaves the appointment of judges squarely in the hands of the President - because by Section 53(3) of the Constitution, the President does not have to act on the advice of anyone. The President has a free hand in appointing judges (since approvals in Parliament are almost invariably a 'rubber stamp' affair). While Presidents in other parts of the world may have appointment powers, they do so within set guidelines and rules, and there are sufficient checks and balances to counter abuse. That does not seem to be the case with Sierra Leone.'[50]

Kaifala further argues that this situation creates a 'tacit agency relationship between the judges and the President who appoints them; they would, therefore, feel obligated to the President and would want to satisfy or protect his interest whenever necessary.'[51]

Furthermore, Section 136 provides that where the office of a High Court judge is vacant, the President may appoint a person who has held office as or qualified for appointment as a judge of the superior court of judicature, even though he has already attained the retirement age or the age at which he shall vacate office. Under the latter provision, there is no need to seek Parliamentary approval, having secured it once. Therefore, this leaves the judge at the pleasure of the President, who has the power to terminate his appointment at will. Since these contract judges only serve at the pleasure of the President, they lack security of tenure and, therefore, cannot be totally independent in the discharge of their official duties, as a judge may be tempted to give in to the dictates of the President to keep his job.[52]

---

49 See Francis Kaifala, The Courts on Trial: The Case against the Existence of Judicial Independence in Sierra Leone, https://old.sierralii.org/sl_internal/blog/The%20Case%20against%20Judicial%20%20Independence%20in%20Sierra%20Leone%20%282%29.docx.

50 Kaifala, The Courts on Trial.

51 Kaifala, The Courts on Trial.

52 Vandi Alieu Koroma, "Analyzing the Code of Conduct for Judicial Officers in Sierra Leone," Centre for Accountability and Rule of Law (CARL), August 11, 2016, https://www.carl-sl.org/pres/analyzing-the-code-of-conduct-for-judicial-officers-in-sierra-leone/.

The TRC noted that:

> 'If judges are not confident that their tenure of office is secure, their independence will be threatened. Judges should not be removable by executive action. It is generally desirable that judges must retire when they reach the retirement age. This reduces the scope for the executive to favour handpicked judges whom they find sympathetic and reduces the temptation, on the part of the judge, to curry executive 'approval' for reappointment.'[53]

The Commission, therefore, recommended that the practice of employing judges on contract should cease, and the retirement age should be extended to 70 without the possibility of extension.[54]

The constitutional arrangement above shows a close relationship between power and justice in Sierra Leone, and the failure to develop credible checks on executive influence over the Judiciary means that justice remains elusive for most Sierra Leoneans. As Kaifala observes, 'Sierra Leone's judiciary over the years has typified the positivist maxim, *'Quod principi placuit, legis habet vigorem'* - translated to mean, 'that which pleases the ruler has the force of law'.[55] We see old patterns of injustice dominating and eroding the small gains made over the past twenty years. For example, in March 2018, the High Court ruled that ten (10) parliamentarians from the All Peoples' Congress (APC) political party were disqualified from Parliament and further ruled that the ruling Sierra Leone People's Party (SLPP) replace nine of them with their party members. Opposition members and lawyers criticised this move as unconstitutional.[56] It was expected that the court would order a re-run following the disqualification of members of parliament. According to the European Union Election Follow-up Mission (EFM) Report, 'several stakeholders from civil society and political parties informed the EFM that they have limited confidence in the judiciary as an impartial and timely solution to election-related disputes.'[57]

---

53 Sierra Leone Truth and Reconciliation Commission, Final Report Vol 2, Ch 3, para. 144.

54 Sierra Leone Truth and Reconciliation Commission, Final Report Vol 2, Ch 3, para 145.

55 Kaifala, The Courts on Trial.

56 BTI Transformation Index, Sierra Leone Country Report 2022, 12, https://bti-project.org/en/reports/country-report/SLE.

57 European Union Election Follow-up Mission, "Sierra Leone 2021 Final Report," November 2021, 30th September 2024 https://ec.europa.eu/info/strategy/relations-non-eu-countries/types-relations-and-partnerships/election-observation/mission-recommendations-repository/mis-

Similarly, on 9 September 2015, the Supreme Court ruled in support of President Ernest Bai Koroma's decision to sack his former vice president Alhaji Samuel Sam-Samuna. The vice president was sacked from his duties by the President, following an alleged request for asylum at the US Embassy. This decision evoked public outrage, with many perceiving the sacking as a breach of Sierra Leone's Constitution and legal process. The vice president had previously been expelled from the ruling APC party because the supposed asylum bid demonstrated a willingness to abandon his duties and office. The court ruled that the President had the constitutional right to relieve the former vice president of his responsibilities without recourse to a parliamentary impeachment procedure set out in sections 50 and 51 of the 1991 Constitution.[58] The case was subsequently taken to the ECOWAS court, which ruled that the removal of vice-president was wrongful and violated his fundamental human rights to a fair hearing and to freely participate in the politics of his country.[59]

This case was a litmus test for the Judiciary, which it failed. After the ruling on 9 September 2015, the former vice president gave his reaction during an interview on BBC's Focus on Africa radio program: 'It's a disgrace in the Judiciary. With a pedigree, I would think that they would stand up to the movement, be independent, and dispense justice as one of the three arms of Government. I'm very much disappointed in the Judiciary that they did not stand up to the moment.'[60]

A Constitutional Review Committee (CRC)[61] set up in 2013 to review the Constitution accordingly recommended that the retirement age of a judge be extended to 70, without the possibility of extension of the tenure after attaining the retirement age, and where there is a vacancy, the appointment of judges who previously held office be subject to the approval of Parliament. However, successive post-conflict governments have rejected this recommendation, including the current Government of President Bio.

---

sions/440.

58 *Alhaji Sam Sumana v Attorney-General & Anor.*

59 *Sam-Sumana v. Republic of Sierra Leone.*

60 Abdul Brima, "Sierra Leone's Constitutional Crisis: The Final Verdict," Peace Insight, 2015, https://www.peaceinsight.org/en/authors/abdul-brima/.

61 [1]Sierra Leone, Constitutional Review Committee, Abridged Draft Report, February 2016, section on political will, https://www.parliament.gov.sl/uploads/other_resources/CRC%20PROPOSED%20CONSTITUTION.pdf.

8. Independence of the Judicial and Legal Service Commission

The Judicial and Legal Service Commission (JLSC), which appoints judges, is also subject to executive interference. Suma explains that:

> 'All members of the JLSC are appointed by the President in some way, either specifically to serve on the Commission or to hold the public office that qualifies them automatically for membership on the Commission. The JLSC framework raises the risk that the ruling political party can dominate the pre-Parliamentary appointments process.'[62]

Accordingly, the CRC recommended that the membership of the JLSC provided for under section 140(1) be expanded to include two lay representatives, a Judge from the Supreme Court and the High Court, a representative from the Human Resource Management Office and the Financial Secretary. [63] The Bio administration accepted to expand the scope of the JLSC by the addition only of the Financial Secretary. It rejected the recommendations to make the Commission more independent by increasing its membership.[64]

9. Budgetary allocation for the Judiciary

In addition to the appointment of the judges, budgetary allocations for the Judiciary are also controlled by the executive. As explained in the 2016-2021 Strategic Plan of the Judiciary, budgetary allocations controlled by the executive make it difficult for the Judiciary to recruit the right support staff and remain operationally independent and impartial.[65] This lack of fiscal independence ultimately undermines judicial autonomy.

The Judiciary previously used a system of self-accounting which enabled it to use the income it received for services provided to fund its operations,

---

62 Suma, "Sierra Leone: Justice Sector" p. 10.

63 Constitutional Review Committee, Abridged Draft Report, 5, p. 77.

64 Report on the Review of the 2017 Government White Paper on the Constitution of Sierra Leone, 1991 (Act No.6 of 1991), December 2021, https://www.thesierraleonetelegraph.com/wp-content/uploads/2022/01/REPORT-ON-THE-REVIEW-OF-THE-2017-GOVERNMENT-WHITE-PAPER-ON-THE-CONSTITUTION-OF-SIERRA-LEONE-1991.pdf.

65 See, Judiciary Strategic Plan 2016–2021 (Sierra Leone), June 22, 2016, https://www.judiciary.gov.sl/wp-content/uploads/2021/07/Judiciary-Strategic-Plan-2016-2021-22062016-1.pdf.

but the practice was abandoned in the 1970s,[66] and the Judiciary became wholly financially dependent on the Ministry of Finance, which controls the Consolidated Fund.[67] The Judiciary asserts in its Strategic Plan for 2016-2021 that without complete control of its human resources and budgets, it is challenging to remain independent, implement reforms and build a culture of transparency and accountability.[68]

The TRC recommended that the Judiciary have financial and administrative autonomy and that the Judiciary itself is best placed to plan for an efficient justice delivery system. Accordingly, the CRC recommended that section 143 be amended to ensure that the Judiciary is self-accounting by providing that any fines or other monies, other than fees paid for filing or the granting of probate, received by the courts shall form part of the Consolidated Fund. The Government rejected this recommendation in the 2022 White Paper, noting that the current provision is adequate.

10. Office of the Attorney General and Minister of Justice

Further, the separation of the office of the Attorney-General and Minister of Justice has been on the cards for reform for many years. The Attorney General was given powers over judicial affairs in 1978. The 1978 Constitution established a one-party republic with President Siaka Stevens at the helm. The Constitution merged the roles of the Attorney General and the Minister of Justice, giving one person the responsibility of representing the state in legal cases and overseeing judicial affairs. The responsibilities of the Minister of Justice are not explicitly stated in the Constitution, but this official acts as the intermediary between the Judiciary and the Parliament/Cabinet while supervising judicial matters.[69]

This structural anomaly diluted judicial independence from the executive by preventing the Attorney-General from exercising his prosecutorial

---

66 See, Niobe Thompson, In Pursuit of Justice: A Report on the Judiciary in Sierra Leone (report, Commonwealth Human Rights Initiative and the Sierra Leone Bar Association, 2002), https://www.humanrightsinitiative.org/publications/ffm/sierra_leone_report.pdf.

67 Ibid. Under that system, revenues generated by the then Judicial Sub-Treasury from court fees and fines were used to fund the Judiciary, and the only returns made to the Public Treasury were in the form of audit reports explaining income and expenditure for a given period. This system was discontinued in the late 1970s as the one-party state was consolidated. Commonwealth human rights initiative.

68 Judiciary Strategic Plan 2016–2021 (Sierra Leone), June 22, 2016, https://www.judiciary.gov.sl/wp-content/uploads/2021/07/Judiciary-Strategic-Plan-2016-2021-22062016-1.pdf.

69 Thompson, In Pursuit of Justice, 34.

authority without bias from the executive branch, of which he is a member as Minister of Justice. The Bio Administration's White Paper, released in 2022,[70] accepted the CRC's recommendation to separate the office of the Attorney General and Minister of Justice. While this is laudable, much remains to be done to ensure its implementation.

Effective separation of the office of the Attorney-General and Minister of Justice would require not only legislative reforms specifying the distinct roles and responsibilities of both offices, but also a transparent appointment process, independent oversight, and strict conflict of interest provisions to ensure that the Attorneys-General carry out their legal functions without undue political influence.

11. Political Will to Address Structural Issues in the Constitution

The TRC identified the inconsistencies in the Constitution that enabled the structural issues that undermined the justice sector and recommended that Parliament considers the adoption of a new Constitution, employing a consultative and participatory process. A Constitutional review process set in motion by former President Kabbah has lasted for over fifteen (15) years, with successive governments cancelling and reviewing previous recommendations. The first constitutional review process initiated by the late President Kabbah started in 2006. The Committee presented its report[71] to the Government of President Koroma, who succeeded President Kabbah, in 2008. However, the Koroma Government believed that the review process was not consultative enough, so in July 2013, it set up an 80-person Constitutional Review Committee (CRC) headed by the Late Justice Cowan. The review process lasted from 2013 to 2017, and recommendations were presented to the Government in January 2017. However, a Government White Paper was released on 10 November 2017, rejecting about 100 recommendations of the CRC out of 134.

The Bio government, succeeding the Koroma administration, established a technical committee to review the Cowan Constitutional Review Committee's recommendations and the Koroma government's White Paper. In January 2022, the Bio government published its own White Paper, adopting

70 Report on the Review of the 2017 Government White Paper.

71 Sierra Leone, Commission to Review the Constitution, Report of the Commission to Review the Constitution of Sierra Leone, 1991, January 2008, https://constitutionnet.org/sites/default/files/peter_tucker_report_2008.pdf.

key recommendations including the abolition of the death penalty, repeal of Part V of the Public Order Act to protect free speech, and establishment of the Independent Commission for Peace and National Cohesion. These reforms aim to address governance issues highlighted by the Truth and Reconciliation Commission (TRC) and promote justice and peace.[72]

The Bio government adopted several Constitutional Review Committee (CRC) recommendations concerning the judiciary, including increasing the number of Supreme Court, Court of Appeal, and High Court judges; authorizing the Chief Justice to establish Court of Appeal divisions via statutory instrument; incorporating court-martial into Section 129(2); expanding the Judicial and Legal Service Commission (JLSC) to include only the Financial Secretary; and replacing the terms 'inferior' and 'traditional' courts with 'subordinate' and 'local' courts.

However, the Government rejected specific recommendations that sought to curtail executive control over the Judiciary. These include, among others, the recommendations to amend section 135 (4) of the Constitution on the appointment and tenure of judges, [73] Section 136 (4) on judicial vacancies,[74] section 143 to ensure financial independence of the Judiciary, Section 141 (1) on the power of the JLSC to appoint and to exercise disciplinary control over persons holding certain Judicial and Legal Offices to the exclusion of any other body or authority.

As shown in the previous section, rejecting these critical recommendations that would have otherwise remedied the structural issues undermining judicial independence in Sierra Leone shows a lack of political will to remove executive influence over the Judiciary.

Many in the judicial sector were hopeful that the constitutional review process would usher in new changes leading to an autonomous and independent judiciary. The Judiciary noted in its 2016-2021 Strategic plan that '*the ongoing constitutional review process ... provides a once-in-a-lifetime*

[72] State House of Sierra Leone, "Sierra Leone's President Julius Maada Bio Launches White Paper on Constitutional Review Process, Accepts Key Recommendations for Major Progressive Legal Reforms," State House, https://statehouse.gov.sl/sierra-leones-president-julius-maada-bio-launches-white-paper-on-constitutional-review-process-accepts-key-recommendations-for-major-progressive-legal-reforms/.

[73] State House, "White Paper."

[74] The CRC recommended that section 136 (4) be amended to include the words '...subject to the approval of Parliament'. See the analysis on the appointment and tenure of judges above. The Institute for Legal Research and Advocacy for Justice noted in its position paper on the Bio Government's White Paper, noted that by rejecting this recommendation, a back door has been provided for Judges to be appointed without the approval of Parliament.

window of opportunity for constitutional changes that should contribute to independence, speedy trials, efficient management of cases, and more control of budgetary processes that will impact the Judiciary in the long term'.[75]

12. Conclusion

The TRC report sheds light on the critical role played by the judicial sector in fueling the conflict and shaping the nation's post-conflict trajectory. The report's findings underscore the pressing need for comprehensive institutional reform and improved governance to prevent future conflicts, protect human rights, and ensure the rule of law.

An important reminder of what post-conflict governments need to do to demonstrate their commitment to tackling the justice issues that led to the conflict is provided in the TRC's preface to its recommendations regarding the rule of law as follows:

> 'In a true democracy, there is no compromise on the supremacy of the Constitution and the rule of law. The rule of law is the expectation of equality of treatment under objective and accessible rules. Discretionary governmental power should be subject to control by the courts. Courts should apply the same law to all, regardless of their standing in society. In short, the rule of law says that nobody is above the law. Inequitable law, separate court systems, lack of access to courts, few lawyers, and a confusion of administrative and judicial roles all conspired to prevent the application of the rule of law in Sierra Leone. Courts rarely protected human rights or policed administrative irregularity. The starting point in establishing the rule of law is the creation of an independent, impartial, and autonomous judiciary.'[76]

Despite two decades since the end of the civil conflict, the expectation of establishing an *independent, impartial and autonomous judiciary*, remains unfulfilled. The post-conflict reforms only provided temporary remedies. There has been slow progress in addressing the deep-rooted issues that initially plagued the justice sector and persists today. Despite the thorough work that

---

75 Judiciary Strategic Plan.

76 Sierra Leone Truth and Reconciliation Commission Final Report, Vol 3A, p. 106.

went into developing the TRC recommendations, successive governments have been reluctant to carry out the recommendations concerning the Judiciary that would allow for long-term structural changes and improvement in the dispensation of justice. The response to the constitutional review recommendations by successive post-conflict Governments further evidences this reluctance.

It is crucial for the Government to remove executive influence over the Judiciary and strengthen the rule of law to build trust among its citizens and sustain the hard-earned peace. Failure to do so will only perpetuate the injustices and grievances that fueled the 11 years of civil war and threaten the country's stability and development. The Government must demonstrate political will to uphold judicial independence and respect court decisions, even when those decisions may be politically unpopular.

Fostering an independent Judiciary is an ongoing, evolving process, necessitating an enduring commitment from the Government. A robust, independent Judiciary is the linchpin for upholding the rule of law, ensuring justice, and promoting a stable, democratic society in Sierra Leone. Therefore, concerted efforts are necessary to steer the nation towards lasting peace, security, and prosperity.

CHARTING THE PATH AHEAD – SUMMATION AND RECOMMENDATIONS

ROWLAND COLE AND ABDUL TEJAN-COLE

1. Bringing the Central Issues Together

This chapter brings together the central issues explored throughout the book, weaving a coherent narrative of the judiciary's pivotal role in Sierra Leone's governance and justice framework. The chapters collectively illuminate systemic challenges, from executive overreach and judicial inefficiencies to the erosion of public trust, while highlighting the judiciary's potential to act as a safeguard of constitutional principles, individual rights, and democratic governance.

In *Under the Gavel: Francis Minah and the Quandaries of Sierra Leone's Legal System*, Mohamed A. Bangura examines one of Sierra Leone's most disputed legal episodes, the treason trial and execution of Vice President Francis Minah. The chapter exposes how procedural flaws, weak evidence, and political interference shaped the case, showing the judiciary's role in enabling injustice. Bangura argues that these failures weakened public trust and undermined the rule of law. He situates Minah's trial within a wider pattern of judicial complicity and presses for reforms to secure judicial independence and redress miscarriages of justice. The analysis links directly to the book's central theme by framing judicial accountability as essential for democratic consolidation.

Victor Idrissa Lansana's *Constitutional Controversy: The Case of Alhaji Samuel Sam-Sumana vs. The Attorney General & Minister of Justice and Victor Bockarie Foh* provides a rigorous examination of the Supreme Court of Sierra Leone's decision to uphold the President's unilateral dismissal of the Vice President, a judgment that has generated sustained debate within constitutional and legal scholarship. The chapter interrogates the judiciary's expansive interpretation of presidential authority, arguing that such an approach weakened constitutional safeguards and raised profound concerns about the erosion of judicial independence. Lansana draws attention to the Court's failure to apply a searching scrutiny of procedural fairness in relation to Sam-Sumana's expulsion from his political party, an omission that undermined both the integrity of the adjudicative process and the broader commitment to the rule of law. By juxtaposing the reasoning of the domestic court with the judgment of the ECOWAS Court, which placed strong emphasis on procedural justice and due process guarantees, Lansana illustrates the divergent judicial approaches to questions of constitutional accountability. In doing so, he underscores the judiciary's central responsibility in safeguarding constitutional boundaries and preventing the overreach of executive power. The chapter's critical insights reflect not only on the deficiencies of the case itself but also on the judiciary's dual capacity either to reinforce or to compromise democratic principles in fragile constitutional orders.

The chapter, *Free Speech, Judicial Independence, and the Cases of Dumbar and Mansaray* by Conrad Lisk, provides a critical analysis of the complex relationship between judicial independence and the protection of freedom of expression within Sierra Leone's constitutional order. Drawing on two landmark cases, the chapter demonstrates how structural vulnerabilities in the legal system, including persistent political interference and the continued reliance on outdated legislative frameworks, have undermined the judiciary's capacity to act as a guardian of fundamental freedoms. The conviction of Reverend Dumbar under colonial-era legislation is examined as an illustration of the judiciary's instrumentalisation in the suppression of dissenting voices, thereby raising serious questions about the compatibility of such practices with democratic norms and constitutional guarantees. In parallel, the case of Michael Mansaray is analysed in the context of emerging challenges posed by digital communication technologies, exposing the judiciary's difficulties in reconciling freedom of expression with the need for regulatory oversight in an evolving technological environment. Through these case studies, Lisk highlights the judiciary's pivotal role in either reinforcing or weakening constitutional protections, and he advances a broader argument for judicial reforms designed to address entrenched systemic deficiencies and to ensure the effective protection of fundamental rights. In so doing, the chapter situates the Sierra Leonean experience within ongoing scholarly debates on the relationship between courts, free speech, and democratic consolidation, thereby aligning with the book's overarching thematic concern with judicial accountability and institutional reform.

Millicent Stronge's, *The Wellington Street Murders: Judicial Independence, Accessorial Liability, and the Common Purpose Doctrine* offers a critical examination of the application of criminal law principles in one of Sierra Leone's most notorious cases. Stronge interrogates the manner in which the doctrine of common purpose was deployed to secure convictions, revealing the judiciary's susceptibility to both public sentiment and political pressure. Her analysis underscores the dangers inherent in expansive judicial reliance on doctrines of collective liability without sufficient attention to individual culpability, thereby raising important concerns about the integrity of criminal adjudication. In advancing her critique, Stronge calls for greater legislative clarity and for the exercise of judicial restraint, arguing that the justice system must be anchored in fairness, impartiality, and a careful balancing of competing interests. This chapter enriches the broader discourse on the judiciary's role in safeguarding the rule of law by probing the intersection of public opinion, substantive legal principles, and the imperatives of judicial independence.

Ronald Gidwani's *Beyond Birthright: Interrogating Sierra Leone's Citizenship Jurisprudence in Akar and Yumkella Cases* undertakes a critical examination of Sierra Leone's exclusionary citizenship laws and their broader implications for equality, democratic participation, and governance. The chapter situates the analysis within the jurisprudence that has emerged from the courts, highlighting the judiciary's ambivalent role in both entrenching and, at times, challenging systemic forms of discrimination. Particular attention is given to cases involving dual citizenship and racial exclusions, which expose the tensions between inherited legal frameworks, constitutional guarantees, and the demands of a pluralistic society. Gidwani argues that the persistence of exclusionary doctrines undermines not only individual rights but also the legitimacy of the state's democratic institutions. By contextualising these debates within international human rights frameworks, he makes the case for comprehensive reforms to construct a more inclusive legal regime capable of reconciling domestic citizenship laws with global norms. In doing so, the chapter contributes to the book's overarching thematic concern with judicial review as an essential mechanism for confronting systemic injustice and for aligning national legal orders with international standards of equality and non-discrimination.

In *Locus Standi as a Smokescreen: How Our Courts Use Locus Standi to Avoid Dealing with Cases on Their Merits*, Yada H. Williams offers a critical appraisal of the judiciary's restrictive interpretation of *locus standi* and its broader implications for access to justice and the development of public interest litigation in Sierra Leone. The chapter demonstrates how the courts' insistence on narrow standing requirements has operated as a procedural barrier, effectively precluding substantive adjudication on matters of significant constitutional and societal importance. The judiciary has contributed to a culture of unaccountability by allowing technicalities to foreclose judicial engagement with pressing legal and political questions, and has, at times, facilitated governmental impunity. Williams argues for a more liberalised and purposive approach to *locus standi*, one that recognises the judiciary's responsibility to ensure that the courts remain accessible to individuals and groups seeking to vindicate rights and challenge abuses of power. In advancing this position, the chapter underscores the vital role of the judiciary in shaping the contours of access to justice and in ensuring that the interpretation of legal doctrines does not operate as an exclusionary device that undermines constitutionalism and democratic governance.

The Non-Assignment of Cases: A Travesty of Access to Justice in Sierra Leone by Augustine Sorie-Sengbe Marrah and Mohamed Jalloh interrogates the entrenched problem of delayed case assignments and its corrosive impact on access to justice and judicial accountability. The chapter critiques the absence of transparent and consistent procedures for the allocation of cases, arguing that this institutional weakness not only frustrates litigants but also reflects deeper failures of governance within the justice sector. By situating the problem within broader debates on judicial integrity and efficiency, the authors demonstrate how opaque allocation practices contribute to perceptions of bias, arbitrariness, and susceptibility to political influence. Drawing on comparative insights and best practices from other jurisdictions, Marrah and Jalloh advance a set of reform proposals, including the adoption of automated case management systems and the establishment of specialised courts, designed to enhance transparency, efficiency, and public confidence in the judiciary. In addressing these internal structural challenges, the chapter reinforces the book's thematic concern with the judiciary's role as a guardian of constitutional principles and underscores the necessity of institutional reform to secure both accountability and the rule of law.

Kadija Kabba's *Judicial Review: An Essential Tool for Curbing the Excesses and Abuse of Executive Action in Sierra Leone* positions judicial review as a cornerstone of accountability. The chapter explores how this mechanism safeguards individual rights, curtails executive overreach, and promotes adherence to constitutional principles. By highlighting barriers to access and proposing practical reforms, Kabba underscores judicial review's potential to restore public trust and enhance governance. This chapter integrates judicial review into the broader narrative of legal and institutional reform, affirming its role in upholding the rule of law.

Kadija Kabba's *Judicial Review: An Essential Tool for Curbing the Excesses and Abuse of Executive Action in Sierra Leone* situates judicial review at the centre of constitutional accountability, framing it as an indispensable mechanism for constraining executive authority and safeguarding the rights of individuals. The chapter examines the jurisprudential foundations of judicial review and demonstrates how, when effectively applied, it serves to limit executive overreach, reinforce adherence to constitutional norms, and promote the rule of law. At the same time, Kabba identifies significant barriers to the effective exercise of judicial review, including restrictive procedural rules, limited access to courts, and broader institutional weaknesses that diminish judicial responsiveness. By advancing proposals for practical reforms aimed at lowering these barriers, Kabba underscores the potential of judicial review to rebuild public trust in state institutions and to strengthen democratic governance. In doing so, the chapter integrates judicial review into the book's broader discourse on legal and institutional reform, affirming its centrality to the judiciary's role in preserving constitutionalism and upholding the rule of law.

In *Reconciling the Past, Reforming the Future: Sierra Leone's TRC and Post-Conflict Reform*, Saramba Kandeh offers a critical evaluation of the justice sector reforms initiated in the aftermath of the country's Truth and Reconciliation Commission (TRC). While acknowledging tangible progress in areas such as infrastructure development and legislative amendments, Kandeh interrogates the enduring structural weaknesses that continue to compromise the effectiveness of post-conflict reform. In particular, the chapter highlights the persistence of executive interference in judicial processes and the chronic underfunding of justice sector institutions as key obstacles to meaningful transformation. By situating these shortcomings within the broader historical trajectory of governance and institutional fragility in Sierra Leone, Kandeh underscores the unfinished nature of the reform project. The chapter advances a call for constitutional reforms aimed at fortifying judicial independence and re-establishing public trust in the justice system. In linking the failures of the past to the challenges of the present, the analysis reinforces the imperative of systemic reform as a necessary condition for accountability, institutional resilience, and the realisation of justice in post-conflict Sierra Leone.

The chapters collectively underscore the judiciary's centrality to Sierra Leone's governance framework, revealing its potential as both a guardian of justice and an enabler of systemic failure. Through detailed case studies and critical analyses, the book highlights the judiciary's role in addressing executive overreach, safeguarding constitutional freedoms, and promoting access to justice. The contributors advocate for reforms to strengthen judicial independence, improve procedural efficiency, and align legal frameworks with democratic principles.

2. Challenges Facing the Justice Sector in Sierra Leone

The justice sector in Sierra Leone is integral to upholding the rule of law, ensuring access to justice, protecting human rights, and fostering democratic governance. Despite its centrality, the sector grapples with a myriad of challenges that undermine its efficacy, accessibility, and integrity. These issues are rooted in historical, institutional, and systemic factors, many of which were exacerbated by the country's decade-long civil war and its aftermath.

Judicial independence is a cornerstone of any functioning justice system, yet it remains in a precarious state in Sierra Leone. The executive branch wields significant influence over judicial appointments, promotions, and funding, creating an environment conducive to interference. The dual role of the Attorney General and Minister of Justice, as both the government's legal adviser and a key figure in judicial matters, further compounds this issue. This structural overlap compromises the separation of powers, leaving the judiciary vulnerable to political pressures.

Notable cases, such as the dismissal of Vice President Alhaji Samuel Sam-Sumana and the treason trial of Francis Minah, underscore how political considerations have historically shaped judicial decisions. Such instances erode public confidence in the judiciary's ability to act as an impartial arbiter of justice. While efforts to reform the justice sector have included capacity-building initiatives and legislative amendments, these measures have yet to address the entrenched executive influence that undermines judicial independence.

Access to justice remains a significant challenge, particularly for marginalised and vulnerable populations. High litigation costs, complex procedural requirements, and an uneven distribution of legal services disproportionately affect those living in rural and economically disadvantaged areas. The lack of legal aid exacerbates this issue, leaving many without the means to seek redress for grievances or defend their rights.

The non-assignment of cases, as highlighted in Augustine Sorie-Sengbe Marrah and Mohamed Jalloh's analysis, further restricts access to justice. Delays in assigning judges or hearing cases create a backlog that clogs the judicial system, denying citizens timely remedies. This procedural inefficiency disproportionately impacts cases of public interest and constitutional importance, perpetuating inequalities and eroding public trust.

Additionally, gender disparities in accessing justice remain prevalent. Women and girls, particularly those in rural areas, face significant barriers in reporting crimes such as domestic violence and sexual assault. Cultural stigma, inadequate legal protections, and a lack of awareness about legal rights further hinder their ability to seek justice.

Corruption pervades various levels of the justice sector, undermining its credibility and effectiveness. Judicial officers, court staff, and law enforcement agencies have all faced allegations of accepting bribes or engaging in other unethical practices. This corruption erodes public trust in the judiciary, as citizens perceive the justice system as favouring the wealthy and politically connected.

Impunity for corruption within the justice sector compounds the problem. Despite periodic efforts to hold judicial officers and public officials accountable, these initiatives have often been inconsistent and lack the necessary institutional backing. The Anti-Corruption Commission has achieved some successes, but its capacity to address entrenched judicial corruption remains limited.

The justice sector suffers from chronic underfunding, which hampers its ability to deliver effective and timely justice. Courtrooms, judicial offices, and correctional facilities are often dilapidated, lacking basic amenities and technological infrastructure. The absence of automated case management systems contributes to inefficiencies, as cases are tracked manually, increasing the likelihood of delays and errors.

Inadequate staffing levels further strain the sector. A shortage of judges, magistrates, and trained court personnel results in significant delays in case resolution. Law enforcement agencies also face resource limitations, including insufficient training and inadequate investigative tools, which compromise the quality of evidence presented in court.

Procedural inefficiencies are a persistent problem within Sierra Leone's justice system. Complex and archaic legal processes create unnecessary delays and confusion for litigants. The slow pace of judicial proceedings, compounded by frequent adjournments, undermines public confidence and frustrates litigants seeking swift resolutions.

The restrictive interpretation of doctrines such as *locus standi* limits access to justice in cases of public interest. As Yada H. Williams argues, this doctrine is often used as a smokescreen to dismiss cases on technical grounds rather than addressing substantive issues. Such procedural barriers discourage public interest litigation, reducing the judiciary's ability to hold the government and other powerful entities accountable.

3. Challenges in Implementing Reforms

Post-conflict reforms, while well-intentioned, have faced significant implementation challenges. Donor-funded initiatives, such as the Justice Sector Development Programme, have contributed to infrastructure development and capacity-building, but their impact has been undermined by a lack of political will and systemic resistance to change. For example, recommendations from the Truth and Reconciliation Commission (TRC) for constitutional amendments to strengthen judicial independence remain largely unimplemented.

The disconnect between legal reforms and societal attitudes also poses a barrier to progress. Cultural norms and traditional practices often conflict with statutory laws, particularly in areas such as gender equality and property rights. Bridging this gap requires sustained efforts to raise public awareness and integrate customary and formal legal systems in a manner that respects human rights.

4. Towards a Resilient Justice System

Sierra Leone's 1991 Constitution, while an improvement over its predecessor, still leaves room for significant reform. The judiciary's independence is compromised by provisions allowing for executive influence in appointments, budgetary allocations, and disciplinary proceedings. Comprehensive constitutional amendments are needed to enshrine judicial independence and protect it from political interference. The challenges facing Sierra Leone's justice sector demand a comprehensive and multi-dimensional response. Any successful reform must address the structural, institutional, and cultural impediments that hinder the delivery of justice. Drawing lessons from comparative jurisdictions and leveraging local contexts, the following non-exhaustive approaches outline pathways to building a resilient justice system.

First, judicial independence is fundamental to upholding the rule of law and fostering public trust in the judiciary. The principle of separation of powers requires that the Judiciary remains independent from the executive branch and free from political influence. In Sierra Leone the executive retains significant influence, particularly through its control over funding and the fusion and occupancy of the offices of Attorney General and Minister of Justice by a single appointee. These offices must be decoupled. Drawing on best practices from other jurisdictions, Sierra Leone could benefit from decoupling the roles of the Attorney General and the Minister of Justice, as seen in countries like Kenya and South Africa. This separation would mitigate conflicts of interest and bolster the judiciary's independence from executive interference. Further, a strong judicial service commission foments institutional independence and impartiality, and promote honesty and integrity among judges.

To strengthen the judicial service commission, it is important to democratize its composition by increasing its size to provide for diversity and public participation. Whereas it may be argued that a commission dominated by judges has better chances of being independent since they would transfer their independence to the commission, the question of judicial independence is highly contested in Sierra Leone. A judiciary dominated by judges could use their majority to represent their interests. This undermines the oversight role that the commission should have on the judiciary. Incorporating lay persons which high integrity tends to provide a balanced approach and thinking that are neutral and do not solely align with the interests of the judiciary. A commission dominated by judicial officers may find it difficult to discipline judges due to conflict of interests. Therefore, while the common approach has been to dominate judicial service commissions with judges or persons with legal backgrounds, that does not necessarily serve the best purposes of a dynamic and evolving society where the judiciary suffers from a trust deficit.

Second, implementing a transparent and merit-based process for judicial appointments and promotions, akin to the United Kingdom's Judicial Appointments Commission, would help ensure that only the most qualified and impartial candidates ascend to the bench. Sierra Leone's 1991 Constitution introduced improvements over the 1978 framework, particularly regarding the appointment of judges. For instance, the judiciary is no longer entirely at the mercy of the executive, with appointments now requiring the President to consult with the Judicial and Legal Service Commission.[1]

Third, judicial independence must also be safeguarded through financial autonomy. Allocating a guaranteed percentage of the national budget to the judiciary, as practiced in Ghana, can provide the resources needed to strengthen judicial infrastructure and attract skilled personnel. In addition to provisions in the national budget, a judicial administration fund should be established to enable the judiciary to retain fines and fees collected. Without financial independence, the judiciary remains vulnerable to executive manipulation, undermining its ability to act impartially.

Fourth, access to justice remains elusive for many Sierra Leoneans, particularly in rural areas where courts are scarce, and legal literacy is low. Expanding legal aid services is essential for ensuring that all citizens, regardless of their economic status, can defend their rights. This can be achieved by increasing funding for public legal aid programmes and fostering partnerships with civil society organisations to deliver pro bono services.

Fifth, simplifying procedural requirements can also make the justice system more accessible. Complex legal processes deter citizens from seeking redress and disproportionately affect marginalised populations. Introducing alternative dispute resolution (ADR) mechanisms, such as mediation and arbitration, in local communities can provide quicker and less intimidating avenues for resolving disputes. ADR also diverts cases away from litigation, thereby reducing judicial caseload and promoting efficiency.

Sixth, decentralising judicial services is critical. Establishing circuit courts or mobile courts in remote areas can bring justice closer to underserved populations. Such initiatives, as seen in Uganda and Bangladesh, have successfully reduced case backlogs and improved access to justice for rural communities.

Seventh, public legal education is vital for empowering citizens. Civil society organisations and legal professionals should collaborate to raise awareness about legal rights and available remedies. Radio programmes, community workshops, and digital campaigns can bridge the knowledge gap, ensuring that citizens understand how to navigate the justice system.

---

1 As to the effectiveness of this provision see Basita Michael, "Reforming the Lame Duck Judicial and Legal Service Commission," in *Thirty Years of the Sierra Leone Constitution: Reflections on its Past and Future*, ed. Abdul Tejan-Cole and Rowland Cole (Freetown, Sierra Leone: Sierra Leone Law Publishers, 2022), 203.

Eight, corruption undermines the integrity of the justice sector and perpetuates inequality. Judicial independence also requires judicial accountability, and the Judiciary must account for the exercise of its mandate. Judicial accountability creates space for legitimate scrutiny of the Judiciary's actions and the establishment of accountability mechanisms to address complaints against individual judges. Strengthening oversight mechanisms is crucial for restoring public confidence in the judiciary. The Anti-Corruption Commission (ACC) should be empowered to investigate and prosecute judicial officers implicated in corrupt practices. Establishing an independent judicial ombudsman to handle complaints against judges and court officials can also enhance accountability.

Ninth, training programmes for judges and court staff should emphasise ethical standards and the consequences of corruption. Incorporating integrity assessments as part of judicial appointments and promotions can further deter unethical behaviour.

Tenth, public access to information is a powerful tool for combating corruption. The regular publication of court decisions, case schedules, and financial reports online increases transparency and reduces opportunities for abuse. Sierra Leone can learn from countries like Estonia and Kenya, where open access to judicial data has improved public trust and accountability.

Eleventh, technological innovation offers a transformative opportunity to improve the efficiency and accessibility of Sierra Leone's justice system. Outdated ways of conducting business make justice slow and is inherently contrary to how courts should function in a democracy. Investing in automated case management systems can streamline court processes, reduce delays, and ensure transparency. To foster transparency and public trust, case allocation should be automated and once allocated, cases should not be withdrawn from judges except for exceptional circumstances. Exceptional circumstances should be clearly defined to include prolonged absence or unavailability of the judicial officer or recusal. Digital platforms can enable litigants to track case progress, file documents, and access court rulings without physical visits.

Virtual courtrooms and online dispute resolution mechanisms, which gained prominence during the COVID-19 pandemic, can enhance access to justice, particularly in remote areas. Sierra Leone could emulate Rwanda's integrated electronic case management system, which has significantly reduced case backlogs and improved judicial efficiency. However, the adoption of technology must be accompanied by capacity-building initiatives. Judges, lawyers, and court staff require training to use digital tools effectively.

Additionally, addressing the digital divide is essential to ensure that technological advancements do not exacerbate inequalities.

Twelfth, reforms should address the integration of customary and statutory legal systems. Customary law remains a significant aspect of dispute resolution in Sierra Leone, particularly in rural areas. Aligning these systems with constitutional principles and human rights norms can ensure fairness and inclusivity while respecting cultural traditions.

Thirteenth, lawyers cannot afford to be complacent about the rule of law. The rule of law cannot be realized without advocacy and the supportive role of the lawyer. They are duty bound to play a leadership role in identifying inadequacies of public institutions, in particular judiciary, and offer solutions for institutional efficiency, effectiveness, and transparency. It cannot be gainsaid, that Sierra Leone needs a formidable lawyers association, that is devoid of political interference and state capture as has been demonstrated in recent years.

Lawyers also play a critical role in strengthening the judiciary in the course of their professional practice. They initiate cases, produce the evidence and frame the issues for determination for judicial consideration. To perform their appointed function, lawyers must be knowledgeable in the law, competent in its application and play a critical role in shaping its evolution. As Justice William J. Brennan, Jr., rightly observed:

> 'Lawyers, before any other group, must continue to point out how the system is really working-how it actually affects people. They must constantly demonstrate to courts and legislatures alike the tragic results of legal nonintervention. They must highlight how legal doctrines no longer bear any relation to reality, whether in landlord and tenant law, holder in due course law, or any other law. In sum, lawyers must bring real morality into the legal consciousness.'[2]

Not only are lawyers bound not only to assist in the elucidation of relevant fact and law they have a duty to defend the impartial discharge of judicial duty. Having said this, judges themselves must have the courage to resist extraneous influence, eschew political pressure and be adaptive to an evolving environment.

---

2 William J. Brennan, Jr., "Are Citizens Justified in Being Suspicious of the Law and the Legal System?," University of Miami Law Review 43 (1989): 986.

Fourteenth, civil society organisations have a pivotal role in advancing judicial reform. By advocating for policy changes, monitoring judicial performance, and engaging in public legal education, these groups can contribute to building a more transparent and accountable justice system. Their involvement ensures that reforms reflect the needs and aspirations of the broader population. As has been noted previously, these approaches are non-exhaustive.

5. Conclusion

Reforming Sierra Leone's justice sector requires bold, coordinated, and sustained efforts across multiple dimensions. Strengthening judicial independence, enhancing access to justice, combating corruption, modernising infrastructure, and implementing comprehensive reforms are critical steps toward building a resilient justice system. These measures must be underpinned by a commitment to transparency, inclusivity, and accountability.

The justice sector in Sierra Leone stands at a crossroads. While it holds the potential to be a guardian of constitutional principles and a bulwark against governance failures, its challenges threaten to undermine its legitimacy and effectiveness. By addressing systemic weaknesses and fostering an environment of transparency, accountability, and inclusivity, Sierra Leone can build a resilient justice system that upholds the rule of law and restores public confidence. Such reforms are not only vital for the judiciary's integrity but also for the broader project of democratic consolidation and national development.

LIST OF CASES

Abdul Rahim v King-Emperor. 48 BOMLR 473, 1946.

African Commission on Human and Peoples' Rights in Social and Economic Rights Action Center and the Center for Economic and Social Rights v. Nigeria. African Commission on Human and Peoples' Rights, 2001.

Alhaji Abdulai Bangura v Sierra Leone National Petroleum Company Limited & Others. SC MISC APP 4/2006, Supreme Court of Sierra Leone, 2006.

Alhaji Samuel Sam-Sumana v The Attorney-General & Minister of Justice & Others. SC 4/2015, Supreme Court of Sierra Leone, 5 May 2015.

Alie Basma v. The Registrar of Companies and Celtel Limited. SLHC 182, High Court of Sierra Leone

Anisminic v Foreign Compensation Commission. [1969] 2 AC 147, 1969.

Associated Provincial Picture Houses Ltd. v Wednesbury Corporation. [1948] 1 KB 223, 1948.

Attorney-General of Lagos State v Attorney-General of the Federation. 8 NWLR (PT 1566) 20, 2017.

Bishop Donald Kisaka v Attorney-General & Others. Civil Appeal No. 280 of 2013, [2014] eKLR, 2014.

Chang Wing-Siu v R. [1985] 1 AC 168, 1985.

Chidi v Minister of Justice. 1992 (4) S.A. 110 (A.D.), 1992.

Civil Liberties Organisation v Nigeria. 45/90, African Commission on Human and Peoples' Rights, 27 Apr. 1997.

Col. Halilu Akilu v Chief Gani Fawehinmi. SC 215/1988 & SC 216/1988, Supreme Court of Nigeria, 5 Mar. 1989.

Cooper v Wandsworth Board of Works. 14 CBNS 180, 1863.

Council of Civil Service Unions v Minister for the Civil Service. [1985] AC 374 (HL), 1985.

David Fornah v Alhaji Kandeh Yumkella and Others. Supt. Ct. Case No. 2/2018, Supreme Court of Sierra Leone.

David Lansana & 11 Others v. Regina. 1970–71 A.L.R. (S.L.) 186, 1971.

Dr. Harry Will v Attorney General & Minister of Justice. SC MISC APP 7/1999, Supreme Court of Sierra Leone.

Dumbar v S. SLCA 1279, Court of Appeal of Sierra Leone, 15 Feb. 1972.

Ex Parte Muctaru Ola Taju-Deen v Commissioner, Anti-Corruption Commission & Ors. SC MISC APP 6/2000, Supreme Court of Sierra Leone.

Federation of African Journalists and Others v The Gambia. ECW/CCJ/JUD/04/18, ECOWAS Community Court of Justice, 2018.

Fraser v HMA. [2011] UKSC 24, 2011.*Government of Malaysia v. Lim Kit Siang*. (1988) 2 MLJ 12, 1988.

Herriott v City of Seattle. 500 P.2d 101, 81 Wn.2d 48, Supreme Court of Washington, 1972.

HKSAR v Chan Kam Shing. [2016] HKCFA 8, 2016.

Hon. Kakpindi Jamiru and Hon. Joseph Sallu Conteh v. Dr. John Karefa-Smart. SC3/97, Supreme Court of Sierra Leone, 2000.

In re: Otugor Gamioba and Others v Esezi II, The Onodjie of Okpe, and Others. FSC 120/1961, Supreme Court of Nigeria, 9 Oct. 1961.

In R (Refugee Legal Centre) v Secretary of State for the Home Department. [2005] 1 WLR 2219 (CA), 2005.

Isatu Kamara v The Attorney-General. SC MISC APP 4/1992, Supreme Court of Sierra Leone, 11 Aug. 1992.

Jabbie v Sierra Leone People's Party and 3 Others. SC MISC APP 1/2011, Supreme Court of Sierra Leone, 28 Feb. 2011.

Jalloh v National Insurance Co. Ltd. SC MISC APP 2/1986, Supreme Court of Sierra Leone, 18 Mar. 1986.

John and Four Others v The State. 1972-73 ALR S.L. 441, 1973.

Kamara v Attorney-General. Supreme Court of Sierra Leone, n.d. (unreported).

Kargbo v R. 1967-68 ALR S.L. 146, 1968.

Liesching and Others v S. and Another. 2017 (4) B.C.L.R. 454 (C.C.), 2017 (2) S.A.C.R. 193 (C.C.), 2017.

London Passenger Transport Board v Moscrop. [1942] 1 All ER 972, 1942.

M v Home Office. [1994] 1 AC 377, [1992] 4 All ER 97, [1993] 3 All ER 537, 1994.

Malaysian Trade Union Congress (MTUC) & 13 Ors v Menteri Tenaga, Air Dan Komunikasi & Anor. High Court of Malaysia, n.d. (unreported).

Marbury v Madison. 5 U.S. 137, 1803.*McAuliffe v. R*. (1995) 183 CLR 108, 1995.

Mc Innes v. HMA. [2010] UKSC 7, 2010.

Minister of Justice of Canada v Borowski. [1981] 2 SCR 575, Supreme Court of Canada, 1981.

Mohamed Sorie Fornah and Others v The State. Cr. App. 31/74, Supreme Court of Sierra Leone, 30 Apr. 1975 (unreported).

Mulcahy v The Queen. 1963 CanLII 1110 (SCC), 1963.

Nagle v Feilden. [1966] 2 QB 633 (CA), 1966.

Oba Lamidi Adeyemi (Alafin of Oyo) v Attorney General, Oyo State. 1 SCNLR 605, Supreme Court of Nigeria, 1984.

Palmer v Stooke & Attorney-General. 1950-56 ALR S.L. 325, Supreme Court of Sierra Leone, 12 Jan. 1953.

Palmer v The Governor. CIVIL CASE 241 of 1952, Supreme Court of Sierra Leone, 18 Nov. 1952.

Presley v DPP (SA). [2016] HCA 30, 2016.*Prosecutor v. Charles Ghankay Taylor*. SCSL-03-01-T-1285, Special Court for Sierra Leone, n.d.,

R. v Anderson and R. v. Morris. [1966] 2 QB 110, 1966.

R. v Betty. (1964) 48 Cr. App. R. 6, 1964.

R. v Bob Jones. 1967-68 ALR S.L. 237, 1968.

R. v Collison. 4 Car. & P. 565, 1831.

R. v Grant and Gilbert. (1954) 38 Cr. App. Rep. 107, 1954.

R. v Greenfield. (1973) 3 All E.R. 1050, 1973.

R. v Gunewardene. [1951] 35 Cr. App. R. 80, 1951.

R. v Jogee. [2016] UKSC 8, 2016.

R. v Macklin. 2 Lew. CC 225, 168 E.R. 1136, 1838.

R. v Nat Bell Liquors Ltd. [1922] 2 AC 128 (PC), 1922.

R. v Reid. (1976) 62 Cr. App. R. 109, 1976.*R. v. Rudd*. [1948] 32 Cr. App. R. 138, 1948.

R. v Smith (Wesley). [1963] 1 WLR 1200, 1963.

R. v Spraggett. [1960] Crim. L.R. 840, 1960.

R. v Thistlewood. 33 St. Tr. 681, 1820.

Republic v High Court, General Jurisdiction, Accra. J7 18 of 2019, Supreme Court of Ghana, 14 Jan. 2020.

Ridge v Baldwin. [1964] AC 40 (HL), 1964.

Roberts v Gwyrfai Rural District Council. [1899] 2 Ch 608 (CA), 1899.

Ruddock v The Queen. [2016] UKPC 7, 2016.

Samuel Hinga Norman v Dr. Sama S. Banya. S.C. No. 2/2005, Supreme Court of Sierra Leone, 2005.

Samuel Sam-Sumana v Republic of Sierra Leone. ECW/CCJ/APP/38/16, ECW/CCJ/JUD/19/17, ECOWAS Community Court of Justice, n.d.

Senator Abraham Adesanya v President of the Federal Republic of Nigeria & Anor. S.C. 1/81, Supreme Court of Nigeria, 15 May 1981.

Sierra Leone Association of Journalists v The Attorney General & Minister of Justice & Another. SC 1/2020, Supreme Court of Sierra Leone, 11 Nov. 2009.

Subramanian v Public Prosecutor. [1965] 1 W.L.R. 965, 1965.

Sze Kwan Lung v HKSAR. (2004) 7 HKCFAR 475, 2004.

The State v Alghassim Jah. SC MISC APP 1/1994, Supreme Court of Sierra Leone, 1 Jan. 1995.

The State v Brigadier John Bangura and Others. Supreme Court of Sierra Leone, n.d. (unreported).

The State v Gabriel Mohamed Tennyson Kaikai and 17 Others. SLSC 9, Supreme Court of Sierra Leone, 29 Sept. 1989.

The State v LT. Col. C. N. Deen. MISC APP 1/95, Supreme Court of Sierra Leone, 1995.*The State v. The Honourable Mr. Justice F.C. Gbow, Judge*. SC MISC APP 6/93, Supreme Court of Sierra Leone, 22 June 1994.

Velásquez Rodríguez v Honduras. Inter-American Court of Human Rights, 1988.

Verein KlimaSeniorinnen Schweiz v Switzerland. European Court of Human Rights, 2024.

Walker v R. 1964-1966 ALR S.L. 144, 1966.

Ward v Holman. [1964] 2 Q.B. 850, 1964.

Zhou Wenje v Pioneer Power Engineering Company SL Ltd & Others. MISC APP 001/2025, High Court of Sierra Leone, 2025.

LIST OF BOOKS

Abdulai, Emmanuel Saffa, and Ina Kubbe, editors. The Diverse Facets of Corruption in Sierra Leone. Springer Nature Switzerland, 2024.

Aïvo, Frédéric Joël. Le Juge Constitutionnel et l'Etat de Droit en Afrique: L'Exemple du Modéle Béninois. L'Harmattan, 2006.

Aleinikoff, T. Alexander, and Douglas Klusmeyer, editors. Citizenship Today: Global Perspectives and Practices. Carnegie Endowment for International Peace, 2001.

Alie, Joe A. D. A New History of Sierra Leone. St. Martin's Press, 1990.

Barnett, Hilaire. Constitutional and Administrative Law. 12th ed., Routledge, 2017.

Baxter, Lawrence. Administrative Law. Juta, 1984.

Benhabib, Seyla. The Rights of Others: Aliens, Residents, and Citizens. Cambridge University Press, 2007.

Berewa, Solomon E. A New Perspective on Governance, Leadership, Conflict and Nation Building in Sierra Leone. AuthorHouse, 2011.

Bickel, Alexander M. The Least Dangerous Branch: The Supreme Court at the Bar of Politics.

Bobbs-Merrill, 1982.Black's Law Dictionary with Pronunciations. 6th ed., West Group, 1991.

Bosniak, Linda. The Citizen and the Alien: Dilemmas of Contemporary Membership. Princeton University Press, 2006.Brooks, George E. Landlords and Strangers: Ecology, Society, and Trade in Western Africa, 1000–1630. Westview Press, 1993.

Cane, Peter. Administrative Law. 5th ed., Oxford University Press, 2011.

Cane, Peter. An Introduction to Administrative Law. 5th ed., Clarendon Press, 1996.

Davis, Kenneth Culp. Administrative Law Treatise. West Publishing Company, 1958.

De Smith, S. A., Hon. Lord Woolf, and Jeffrey Jowell. Judicial Review of Administrative Action. 5th ed., Sweet & Maxwell, 1995.

Dyzenhaus, David. The Constitution of Law: Legality in a Time of Emergency. Cambridge University Press, 2011.

Ely, John Hart. Democracy and Distrust: A Theory of Judicial Review. Harvard University Press, 1980.

Fordham, Michael. Judicial Review Handbook. 5th ed., Hart Publishing, 2008.

Forna, Aminatta. The Devil That Danced on the Water: A Daughter's Quest. Atlantic Monthly Press/HarperCollins, 2002.

Fransman, Laurie, Adrian Berry, and Alison Harvey. "Sierra Leone."

Fransman's British Nationality Law, 3rd ed., Bloomsbury Professional, 2011, pp. 500–501.

Fyfe, Christopher. A History of Sierra Leone. Oxford University Press, 1962.

Fyle, Magbaily C. Historical Dictionary of Sierra Leone. 3rd ed., Scarecrow Press, 2006.

Harlow, Carol, and Richard Rawlings. Law and Administration. Weidenfeld and Nicolson, 1984.

Hobbes, Thomas. Leviathan. Edited by C. B. Macpherson, Penguin Classics, 1985.

Kup, Alexander Peter. Sierra Leone: A Concise History. Douglas David and Charles Limited, 1975.

Manby, Bronwen. Citizenship in Africa: The Law of Belonging. Hart Publishing, 2018.

Manby, Bronwen. Citizenship Law in Africa: A Comparative Study. 3rd ed., Open Society Foundations, 2016.

Marshall, T. H., and Tom Bottomore. Citizenship and Social Class. Pluto Press, 1992.

Obama, Barack. Dreams from My Father: A Story of Race and Inheritance. Three Rivers Press, 1995.

Postema, Gerald J. Law's Rule: The Nature, Value, and Viability of the Rule of Law. Oxford University Press, 2022.

Rawls, John. Political Liberalism. Columbia University Press, 1993.

Russell, William Oldnall. A Treatise on Crimes, and Indictable Misdemeanors. Vol. 1, J. Butterworth, 1819.

Thio, S. M. Locus Standi and Judicial Review. University Press, 1971.

Thompson, Bankole. The Criminal Law of Sierra Leone. University Press of America, 1999.

Van Zyl Smit, Jan. The Appointment, Tenure and Removal of Judges under Commonwealth Principles: A Compendium and Analysis of Best Practice. British Institute of International and Comparative Law, 2015.

Wade, Henry William Rawson. Administrative Law. 2nd ed., Clarendon Press, 1967.

Woolf, Harry, Jeffrey Jowell, and Andrew Le Sueur. De Smith's Judicial Review. 6th ed., Sweet & Maxwell, 2007.

STATUTES, CONVENTIONS, AND LEGAL DOCUMENTS

Abolition of the Death Penalty Act, 2022. Act No. 6 of 2022, Sierra Leone, 2022.

African Charter on Human and Peoples' Rights. Organization of African Unity, 1981.

American Convention on Human Rights. Organization of American States, 1969.Citizenship Act, 1973. Act No. 4 of 1973, Sierra Leone, 1973.

Constitution of Ghana, 1992. Government of Ghana, 1992.

Constitution of Sierra Leone, 1961. The Sierra Leone (Constitution) Order in Council, 1961.

Constitution of Sierra Leone, 1978. Act No. 12 of 1978, Sierra Leone, 1978.

Constitution of Sierra Leone, 1991. Act No. 6 of 1991, Sierra Leone, 1991.

Constitution of the Federal Republic of Nigeria, 1979. Federal Republic of Nigeria, 1979.

Constitution of the Republic of South Africa. Republic of South Africa, 1996.

Convention on the Rights of Persons with Disabilities. United Nations, 2006.

Criminal Procedure (Amendment) No. 3 Act, 1973. Act No. 25 of 1973, Sierra Leone, 1973.

Criminal Procedure Acts, 1965. Act No. 32 of 1965, Sierra Leone, 1965.

Cybersecurity and Crime Act, 2021. Act No. 12 of 2021, Sierra Leone, 2021.

European Convention on Human Rights. Council of Europe, 1950.

Human Rights Committee, Rules of Procedure. United Nations Human Rights Committee, 1977.

Larceny Act, 1916. S. 23, as amended by Imperial Statutes (Criminal Law) Adoption (Amendment) Act, 1971, United Kingdom, 1916.

National Drug Control Act, 2008. Act No. 10 of 2008, Sierra Leone, 2008.

Offences Against the Persons Act, 1861. United Kingdom, 1861.

Political Parties Act, 2002. Act No. 3 of 2002, Sierra Leone, 2002.

Public Order Act, 1965. Act No. 46 of 1965, Sierra Leone, 1965.

Rules of Procedure and Evidence of the Special Court for Sierra Leone.

Special Court for Sierra Leone, 2002.Sierra Leone Citizenship (Amendment) Act, 2006. Act No. 11 of 2006, Sierra Leone, 2006.

Sierra Leone Citizenship (Amendment) Act, 2017. Act No. 17 of 2017, Sierra Leone, 2017.

Sierra Leone High Court Rules, 2007. Sierra Leone, 2007.Sierra Leone Supreme Court Rules, 1996. Sierra Leone, 1996.

South Africa Criminal Procedure Act. Act No. 51 of 1977, Republic of South Africa, 1977.

United States Constitution. Amend. XIV, § 1, cl. 1, United States, 1787.

Universal Declaration of Human Rights

LIST OF REPORTS

Albrecht, Peter, and Paul Jackson. Security System Transformation in Sierra Leone, 1997–2007. GFN-SSR, 2009.

Amnesty International. Sierra Leone Government Urged to Implement the Recommendations of the Truth and Reconciliation Commission (TRC). Amnesty International, 2005.

Atlantic Council. Why the Rule of Law Is the Key to Prosperity: Lessons from Thirty Years of Data. Atlantic Council, 2025.

BTI Transformation Index. Sierra Leone Country Report 2022. BTI Project, 2022.

European Union Election Follow-up Mission. Sierra Leone 2021 Final Report.

European Union, Nov. 2021.

Gross, Samuel R., et al. Race and Wrongful Convictions in the United States. National Registry of Exonerations, Newkirk Center for Science and Society, U. of California Irvine, 7 Mar. 2017.

Institute of Human Rights and Development in Africa. Judicial Colloquium on Locus Standi in Administrative Justice and Human Rights Enforcement. Judicial Colloquium, May 26, 2001.

Judiciary of Kenya. State of the Judiciary & the Administration of Justice: Annual Report, 2023–24. Judiciary of Kenya, 2024.

Judiciary of Sierra Leone. Judiciary Strategic Plan 2016–2021. Judiciary of Sierra Leone, 22 June 2016.

Kaldor, Mary, and James Vincent. Evaluation of UNDP Assistance to Conflict-Affected Countries: Case Study Sierra Leone. United Nations Development Programme, 2006.

Khan, Amadu Wurie. Country Report on Citizenship Laws in Sierra Leone. European University Institute, 2021.

Leboeuf, Aline. Sierra Leone: List of Extremely Violent Events Perpetrated during the War, 1991–2002. Online Encyclopedia of Mass Violence, 2008.

Satterthwaite, Margaret. Report of the Special Rapporteur on the Independence of Judges and Lawyers: Safeguarding the Independence of Judicial Systems in the Face of Contemporary Challenges to Democracy. A/HRC/56/62, United Nations Human Rights Council, 2024.

Sierra Leone, Commission to Review the Constitution. Report of the Commission to Review the Constitution of Sierra Leone, 1991. ConstitutionNet, Jan. 2008.

Sierra Leone, Constitutional Review Committee. Abridged Draft Report. Sierra Leone Parliament, Feb. 2016,

Report on the Review of the 2017 Government White Paper on the Constitution of Sierra Leone, 1991. The Sierra Leone Telegraph, Dec. 2021.

Special Court for Sierra Leone. Overview of the Sierra Leone Truth & Reconciliation Report. ReliefWeb, Oct. 2004.

Suma, Mohamed. Sierra Leone: Justice Sector and the Rule of Law. AfriMAP and the Open Society Initiative for West Africa, 2014,

Thompson, Niobe. In Pursuit of Justice: A Report on the Judiciary in Sierra Leone. Commonwealth Human Rights Initiative and the Sierra Leone Bar Association, 2002,

Truth and Reconciliation Commission of Sierra Leone. Witness to Truth: Report of the Truth and Reconciliation Commission. 2004.

Tucker, Peter L. Report of the Constitutional Review Commission. Sierra Leone Parliament, 2008.

United Nations Integrated Office in Sierra Leone (UNIOSIL). Summary of the Findings and Core Recommendations of the Sierra Leone Truth and Reconciliation Commission. ReliefWeb, 24 May 2007.

U.S. Committee for Refugees. World Refugee Survey 2002: Sierra Leone. Refworld, 10 June 2002.

World Justice Project. WJP Rule of Law Index 2023. World Justice Project, 2023,

INDEX